WHAT
MONEY
WANTS

D0916566

WHAT MONEY WANTS

AN ECONOMY OF DESIRE

NOAM YURAN

STANFORD UNIVERSITY PRESS ∗ STANFORD, CALIFORNIA

To my parents, Hava and Yossef

Stanford University Press
Stanford, California

©2014 by the Board of Trustees of the Leland Stanford Junior University. All rights reserved.

This book was published with the support of the Israel Science Foundation.

This book has been partially underwritten by the Stanford Authors Fund. We are grateful to the Fund for its support of scholarship by first-time authors. For more information, please see www.sup.org/authorsfund

No part of this book may be reproduced or transmitted in any form or by any means, electronic or mechanical, including photocopying and recording, or in any information storage or retrieval system without the prior written permission of Stanford University Press.

Printed in the United States of America on acid-free, archival-quality paper

Library of Congress Cataloging-in-Publication Data

Yuran, Noam, author.
  What money wants : an economy of desire / Noam Yuran.
      pages cm
  Includes bibliographical references and index.
  ISBN 978-0-8047-8592-1 (cloth : alk. paper) — ISBN 978-0-8047-8593-8 (pbk. : alk. paper)
  1. Money—Philosophy. 2. Desire—Economic aspects. 3. Economics—Philosophy. I. Title.
  HG220.3.Y83 2014
  330.01'9—dc23

                                    2013021463

ISBN 978-0-8047-8889-2 (electronic)

Typeset by Bruce Lundquist in 10.5/15 Adobe Garamond Pro

CONTENTS

ACKNOWLEDGMENTS

The economy teaches us that having sufficiently large debts that can no longer be settled is actually a blissful situation. I acknowledge such happy debts to the many people who have helped me during the work on this book.

Haim Marantz, who supervised my PhD dissertation on which this book is based, is endowed with a generous spirit, which only true teachers have. This book could not have materialized without him. His insistence that I add a chapter on Veblen proved essential to the project. I thank him for his wise and patient advice. I wholeheartedly thank Slavoj Žižek, who also supervised my work. Apart from being a source of intellectual influence, Slavoj took the time to read and comment on several versions of the manuscript.

Keith Hart encouraged me to publish the work. I greatly benefited from the long conversations we had and from his wide perspective on economic thought. I thank Arjun Appadurai for his invaluable advice after reading the manuscript. His thoughtful comments helped me clarify the notion of history that underlies this book. Arjun's invitation to visit the Cultures of Finance group at the Institute for Public Knowledge at New York University provided me with an opportunity for an inspiring intellectual engagement. I especially want to thank two members of the group, Robert Wosnitzer and Benjamin Lee, for their interest and advice on the project. They helped me to better understand the connections between finance and consumer culture.

While working on the book, I received a research fellowship from the Minerva Humanities Center at Tel Aviv University. I thank Adi Ophir, the co-director of the center, for many years of dialogue and support. The collective work at the center is an ongoing stimulation for me. I especially enjoyed three years of lively discussions with the political economy research group there. I thank the members of the group: Yuval Yonay, Dotan Leshem,

Anat Rosenberg, Roy Kreitner, Oz Gore, Michael Zakim, Shaul Hayoun, Uzi Livneh, Oleg Komlik, Tahel Frosh, and Rami Kaplan. I especially want to thank my friends in the researchers' room at the center Dikla Bytner—Tali Friedman, Uri Eran, Ori Rotlevy, Moriya Ben Barak, and Yael Atiya—for their jolly company and for enduring my pointless complaints during the work on the book. Remember, there is no despair in the world whatsoever.

Many colleagues and teachers kindly shared their knowledge and thoughts with me. I especially thank Moshe Zuckermann, Arie Arnon, Gideon Freudenthal, Anat Matar, and Eva Illouz.

I am thankful to Evergreen Venture Partners, which accepted me to its fellowship program. The turbulent seminar headed by Doron Avital was an intellectual challenge. I thank the members of the seminar: Elad Mentovich, Oriel Bergig, Romi Mikulinsky, and Roly Belfer.

Thoughts about money are of an obsessive nature as many of my friends have learned. I am grateful to good friends with whom I shared my thoughts. I thank Eyal Dotan for the conversation that sprouted the idea for this book. I thank my friend Oded Shechter for many years of common thought and shared ideas. I thank Joshua Simon, partner on many roads, and Yitzhak Laor, Gavin Steingo, and Yuval Kremnitzer. I thank my fellow PhD students in the Philosophy Department at Ben Gurion University: Ariel Sarid and Sergeiy Sandler.

The staff at Stanford University Press made the publishing process a pleasant experience. Emily-Jane Cohen put her trust in the project from the beginning. I thank her for her kind support and care. I thank Emma S. Harper and Judith Hibbard for making all procedures so easy. Many of the words in this book are Leslie Rubin's. Her work went beyond copyediting, and she provided valuable insights to the book.

Finally, I would like to thank my family. My brothers Hanan and Nadav Yoran were involved with my work, and I thank them for their constant care. I thank my wife Sivan for her love and patience during the long project and my children Itamar, Alona, and Omer for being there.

PREFACE

KEITH HART

During a period around 1900, five books came out, each of them offering a radically new perspective on the modern economic system that was then given a name, "capitalism." They were V. I. Lenin's *The Development of Capitalism in Russia* (1899), which is still the best available account of capitalist development in backward areas; Thorstein Veblen's *The Theory of the Leisure Class* (1899), which launched the study of consumption and institutional economics; Georg Simmel's *The Philosophy of Money* (1900), which has a claim to being the most profound meditation on the topic since Karl Marx; Werner Sombart's *Der Moderner Kapitalismus* (1902), which is the original source for the name of our economic system; and Max Weber's *The Protestant Ethic and the Spirit of Capitalism* (1904–5), which is possibly the most famous essay in sociology ever written.

All of these were in some kind of dialogue with Karl Marx's work that was published in the mid-nineteenth century. This was also a time when the theory of relativity, quantum mechanics, and cubism were being formed. Not much later the Federal Reserve and the first fully-automated production line saw daylight in 1913, and twentieth-century capitalism was born.

Noam Yuran's book is likewise in dialogue with Marx, and it draws heavily on Veblen and Weber, but only indirectly or not at all on the others. We are living through a watershed in world economic history when the doctrines of orthodox economics have been discredited by financial crisis. It ought to be a time of intellectual renewal and discovery, but the contours of such change are not yet obvious. By revisiting that epoch just over a century ago and, especially, through his interpretation of Marx's theory and method, Yuran may well have produced a classic of our era. His argument is by no means solely an exercise in intellectual archaeology, nor is it an explanation of the current historical transition. It is steeped in a contemporary critique of the consumer economy of our day, which he analyzes through vivid anecdotes of brand names, celebrities, television, and advertising with which we are all familiar.

What Money Wants is in truth a work of economic philosophy whose aim is to develop a toolkit and a strategy for understanding the modern economy that differ radically from those of orthodox economics. As a startlingly new version of heterodox economics, it aims to challenge the mainstream discipline from the inside, not through some external perspective drawn from sociology, psychology, or anthropology.

Yuran's approach has two anchors, each a dialectical negation of the twin foundations of orthodox economics: its utilitarian focus on individual subjectivity and its ahistorical method. His topic is the impersonal economy that is foreign to the subject's point of view and often invisible to him or her; he aims to reveal the historicity of economic action by showing how the past persists in economic objects. For Yuran the essence of history is story (indeed, for the Greeks they were the same word), and this takes him into an intense engagement with the philosophy of history through the three principal authors examined here.

How else to address questions of this magnitude than through money? Economists are notoriously weak when it comes to studying money. They can tell us what it does, but not what it is or why it occupies its dominant place in our lives. For economists money is mainly a means of satisfying consumer utilities through the purchase of commodities. No one ever asks what rich men want money for; to accumulate thousands of pairs of shoes is pathological, but to keep on accumulating money is unremarkable. Yuran argues that money is the economic object par excellence. It represents the impersonal, historical economy that lies beyond our comprehension or reach and is marked by lack or absence. The word "want" means both something missing and the desire for it. Hence Yuran emphasizes money as an object of desire. The Germanic "want" retains a dialectic that is missing from the Latinate "desire."

Yuran writes with a logical clarity that is enlivened by his ability to find unexpected meaning in familiar cultural artifacts and by a well-founded belief that works of literature are better suited to his subject matter than the pseudoscientific style of contemporary economics. Charles Dickens features prominently as a source that duly complements Marx's writing of the same period.

Indeed, an idea is gaining acceptance that Marx had to be a great novelist to succeed in his critique of the political economy (the discipline).

Yuran's juxtaposition of Dickens with Adam Smith is particularly reveal-ing. (Smith taught rhetoric and belles lettres for fifteen years before eventually using them to write *The Wealth of Nations*.) In today's supersaturated world of telecommunications, Yuran provides interpretations of car commercials and reality TV that are at once a revelation and hilarious. But this cannot disguise the difficulty most readers will have in trying to digest his unfamiliar ideas. For orthodox economics is not just a specialist academic discipline; it is a cultural expression of the Anglophone societies that did most to pioneer capi-talism as well as thinking about it. Most of us have to dismantle deep-seated sources of cultural resistance to his message to receive even part of it.

If there is a contemporary link to Yuran's highly original approach, it is Slavoj Žižek's reading of Marx through Jacques Lacan, generously acknowl-edged here. I can't begin to summarize that link beyond pointing to its signifi-cance in the text. Less obvious—and more immediately accessible—is Yuran's use of Max Weber to provide a satisfying illustration of his core argument concerning money. Usually, aficionados of Marx consign Weber permanently to the opposition camp. Yuran begins unpromisingly by claiming that Weber's thesis on the significance of religious ideas for the origins of capitalist econ-omy has a uni-directional causal logic: the austere imperatives of a salvationist ideology made entrenchment of a rationalist economic ethos possible.

I always thought that Weber harnessed Goethe's idea of "elective affinity" to a probabilistic approach so that two correlated things may be said to rein-force each other in selective ways without one causing the other. Fortunately, Yuran's alternative also shows how religion and economy were intertwined in this case. At first, the overt religious doctrine made its economic corollary invisible. Later, when capitalism had turned society itself into a profit-making machine, religion passed from view. But there was always an economic aspect to religion, and there is now a religious dimension of the economy. Yuran pro-vides a powerful demonstration of this vision of history through his analysis of money.

If orthodox economics is the villain in this story, Marx is undoubtedly its hero. There are two types of intellectuals, which I prefer to identify as intel-lectuals of structure and intellectuals of transition. The first reveals the logic of a persistent form, and the second addresses the movement from one form to another. For all his credentials as the founder of a revolutionary movement, Marx belongs in the first category. He really nailed Victorian capitalism as a system. Lenin devoted himself much more effectively to the second question. But Marx (and let us not forget Engels, whose empirical knowledge of industrial capitalism was crucial to their early partnership) went further. He claimed that what they were witnessing in one particular place would change the whole world irreversibly. And it did. How did he do that? He developed a method of structuralist (or, perhaps, I should now say "ontological") history of which Yuran's book is the best contemporary example I have encountered. This is not history of the kind I alluded to in the opening paragraph of this Preface, an attempt to situate linked social phenomena in a pattern of movement such as our own historical crisis.

One of the most strikingly original features of this book is its engagement with the narrative aspects of history. If the past is approached in terms specific to itself, there is nothing uniquely historical about the method. It is rather an exercise in economics, sociology, or anthropology using facts gathered from the past. Yuran insists that historical method must acknowledge the dialectical relationship of the past to the present when constructing a story and for many this implies the dreaded threat of "teleology." The way he develops and applies his own approach to this problem is extremely subtle; it offers an incisive guide to Marx (whose own historical method is still poorly understood), and it does illuminate how we might think about economy currently and in world history over the last few centuries. The key to the method is the substance of Yuran's take on money, and I balk at trying to summarize that here.

Yuran has little to say about the modifications of capitalism that occurred in the twentieth century or are occurring now: welfare states, transnational corporations, Brazil, Russia, India, China and South Africa (the BRICS), the return of rentier finance. Nor does he offer any vision of what might replace it. He obviously believes that Western capitalism over the last three centuries or so is one thing, more than any of its historical variations. He acknowledges that, in some ways, the emphasis has shifted from production to consumption and this contrast underpins his desire to bring Marx up to date by integrating the two sides more explicitly than his great predecessor did. He therefore cuts through the debate about the respective role of states and markets as sources for money and argues for a view of money as defined by its relationship to the circuit of commodities. I think he succeeds in this brilliantly. But his argument for the singularity of our world closes off perspectives that would rather emphasize its diversity and movement.

The hero has a sidekick in this story. The prophet of the consumer economy was Veblen, and Yuran enlists the ideas of Veblen's most famous book for the task of updating Marx as a critical guide for our times. Veblen, in turn, is shown to be much more compatible with a Marxist approach than its adherents would normally imagine. This hinges on demonstrating that his alleged evolutionism is in fact better understood as a form of historicism in Yuran's terms. On the other hand, the orthodox economists of our day are more faithful to a sterile version of evolutionism, which only highlights their inability to make sense of the history residing in economic objects. Both Veblen and Marx were highly satirical of their own society and especially of their opponents. Taken together they inform Yuran's unique intellectual style, which both is open to literature and aspires to being scientific, as they were. The flipside of scientism is a fear of fiction. We may be entering a phase when they can become more comfortable bedfellows again.

I have spent the last several decades studying and writing about money. I first encountered this book as a precocious PhD thesis three years ago. I am still learning from it. I appear in the present text on three occasions. On the first, my book is dismissed as missing the point: I identify money with memory, whereas Yuran identifies it with oblivion. On the second, we agree about the unity of the two sides of money: heads and tails, states and markets. On the third, he takes issue with one of my stories about prostitution in an engagingly different way. We are obviously contrasting intellectual personalities. When I read this book, I am alternately thrilled and enlightened, confused and frustrated. So will you be. I hope that some of you will stay the course, as I have. You just might be reading one of the formative tracts of our time.

Paris, January 2013

WHAT
MONEY
WANTS

INTRODUCTION

If you ask an economist the trivial question: What does Bill Gates want? she probably has a ready answer. What Bill Gates *really* wants is power—or, perhaps, influence or prestige or social status or fame. Common to all these answers is the way they substitute a vague, intangible, and immeasurable benefit for what appears prima facie as the most obvious and concrete reply: Bill Gates appears to want money. He behaves as if what he wants is money. His business conduct seems to be primarily aimed at increasing the already unimaginable worth of Microsoft. Why, then, should we not see his conduct as a manifestation of desire for wealth? Why not see it as an extreme example of the *way* people want money (a way that may include as justifications those colloquial explanations of the endless race for wealth—power, honor, prestige, etc.)? In addition to the dubious nature of this overconfident naming of vague substitutes for the most obvious answer, each of the possibilities listed by the imaginary economist raises additional and more concrete questions.

What does the will to power mean if Gates seldom appears to use this power? What might this power achieve that his wealth alone cannot? Is there any real sense in which prestige is increased by adding a few more billions to the dozen billions of dollars that Gates already possesses? (Note that this question does not apply to monetary values: fifty billion is exactly one billion more than forty-nine billion.) Can one really draw pleasure from being famous? As Andy Warhol noted, "You can only see an aura [of fame] on people you don't know very well or don't know at all."[1]

I dwell on these absurdities of the economic mind, not usually suspected of inaccuracy, to underline the strange theoretical difficulty that money poses for economics. What in everyday parlance is an obvious truth, namely, that in some sense or another, people want money, is basically unthinkable in economic terms. Herein lies the starting point for the main argument of this book. If desire for money in itself is comprehensively rejected by economic thought, then the idea of money as an object of desire can serve as a starting point for an elaboration of a comprehensive alternative to contemporary economics. Conceiving of a desire for money not as an aberration but as a fundamental economic reality necessitates a radical shift not only in the concept of money, but also in the conceptions of what a commodity is, what economic behavior is, what an economic subject is, and what an economy is. It necessitates, in other words, a radically different economic ontology.

This is the gist of this book: it argues that money should be conceived of primarily as an object of desire, and it elaborates the wide-reaching theoretical shifts entailed by this conception. It can be read as a thought experiment: what would economics look like if it acknowledged desire for money? It anchors this conception in the works of thinkers who were banished from economic discourse throughout the crystallization of orthodox economics during the twentieth century, drawing mainly on the works of Karl Marx, Thorstein Veblen, and Max Weber, with some insights from Georg Simmel. Using the concept of a desire for money as a key to reading these thinkers enables me to formulate the controversy between orthodox and heterodox economics in terms of economic ontology. Marx and Veblen are no longer read by economists—and in the rare occasions they are read, they are misunderstood—because their conceptions of the economy, of economic things, and of economic behavior are radically foreign to those of orthodox economics. What I will show is that this difference can be highlighted by the fact that their theories are compatible with a notion of the desire for money.

Here I briefly outline the dimensions of this alternative ontology. The desire for money is incomprehensible in an individualist, utilitarian framework such as the one that dominates orthodox economics. Money itself is rendered a marginal issue in this framework. This theoretical setting is inverted once we conceive of economy as an impersonal context of action. In that case, money can be thought of as embodying the dimension of impersonal action fundamental to economy. Furthermore, it is when we conceive of money as an object of desire that the economic drive appears in its most alien form.

According to the orthodox economic perspective, people may want things that money can buy—tangible things like food and drink or intangible things like prestige, beauty, or a sense of certainty regarding their future—but they cannot want money itself. That is why economists tend to see money as a "neutral veil" over the "real" economy or a lubricant in its machinery.[2] The distinction between money and *real* things already is rooted in the individualistic view of economics. In a strictly individualist environment, money simply has no meaning. Abandoned like Robinson Crusoe, an individual has no use whatsoever for money. Indeed, Crusoe himself acknowledged this at length when he found a drawer full of money after his shipwreck: "I smiled to myself at the sight of this money: 'O drug!' said I, aloud, 'what art thou good for? Thou art not worth to me—no, not the taking off the ground; one of those knives is worth all this heap; I have no manner of use for thee; even remain where thou art, and go to the bottom as a creature whose life is not worth saving.'" Nevertheless, as a reminder of an advantage that literary imagination sometimes has over economics, Crusoe immediately adds: "However, upon second thoughts I took it away."[3]

Why or, more precisely, how does Crusoe take the money after all? He takes it despite his own internal monologue, which conveys a somewhat complacent blend of self-pity and pride. This play, between an articulated contempt for money and the decision to take it after all, reflects the relation between orthodox and heterodox economic thought. If one's actions are seen to be grounded solely on one's subjectivity, then desire for money in itself makes no sense. By contrast, the inexplicable backtracking, "upon second thoughts I took it away," situates the relation to money at the limits of subjectivity. Crusoe takes the money in spite of the perception he has of his own activity. He acts against his own self-perception. This act reflects the reason why heterodox economics can indeed account for the desire for money.

The works of Marx, Veblen, and Weber share the idea of the economy as an impersonal framework, namely, a framework in which one's activity is situated from the outset against one's own self-perception. This idea pervades Marx's economic thought from the beginning in the concept of alienation and, throughout all its theoretical levels, in his conceptions of commodities, exchange, and money. It is epitomized in the concept of capital as embodying a drive or a movement of accumulation that goes beyond any subjective end. In Veblen a similar notion of economy is explicitly stated in his emphasis on man as "an agent seeking in every act the accomplishment of some concrete, objective, impersonal end."[4] His formulation is steeped in an ostensibly different terminology, namely, in Veblen's predilection for an evolutionary approach to the economy. Yet its meaning for economic theory dovetails with Marxist thought.

If *Capital* elaborates the workings of the drive for profit as an impersonal formation, Veblen's *The Theory of the Leisure Class* elaborates on waste as an impersonal phenomenon. Conspicuous gestures of expenditure on unproductive efforts enter Veblen's economic theory insofar as they suspend the individualist, utilitarian calculus of gains and losses. In Weber's *The Protestant Ethic and the Spirit of Capitalism*, the impersonal dimension is still more evident in the transformation of a divine, austere injunction into an economic drive. In all these conceptions, far from being marginal, money occupies a central place as an object that embodies the impersonal nature of the economy as such. This line of reasoning becomes clearest when desire is brought into account. It is in relation to desire that money most fully assumes its position as embodying the economic in its foreignness to subjectivity.

In the individualistic framework of orthodox economics, the fact that money cannot directly serve subjective ends renders the desire for it a pathological tendency, if not a complete theoretical impossibility. In the impersonal framework of heterodox thought, the same fact allows us to posit the desire for money as an objective reality in the sense that it cannot be fully subjectivized. In joining money and desire, money takes on its most unfamiliar shape when the subject's own desire confronts it as an incomprehensible force. To return to Crusoe—formally speaking, his speech is actually a dialogue because his contemptuous words are actually addressed to the money he found. His additional remark "upon second thoughts I took it away" can be considered as money's mute reply.

A direct representation of this notion of economy as transcending the individual's perspective can be found in the reality-television show *Survivor* in the interesting use the contestants make of the expression *to play the game*. The first thing to note is that here the game does not signify the opposite of reality but rather comprises a hard kernel of reality—a kernel that cannot be revealed except in the guise of a game: the hypocritical, treacherous conduct of the participants in their fight for the one-million-dollar prize. In this usage, the game allows one to suspend in practice one's self-perception, namely, "In my real life I am a conscientious citizen, a good friend, and a loving family man, but in the game I am a jerk." The heterodox view of the economy as an impersonal framework takes this suspended, unreal player as the real economic subject. Furthermore, this view enables us to see the gesture of bracketing as related to the economic object of money—as part of the practices that surround money and sustain it. Money is the embodiment of impersonal economic activity insofar as it enables us to behave as though we are alien to ourselves.

A parallel dimension of the difference between heterodox and orthodox economic ontologies concerns the question of history. The individualistic framework of orthodox economics entails an ahistorical conception of the economy. In this framework, any economic situation can be eventually reduced to individuals and their preferences. These preferences may indeed change over time, with shifts in fashions and tastes; yet, preferences themselves are *not* an object of economic knowledge. Economics only studies the mechanisms of allocating resources according to given preferences. For that reason orthodox economic knowledge lacks, in principle, any meaningful historical dimension.

The heterodox view, in contrast, allows us to bridge the conceptual gap that ostensibly separates economics and history. The view of the economy as impersonal, as a foreign context of action confronting the subject, makes room for history in the sense of an aspect of social reality that surpasses the points of view of individuals. It allows a conceptualization of that aspect of social reality that is blindly inherited from the past. In heterodox economic thought we can find reference to this aspect through the question of persistence, of the way economic systems perpetuate themselves.

The answers we find in Marx, Veblen, and Weber are similar in that they all point to the economic object as a medium or carrier of history. In this sense, their theories historicize the economy not in the trivial manner of viewing any specific economy as embedded in its historical context, but by conceiving of economic objects as historical objects. Weber's "iron cage" metaphor points to this. It suggests that the Protestant ascetic religious ethic that gave rise to the spirit of capitalism has become congealed in the ostensibly neutral economic cosmos, embedded in things and in the practices that surround them. Marx's concept of fetishism addresses the same idea in a systematic manner, as it explains how an antagonistic social order persists as it is mediated through objects: social relations appear to agents as "material relations between persons and social relations between things." Finally, Veblen's institutional economic theory refers to practices and things as they are habituated: things that are associated with power or wealth, such as refined manners, but become appreciated for their own sake. For that reason, a thing enters the economy of conspicuousness precisely by the same movement that makes it a historical thing—it is an economic object insofar as it becomes a remnant of the past, combining persistence with effacement of origin.

This book ponders the possibility of weaving desire into this conjunction of economy and history. It explores the possibility that among the other vestiges that the economic object carries from the past, and with which it confronts the subject, is a social structure of desire that sustains money. If this possibility seems farfetched, one should examine it with respect to the era of gold-based money. In such a system, money is quite clearly entangled with both a misconception and a form of desire. Gold appears as if it is the pure embodiment of economic value and that is also how it is desired. Desire attaches to the untraceable quality that allocates to gold the special function of money, despite the apparent fact that it is but an ordinary commodity.

What should be emphasized is that this conjunction of erroneous belief and desire that surrounds gold is not simply an error in the conception of money. Rather, it *is* money. It is precisely the way that gold assumed, in its time, the function of money. Marx notes this in his *Comments on James Mill*, where he suggests that the efforts of political economy to dispel the mercantilist superstition that gold is the essence of wealth are futile despite their cleverness because this superstition is part of the structure of a monetary economy.[5]

Thus, in this sense, the desire for gold may be conceived as part of the historical reality of money. It is historical precisely because it is related to a misconception of economic agents and, therefore, to that which transcends the purely individualistic perspective. History, in this sense, is a horizon that allows us to grant reality to the erroneous beliefs of agents, and money is a historical object in that it carries an incomprehensible remainder through time.

Some may doubt the relevance of this last consideration for our own time. One objection might be that gold-based money may indeed have been sustained by an erroneous belief and an adjoining pathological desire, but these are precisely the superstitions that were overcome when modern money finally was detached from gold to become a purely technical tool in the administration of goods. This position lies at the basis of the notions of real economy of contemporary economics and the clear-cut distinction between money and things, all the more emphasized by the question of desire (things can be desired while money cannot). Naturally, this position runs contrary to the distinct feeling that contemporary, affluent societies are evermore obsessed with money. To paraphrase F. Scott Fitzgerald's Gatsby who says of

Daisy, the object of his unrequited love, that "her voice is full of money," it seems that our public sphere has become thoroughly moneyed. While money itself has become invisible, consumer culture increasingly strives to make wealth visible.

To provide theoretical support for this intuition, the book introduces a third dimension of the alternative economic ontology that heterodox thought entails. The book draws on Marx and Veblen to consider the idea that in some sense of the term, our monetary systems are still a variant of commodity money. Marx and Veblen offer us complementary ways to overcome the distinction between money and things, which can be brought to bear upon contemporary monetary systems. Marx's concept of capital suggests a way to view things as effects of money. In his M-C-M′ formula (**m**oney is exchanged for **c**ommodities and then exchanged back to **m**oney of a greater sum) for the circulation of capital, things are seen as necessary placeholders in the movement of increasing monetary value. This idea concerns the sphere of production, allegedly distant from the everyday presence of money.

The same idea is mirrored in Veblen's work, where money emerges as a hidden principle behind the objects of conspicuous consumption. Veblen's frequent use of the adjective *pecuniary*, defined by the Merriam-Webster dictionary as "consisting of or measured in money" or "of or relating to money," is symptomatic in this respect. Veblen uses this adjective to qualify a vast array of things and practices, from "pecuniary reputability" and "pecuniary culture" to "pecuniary beauty." This latter expression is a poignant example of the way money can be seen as a hidden principle commanding visual effects. It has to do with the beauty of expensive things; to things that appear to us, wholeheartedly, as beautiful, yet the hidden logic of their beauty is expensiveness. If we take Veblen's and Marx's positions to be complementary, we can come up with a unified theory of the consumer economy in which things are effects of money: from the perspective of capital, things are necessary placeholders in the drive to increase capital; but in the spaces of consumption, they are necessary placeholders in the similarly strange drive to spend money.

A Note on Desire

This book grounds money in desire without committing itself to a precise conception of desire. It does include some references to Lacan and Freud but only where these seem to be required by the economic subject matter. In a way, applying a ready-made concept of desire to economic phenomena would simply be too easy. For example, the Lacanian idea that the aim of a drive is not to reach a goal—but to indefinitely reproduce the movement toward the goal—seems like the perfect conceptual tool for describing the desire for money not simply as an end, but as a means that indefinitely defers realizing its end.[6] Yet because economic discourse has little commitment to psychoanalytic insights, working with such notions might be an exercise in futility. Instead, this book aims to infer a concept of desire for money from economic subject matter. It attempts to extract this concept from a wide range of economic texts and phenomena. It reconstructs a concept of the desire for money mainly from heterodox thought and confronts it with both classical and contemporary economics.

The book outlines the theoretical reasons for the rejection of the desire for money by orthodox economics. It traces the points where orthodox economics seems to approach this concept, as well as the strategies it employs to evade it, and it shows how this concept highlights some peculiar failures of economic thought, especially with reference to the modern consumer economy. With this, my aim is not only to elaborate a critical discourse about economics and the economy, but to tackle a much more difficult task: the initiation of a critical discourse *in* economics.

Moreover, rather than bringing some random concept of desire to bear on economics, the book suggests that a study of money can teach us lessons about desire. As an object of desire, money underscores the extent to which our own desire is foreign to us. It shows how desire can confront the subject as a foreign body. Further, it shows how this desire can be conceived of as social in nature, and how it can be entangled with history. That is to say, a study of money shows how an object can historically carry a social formation of desire that confronts the subject as an alien drive.

The Organization of the Book

Chapter 1 lays the theoretical foundations for grounding money in desire. It suggests replacing the well-known formula that *money is an object believed to be money* with the less obvious one that *money is an object desired as money*. The chapter explores the reasons for the economic rejection of any notion of desire for money and, in parallel, constructs such a notion from Marx's *Capital*. It finds in Marx a theoretical formulation for something already hinted at in the myth of Midas, according to which the desire for money entails a transferal to the object. Marx's capitalist is someone who submits to the object, who acts *as if* money itself wants to grow. The chapter shows that this gesture is necessary for capital to have an objective reality.

A complementary discussion compares Marx's concept of the social object and John Searle's concept of institutional fact. Both concepts refer to the way things, such as money, can partake in social relations. However, Searle's *naturalist* ontology does not afford him a real historical view and leads him to ground the social function of things in agreement (a piece of paper functions as money because people agree to use it as such). By contrast, in Marx, the social object culminates in the idea of commodity fetishism, where the object stands for disavowal, for what cannot be agreed upon, and for social antagonism. The background for this reversal is Marx's historical ontology, in which the object congeals social relations to the extent that they are antagonistic and opposed to subjectivity. In this approach, the object stands for the social insofar as it cannot be subjectivised. This idea is relevant to the question of the desire for money as a drive located at the limit of subjectivity.

At the heart of the second chapter is a literary excursus, based on the assumption that literature can hold real knowledge of money that systematically escapes the reach of orthodox economics. Literature can approach the elaborate social relations and intense fantasies surrounding money that cannot be incorporated into the neutral economic view of it. The chapter uses Dickens's *Hard Times* to confront Marx with classical economics. It finds in the novel a phenomenological account of money's social ontology, in which the money-object involves real and imagined relations with others. The formation of desire in Dickens evokes Adam Smith's account of the emergence of money, in which the money-object involves the imaginings of other people who desire it. The chapter goes on to argue that the structure of desire embedded in money is its historical substance: it is what sustains it in its function and what gets carried along with it through time.

Chapter 3 addresses the contemporary consumer economy. It maintains that we should apply Marx's concept of commodity money to modern fiat money. This goes against the widely accepted view that with the dissolution of the gold standard, money has detached itself from the circle of commodities to become a pure means in their administration. Viewed on its own, the emergence of purely symbolic money may indeed support this accepted narrative. However, if we consider the parallel shift, from material to primarily symbolic objects, which occurred in the field of commodities with the emergence of brand names, an alternative narrative emerges, in which the *relation* between money and commodities persists throughout the shift in their forms. Furthermore, the chapter argues that in contrast to the apparent distancing between money and commodities, the consumer economy is characterized by an ever more intimate entanglement of money and commodities.

The brand name can actually be seen as made of money in a double sense: on a macro-economic level, the price of the branded item is what prevents its endless reproduction; in a local context, the price has become a *quality* of the item because a low price suffices to render the item fake or inauthentic. In both these senses, money can be seen as the substance of the brand name if we conceive of substance as what vouches for identity and irreproducibility. The intriguing point is that this possibility is already foretold in *Capital*, where Marx comments that the fact that one commodity assumes the place of direct exchangeability with all other commodities is "intimately connected," like the two poles of a magnet, to the fact that all other commodities are non-directly exchangeable. The price becoming a quality of a thing marks precisely the extent to which a thing is directly unexchangeable. It marks the loss of an exchange value that results from the mere purchase of the thing.

From this perspective, the emergence of brand names and symbolic money does not represent a break with the system of commodity money but rather a folding of it into itself. In their use value, brand names assume more directly the place allocated to commodities in the system of commodity money. This argument is highly relevant to the question of the desire for money because it becomes most evident when brand names are considered from the point of view of desire. Brands are desired *as* unique and irreplaceable. The excess of desire that differentiates them from mere products is precisely the extent to which they are non-money or the extent to which they partake in the structure of commodity money.

Chapter 4 offers a reading of Weber's *The Protestant Ethic and the Spirit of Capitalism* that posits the notion of desire for money as fundamental to this seminal work. Weber famously argued that the Calvinist ethic gave rise to the capitalist spirit of an endless, calculated pursuit of profit, detached from any notion of direct enjoyment of one's wealth. But beyond this strictly causal explanation, we discern a reverse perspective that Weber actually suppresses.

There, the main question is not how a religious ethic caused a shift in the allegedly remote realm of economic behavior. Rather, it is quite the opposite, namely, why was the religious ethic the appropriate medium for the articulation of the capitalist mindset of the quest for profit for its own sake? The key to answering this inverse question lies in the view of the desire for money as a traumatic drive, analogous to the divine voice of the Protestant god. The inverse narrative thus blurs the causal view's distinction between economy and religion. It enables us to see the Calvinist ethic as having always been an economic phenomenon and the spirit of capitalism as still being a religious one.

The fifth and final chapter revisits some of the book's central themes from a Veblenian perspective based on a reading of *The Theory of the Leisure Class* and other early works. It argues against a longstanding misreading of Veblen. This standard reading sterilizes Veblen's thought in order to incorporate it into a utilitarian economic framework. In this reading, the acts of conspicuous waste that Veblen studied are motivated by an aspiration for a higher social status. But in truth, Veblen analyzes gestures of waste that are completely gratuitous. Status, in his conceptual apparatus, is not a benefit derived from conspicuous waste but, rather, it is the code that enforces waste without benefit in the name of some sublime quality, from decorum to religious taboo. Setting aside the utilitarian framework forced upon it enables us to read Veblen's thought, focused on the category of *what money cannot buy*, which ties waste to the sublime. And through this category, we can read Veblen's thesis as a monetary theory that explores the presence of money in the field of consumption.

Chapter 1

ONTOLOGY
The Specter of Greed

PART I: BETWEEN ORTHODOX AND HETERODOX ECONOMICS

We start with an example from my teacher Haim Marantz. Occasionally we hear of an eccentric and rich person who has acquired an enormous collection of things. I have in mind the former first lady of the Philippines Imelda Marcos who was reported to own three thousand pairs of shoes in 1986 (the year her husband's regime collapsed). Such anecdotes usually serve to illustrate a quirkiness of the rich. "Who could wear three thousand pairs of shoes in a life time?" we might feel compelled to ask.

In contrast, without implying that anything is out of the ordinary, the media inundates us with a stream of information about people who acquire enormous amounts of money. It is considered a sign of craziness to collect shoes in excess of a certain number, whereas it is considered perfectly normal to amass an unlimited amount of money. Moreover, in these media stories, it goes without saying that a person with three thousand pairs of shoes is obsessed with this particular item. The mere possession of the collection attests to a somewhat pathological desire. However, in the same media space, rarely is it automatically assumed that a person in possession of millions or billions of dollars is obsessed with money.

What are we to make of this contrast? I do not think this difference in treatment is simply an indication of a bias in favor of the rich on the part of the mass media. Instead, I think that the distinction should be viewed seriously as an indication of an actual property of money. Drawing on Geoffrey Ingham's term, I propose to see this distinction as indicative of "the social ontology of money."[1]

Perhaps the real point of the difference is that a person can have billions of dollars without actually being greedy. This does not necessarily mean that billionaires do not want money. It might mean that crazy and insatiable greed is encoded in the rules of the game. According to this view, the desire for money is not simply a psychological affect but, in a way, is embedded in the object itself. The fact that people can have billions of dollars without being greedy could simply be considered a minimal description of the way desire is ontologically related to money.

This idea, that greed is not just a desire for money, but embedded somehow in the object itself, is suggested by a comment of Karl Marx in the *Grundrisse*:

> Greed as such [is] impossible without money; all other kinds of accumulation and of mania for accumulation appear as primitive, restricted by needs on the one hand and by the restricted nature of products on the other.[2]

At first glance this may seem like a trivial observation: there is no greed without money, just as there is no desire for salted peanuts in a world that does not know of salted peanuts. But Marx is actually suggesting much more. What he suggests is that the form of the desire for money is inherently related to money as an object. A desire for things is limited by its object, whereas money is an object that allows infinite desire. For ordinary things, there is the possibility of satisfaction or even a limit beyond which the pleasure of use or possession turns into an annoyance, but money can be incessantly acquired; in other words, there is never too much money.

The radical aspect of this distinction between the wish for things and the desire for money is the inversion of the commonsensical relation between desire and the object. We can agree that peanuts are conceivable apart from the manner in which they are desired; however, what Marx suggests is that in the case of money, the desire for the object is intimately connected with the object itself. Taking this concept to its extreme, this idea may mean that in the case of money, it is not the object that arouses desire but instead that the object is constituted by desire. Money is the object that makes possible a certain form of desire. This could be read as a definition of money: money is the thing that can be infinitely desired. A well-known view suggests that money is an object believed to be money. Paraphrasing this concept, Marx's comment suggests that what constitutes a certain object as money is a certain form of desire attached to it, that money is an object desired as money.

A second reading brings to mind another possibility suggested by this formulation that in a way transcends the first one. There is a way in which things can be desired endlessly, that is, desired as if they are money; this is the case of luxury goods. In an example that I explore in more detail in the section called "Desire as Substance" in Chapter 3, the firm Patek Philippe sells luxury wrist-watches at prices as high as two million dollars. According to Marx's distinction between the restricted desire for things and the limitless desire for money, an expensive watch is a thing desired as if it were money. (There is no real reason to stop at a few million dollars. If necessary, the market could produce a watch that would cost dozens of millions.)

Later I develop this insight more systematically and argue that we can view things as embodiments of the desire for money. At this point, we already can find within the object itself the distinction that Marx makes between the desire for things and the desire for money. What justifies the outrageous price of such a wristwatch? Diamonds are not an elegant solution for the watch-maker company because they bear no special relation to watches. One can put diamonds on any object.

In the case of the Patek Philippe watch, the price is justified, to a large extent, by special mechanisms such as those that ensure a high degree of accuracy.[3] Of course, the point is that such a precise measure of accuracy—an error of less than one second over a period of twenty-four hours—is something that the watch owner cannot experience concretely. This level of accuracy stretches the logic of luxury to an extreme; this luxuriousness is in contrast to the *thing-ness* of things, to the possessor's immediate experience. In a sense, we see here Marx's distinction between things and money enfolded into the thing itself: a thing may be desired as money insofar as its thingness is somehow cancelled.

This shadow of money in the realm of things provides a key to a remark-able blindness in contemporary economic thought. In our feverishly *economic* era that is haunted by images of wealth, economics consistently fails to ac-count for a notion of the desire for money. Money, it insists, is but a means and, as such, cannot be desired for itself. Indeed, a notion of desire for money upsets the categorical distinction of economics between money and things. This notion permeates the domain of commodities and presents certain things or certain qualities of things as effects of money. It is for this reason that the notion of a desire for money can serve as an Archimedean point for a multidimensional shift in our conception of the economy. The theoretical im-plications run much deeper than the nature of money. They also affect our concept of commodities, private property, economic action, the historicity of the economy, and more.

This chapter explores the reasons for this oversight and many of its implications. It shows how the basic tenets of the economic worldview exclude the possibility of conceiving of money as an object of desire. Indeed, the exclusion of this possibility is fundamental to what can be termed the economic worldview because it bypasses the debates between right and left within the circle of orthodox economics. Monetarists and Keynesians do not disagree about the commonsense assumption that for the individual agent, money is basically a means.[4] To arrive at an alternative economic ontology based on the thinking of Marx and Veblen, we must first explore the current blindness of economics to the concept of the desire for money.

Why Economics Fails to Account for Greed

The idea to base money on desire is radically foreign to orthodox economics. However, it is not the crossing of the difference between subject and object that is problematic for economics. When economists must account for money's value philosophically, they can ground it in a subjective relation. The question is what type of relation they choose. Thus, for example, Milton Friedman bases the value of paper money on thought or belief:

> Private persons accept these pieces of paper because they are confident that others will. The pieces of green paper have value because everybody thinks they have value. Everybody thinks they have value because in everybody's experience they have had value.[5]

What must be acknowledged is that basing the value of money on a belief bypasses, from the very beginning, the possibility of the desire for money. This theoretical basis presupposes that the idea that people want money is something that requires an explanation in contrast to the idea that people want goods, which is considered a fact and self evident.[6] For this reason, the idea of grounding money in thought refers to the basics of the economic worldview, that is, to what economics purports to study and, what is more important, to that of which it refuses to have any knowledge. The obviousness of the desire for goods does not mean that economics knows everything there is to know about this desire but, on the contrary, that economics purposefully refuses to have any type of positive knowledge about this desire.

In her anthropological study of consumption, Mary Douglas points out this peculiarity, claiming that economics cannot answer what appears as the most basic question, namely, "Why do people want goods?"[7] This peculiarity is not at all coincidental. It is in fact implied by the concept of utility, which governs the view of human action held by economics. To sustain a concept of utility, economics must assume that the utility of qualitatively different things can be quantitatively compared, that is to say, one can compare the utility of a certain medicine with that of, for example, a car. But this means that, in theory, utility must ignore any positive knowledge of the enjoyment or use of things. This means that the knowledge of utility itself—like the knowledge a physician has of a medicine or an engineer has of a car—cannot, in principle, be economic knowledge. This is a basic but paradoxical characteristic of contemporary economic thought: utility plays a central role in its philosophy, yet economics can sustain the concept of utility only insofar as it knows nothing positive about it.

Economics does not see this paradox as a weakness but simply as a formulation of the discipline's assumption that economics is a science of means. Returning to Friedman's grounding of money in thought, we can formulate the underlying logic in terms of utility. When Friedman explains the value of money by the goods it can buy, he actually explains what he does not know (why people want money) by what he cannot, in principle, know (why people want goods).[8]

Paradoxical as it may seem, there is actually something convenient in this theoretical position, which opens a black hole within the theory and in which one can ground any imaginable human behavior. This may be one of the reasons for the unequivocal dominance of the concept of utility over the economic view of human action. It is its discord with the concept of utility that explains why economics cannot account for the notion of a desire for money. This point cannot be overemphasized. The specter of greed and other obsessions with money haunt our popular imaginings of the economy, yet economic theory cannot even begin to conceptualize this desire.

Following the 2008 financial meltdown, Wall Street itself became synonymous with greed. Titles such as *And Then the Roof Caved In: How Wall Street's Greed and Stupidity Brought Capitalism to Its Knees* identified greed as the cause of the crisis. A symptomatic point is the way an official economic view engaged the subject. In the public atmosphere that surrounded the crisis, even the report of the governmental inquiry commission could not ignore the question of greed. The majority report mentions the term at a strategic point.

Immediately following the list of summary conclusions, the report suggests that the conclusions should be viewed "in the context of human nature and individual and societal responsibility" and then states that "to pin this crisis on mortal flaws like greed and hubris would be simplistic. It was the failure to account for human weakness that is relevant to this crisis."[9] However, throughout the four hundred pages of the rest of the majority report, the term is not mentioned again, which makes one wonder whether the commission is reiterating what it warns us about, namely, the failure to account for greed.

This failure is not accidental but actually implied by the terminology of the report, that is, by the categorizing of greed as "a human weakness." What this reflects is an inability of economic discourse to envision greed as an economic phenomenon—to conceive of greed not as an aberration but as embedded in the normal course of action and in economic institutions, practices, and habits of thought. The dismissal of this possibility should not come as a surprise because the idea of economic action oriented toward money, so central to the lay view of the economy, is rejected completely throughout the political spectrum of orthodox economics. To see how this rejection traverses what is considered to be the main lines of polemics within orthodox economics, I mention just two examples from the opposite extremes of this spectrum: Friedrich von Hayek, the spiritual father of neo-liberalism to the right, and John Maynard Keynes, a pillar of the idea of the welfare state, to the left.

In his most explicitly ideological book *The Road to Serfdom*, Hayek conflates political freedom with economic freedom. For that purpose he rejects the tendency to undermine economic issues as *merely economic*. This approach, he writes,

> is largely a consequence of the erroneous belief that there are purely economic ends distinguished from the other ends of life. Yet apart from the pathological case of the miser, there is no such thing. The ultimate ends of the activities of reasonable beings are never economic. Strictly speaking there is no "economic motive" but only economic factors conditioning our striving for other ends.[10]

Hayek dismisses activity directed at money as an economically pathological behavior. Behind this dismissal one can see how ideology permeates theory in economics. Here the rejection of the possibility of economic ends is related not only to the concept of utility, but also to the moral affirmation of the market.

This becomes evident if we consider how Hayek affirms the economic sphere as a tool for managing causes. "So long as we can freely dispose over our income and all our possessions," he writes, "economic loss will always deprive us only of what we regard as the least important of the desires we are able to satisfy."[11] What Hayek invokes here is nothing but the basic principle of diminishing marginal utility. But what should be noted is how easily this allegedly technical tool of economic analysis is transformed into an ethical claim.

The concept of *marginalism*—which brought on the birth of neo-classical economics at the end of the nineteenth century and that dominates microeconomic theory to this day—posits that prices are set by what happens *at the margin*, not by an internal quality of goods, but by their marginal utility, that is, by the utility of the last unit purchased. To express this concept in concrete terms, one could say that the utility one obtains from an additional T-shirt is diminished by the number of T-shirts one already has. For this reason there is a point at which one will stop spending money on T-shirts and start purchasing something else instead, for example, bread.

The whole drama of price setting is located at this marginal point, in the interplay between diminishing marginal utility and rising marginal cost. Undoubtedly, the economic point of view owes much of its *imperialist* power to its ability to construct a magnificent theoretical edifice upon such a simple intuition regarding human activity. Hayek's formulation reveals how an entire ethic is ingrained in this allegedly technical tool of economic analysis. Because any cause, noble as it might be, can be subjected to this mechanism, the market is the ethically responsible way to commit to causes. As noble as our values might be, it is only this market mechanism that forces us to prioritize them and to determine what we are willing to sacrifice for them.

In this theoretical context, far from being a despicable haggle, pricing a value is the only ethically responsible way to commit to it. Thus, if we believe, for example, in the promotion of world peace, the protection of wildlife, and the elevation of modern human spirituality, it is only a market mechanism that forces us to show a real commitment to any of them. But note that if, in addition to these causes, we also want money, then the whole edifice is jeopardized: the authenticity of noble causes is endangered once they are suspected of masking a will to profit or of being motivated by considerations of profit.

It is no coincidence, therefore, that when utility is confronted by the more direct manifestations of desire for money, the ideological nature of the concept of utility emerges. The economic mind can always supply a specific type of utility that lies behind the endless pursuit of wealth: what Bill Gates really wants is honor, respect, social status, influence, power, or anything but money. But, of course, what this invocation really reveals is the empty nature of the concept as a theoretical patchwork that enables theory to dispense with the need to confront reality. Recalling Karl Popper's falsifiability principle, this infinite flexibility of the concept of utility and the fact that it is all too easy to apply to any imagined circumstance testifies to the fact that it is not a scientific concept at all.[12]

The link between the rejection of greed and this pivotal concept of utility may explain why we find a similar position at the opposite end of the political spectrum, namely, in Keynes. Indeed, one finds in Keynes's macroeconomic theory a counterweight to the rigid utilitarian microeconomic framework that is centered on utility-seeking individuals. But because macroeconomics failed to elaborate a full alternative view of human action, even Keynes is susceptible to the basic assumptions implied by the concept of utility.

Thus, in his famous utopian essay "Economic Possibilities for Our Grandchildren," Keynes famously describes greed as a "disgusting morbidity." In this essay, written during the great depression of the 1930s, Keynes speculates on a future when humanity will completely overcome the problem of scarcity. In fact, he declares at the outset that the predicaments of his times are a consequence of the difficulties of humanity in adjusting to the upcoming state of affluence. It will take a hundred years or so to become accustomed to this state, and it will require deep changes. Thus, he writes that in this future time,

> [t]he love of money as a possession—as distinguished from the love of money as a means to the enjoyments and realities of life—will be recognised for what it is, a somewhat disgusting morbidity, one of those semi-criminal, semi-pathological propensities which one hands over with a shudder to the specialists in mental disease.[13]

If one is struck by the specificity of this imagining of greed, one should turn to the next page of the essay, where Keynes hints that he indeed has the Jew on his mind while he is writing. He suggests there that

> perhaps it is not an accident that the race which did most to bring the promise of immortality into the heart and essence of our religions has also

done most for the principle of compound interest and particularly loves this most purposive of human institutions.[14]

What should be noted is that this prejudice of Keynes actually fulfills a theoretical role. Unlike Hayek, and precisely because he holds such a broad historical view, Keynes is forced to attribute a positive function to "purposive" economic action, which prefers some future gain to present "enjoyments and realities of life." Four hundred years marked by such action brought humanity to the verge of prosperity. However, in the current state of affairs, this type of action, epitomized in the principle of compound interest, has become an obstacle rather than a tool on the road to real prosperity. Like the Jew in various anti-Semitic fantasies, this type of action has accomplished its historical role and must pave the way to a new economic framework. The identification of compound interest with the Jew enables Keynes to both attribute a positive function to the desire for money and to exclude it as pathology.

In fact, Keynes actually brings us a long way toward the position that is necessary to render greed as an economic phenomenon. If we clear away the prejudiced overtone, we find that what he suggests is that greed is a necessary pathology. As a human behavior, it is pathological but nonetheless is steeped in the most basic economic practices such as compound interest. Taking this one step further, what is required is a way to conceive of greed in the context of a pathological object rather than a pathological subject.

The Pathological Object

Setting aside Hayek and Keynes, there is one crucial text in the orthodox economic tradition that provides a brilliant moral affirmation of the motive of pure profit-seeking activity. It is Friedman's famous critique of the idea of corporate social responsibility—the idea that businesses should be involved in the community and support social causes such as ecological aims. Friedman argues that the sole social cause to which business should be committed is that of making money—"The Social Responsibility of Business Is to Increase Its Profits," as the title of the article declares.

Friedman's acute assertion is that a corporate manager who speaks of the social responsibility of a firm is either stealing from someone or lying to everyone. To submit resources of the organization to social causes, a corporate manager must draw them from somewhere. And there are only three possible sources, none of which willingly chose to contribute to the cause: (1) the workers who must devote extra, unpaid labor for the cause; (2) the customers who must pay more for the product; or (3) the stockholders who must forgo potential profit. Friedman admits to one additional possibility, namely, that the manager is actually striving to acquire a good reputation for his organization in order to increase its profits in the long run. In that case there is no specific economic sense to his moral flaw; he is simply lying: he is speaking about social responsibility whereas his real goal is profit.[15]

There is something unshakeable in Friedman's argument. The key is to read it side by side with Hayek's and Keynes's denunciations of greed. Recalling Friedman's ideological alliance with Hayek, the point is not to decide between them, but to accept them both as two parts of the same picture. The picture in this case is that what is pathological, irrational, and ethically disgusting when manifested by a person becomes the complete opposite when attributed to the—to use Friedman's term—"artificial person" of the corporation.

Any theoretical account of greed must take as its starting point the way greed is suspended between these two persons: real people can only want things, whereas artificial persons can only want money. The complete picture suggests that to conceive of greed as an economic phenomenon, we must posit it at the limit of subjectivity or consider it by transcending the opposition between subject and object. The term "artificial person" implies a crossing of this opposition. The artificial person is an economic subject that has some sort of objective existence. Its conduct is steeped in objective, impersonal laws. We usually refer to it as a subject in legal contexts (corporations that bear legal responsibility, etc.). However, when we read Friedman's argument against the background of the economic abhorrence of greed, we must also consider the corporation as a moral subject and as a subject of desire, as a subject having a drive or will.

The corporation wills that which is impossible for people to will. This situation also can be described the other way around, namely, from the perspective of real people. The corporation is not only a subject having an objective existence; it is also an organization comprising real people—workers, managers, stockholders. And the marvelous point is that when these real people are viewed through the lenses of the artificial person, they emerge as the mirror image of the way economics conceives of people: whereas a real person wants *real* things, when we abstract all concrete properties of the person and arrive at the anonymous stockholder, the only thing we can legitimately assume that he or she wants is money.

The distinction between subject and object is thus traversed in two complementary ways. On the one hand, we find an echo of the subject in the object or an object that should be conceived of in terms of a subject: the corporation wills what a real person cannot will. On the other hand, we find the object in the subject: viewed as nodes in the impersonal, objective entity of the corporation, real people want what they cannot will when apprehended directly.

This confrontation of the abhorrence of greed as a personal attitude with its affirmation as an impersonal phenomenon points to the way to incorporate it in economic theory. Greed can be conceived of as an economic phenomenon when it is viewed not as a subjective attitude or a psychological fault but when it transcends the distinction between subject and object. Desire for money can take effect only when it is mediated, in various ways, through the object. The corporation is one such way. However, we can point to others as well, such as the repeated gesture of the participants in the reality-television show *Survivor*, who suspend their personalities in playing the game, committing deeds opposed to their values in order to win the big money prize.

The formal parallel of this type of action to economic conduct testifies that in this case, the game is not simply a suspension of social reality but is in itself a unique social reality, proper to economic conduct. The contender who nullifies his or her own beliefs to win the game corresponds with the corporate stockholder who, once abstracted from any subjective attributes, is assumed to want only profit. This contender also corresponds with a manager who justifies a cruel act, such as cutting back jobs to maximize profitability, by invoking the objective laws of the economy. The ultimate masquerade of *Survivor* is found in the invocation of nature. The reality it conveys is not that of bare nature but the social reality of money.

The ideal representation of this type of action already can be found in the paradigmatic representation of greed in the Greek myth of Midas. King Midas wished that everything he touched would turn into gold, only to witness the horrid literal fulfillment of his wish as his food and drink turned to gold in his mouth. (In Nathaniel Hawthorne's harsh version, Midas turns his daughter Marigold into a statue of gold.)

More than a grain of truth is encoded in the myth. First, it sets an opposition between greed and mundane wishes for things and makes greed conditional on the annulment of wishes for things (even a simple enjoyment of breakfast becomes impossible for Midas). But second, and more importantly, what the myth reveals is that the desire for money, in its pure form, can take effect only when it is transferred to the object. Midas reveals the true nature of his wish only when it confronts him as an animate, external object that threatens his very existence.

These are actually two complementary conditions. A desire that annuls all subjective ends can appear only as emanating from the object. In this sense, the myth of Midas provides the basic matrix for the countless texts that associate the desire for money with death. Midas's myth is indeed an imaginary artifact, yet it can be read as the vanishing point that confers meaning to the opposition between the rejection of greed by economics as a personal, subjective attitude and its affirmation as an impersonal, objective reality. In a sense, like Midas, we evidence the desire for money materialized in the form of an ominous object, precisely in Friedman's artificial person of the corporation.

In theoretical terms, the lessons from the myth require a new formulation of the meaning of objects and objectivity in the economy. In the commonsensical economic view, objectivity refers simply to conditions that are external to the subject and independent of it. The confrontation between Friedman and Hayek suggests a different view, in which objectivity is not simply external to the subject but refers to an aspect of economic reality that resists subjectivization and cannot be incorporated within the subject's perspective. It suggests objectivity not as external but as exteriorized. It requires, in other words, a consideration of topology, best captured in Jacques Lacan's idea of "extimacy," where an innermost kernel of the subject appears external to it. That is precisely the status of Midas's wish: his real desire appears to him in the form of an external, ominous object.

The need to account for this topology leads us to the strange situation, where to read Friedman and Hayek together, we must turn to Marx. We can find a theoretical support for the topology of greed in Marx's notion of *personification*, which often accompanies his reference to the capitalist. We can find it first in his foreword to *Capital*, were he guides us, saying,

> I do not by any means depict the capitalist and the landowner in rosy colours. But individuals are dealt with here only in so far as they are the

personifications of economic categories, the bearers of particular class relations and interests.[16]

This may seem to be a simple didactic remark, but it actually points to an alternative economic ontology that goes beyond the orthodox framework.

By referring to the capitalist as a personification of the abstract category of capital, Marx is not simply using an acronym or a didactic illustration for the impersonal forces of the economy. Rather, personification points to a mode of being for both economic categories and economic agents. On the one hand, abstract, impersonal economic categories, such as class or capital, can only exist insofar as they are carried by persons. But more importantly, personification refers also to the manner in which a person carries an abstract, impersonal category. It suggests a fundamental distance between the individual and the economic role he plays. It suggests that the economic agent is constituted by a gesture of distancing from oneself; that in the economy, people behave precisely as when playing a role, which is far from the economic conception of the agent whose behavior is guided solely by preferences and satisfactions.

In other words, capital can exist only insofar as people conduct their business as capitalists—that is the obvious half of the picture—but conducting business as capitalists implies a sense of role playing, of suspending one's immediate wants and satisfactions. Most literally, the notion of personification means that a capitalist is one who behaves *as if* one is a capitalist (just like Friedman's corporate manager, who behaves as if his sole purpose is profit).

What Money Wants

The idea that desire is not simply a relation to a given object, but inscribed on the object itself, runs through Marx's work from his early writings to *Capital*. In the early *Economic and Philosophic Manuscripts of 1844*, we find a comment that situates desire in the basic structure of the monetary economy. Marx notes that "*Money*, inasmuch as it possesses the *property* of being able to buy everything and appropriate all objects, is the *object* most worth possessing."[17]

This comment seems trivial since it pertains to nothing more than the basic structure of any monetary economy. Two points must be emphasized relating to Marx's remark. First, here Marx indeed refers to the only thing we can know for sure about money if we purge from our thought shady metaphysical ideas such as utility. If it is not utility that distinguishes between money and things, then the only thing we know is that in a monetary economy, one can buy anything with money, but it is much harder to buy money with things. Second, Marx outlines a notion of the desire for money on the basic structure of objects and their relations.

His comment points to the difference between the desire for things and the desire for money; or better, it distinguishes between things and money according to the forms of desire related to each. The first form of desire is the commonsensical one, in which money serves our desire for objects. However, beyond this appears another form, a dimension where precisely because money can buy any object, it is more desirable than any object. There is actually something quite reasonable in this form of desire. There is a sense in which money is worth more than any specific object that it can buy precisely because it can buy other objects as well.[18] However, this sense does not allow for a conceptualization in economic terms. However, it captures quite clearly the difference between the desire for things and the desire for money. Whereas the former ideally aims at some horizon of satisfaction in the object desired, the latter, implicated with the infinite potential embodied in money, involves indefinite deferral for which any concrete object is but a frustration.

This implied structure of desire strictly parallels the Lacanian concept of desire in its difference from demand. The fundamental similarity is found in the way desire as an abstract, insatiable thrust appears through the frustration entailed with the satisfaction of every concrete, specific wish/demand. In Lacan's thought, demand is the verbal expression of pre-verbal need. As such it can never be identical with need: the very act of articulating need creates a gap between demand and need, a gap that Lacan terms "primal repression." This gap then reemerges *beyond* demand, in the form of desire.

Demand implies a certain residue that on another level enters an intersubjective framework between the subject and the addressee of its demand. Thus, a thing can satisfy demand but in the intersubjective context, it is perceived as a failed proof of unconditional love. Thus, Lacan writes, "desire is neither the appetite for satisfaction nor the demand for love, but the difference that results from the subtraction of the first from the second, the phenomenon of their splitting."[19] To give a simple example, when a child asks his parents to buy a toy, there is so much more the child may actually be requesting—the toy itself, that *you* buy him or her the toy, that you buy the toy *for him* or *her* and *not* for his or her brothers or sisters—that it is no wonder that the actual toy may prove disappointing.

These main lines of the interplay between demand and desire can be traced in the relation between the desire for objects and the desire for money that Marx finds in the basic structure of the monetary economy. Money can buy different concrete things, but it is the concreteness of these things that gives rise to the indefinite desire for money. The desire for money emerges through the frustration that accompanies anything that money can buy, precisely because of its concreteness.

Returning to Marx, the comment from the *Manuscripts* may seem typical of his early, humanist thought. But a close consideration reveals in it the beginning of a stubborn theoretical effort that runs throughout Marx's thought to his mature work. In *Capital* we find the most elaborate formulation of the idea that the subject's desire is encoded in the system of objects. This idea informs the overall makeup of chapter 4 in *Capital*, titled "The General Formula for Capital," in which Marx elaborates for the first time this pivotal concept. The point to note is that the chapter begins with a long account of objects, and the ways in which they are exchanged, with little reference to people.

Marx defines capital by the difference between the two forms of circulation of things. The first is the direct form, denoted C-M-C, in which commodities are exchanged for money only to be exchanged into other commodities. This form of circulation still represents the orthodox conception of money and economy, in which money is but a means for accelerating the exchange of goods. It conforms to the idea of a logical primacy of the real economy, with the bottom line being that the economy is concerned with the distribution of things. However, in Marx's thought this form of circulation serves only as a theoretical background against which we can pose the defining feature of capitalism, namely, the famous M-C-M' circulation, where money is exchanged for commodities, only to be exchanged back to money of a greater sum.

This circulation describes, for example, the mode of conduct of an entrepreneur who buys commodities (possibly including labor power) to obtain profit. The difference between the two circulations is far from technical. The capitalist form of circulation entails a radical alternative to the orthodox economic view. From the perspective of the circulation of capital, that which is *real* in the economy is the money movement, whereas *things*—commodities—are mere effects. What should be noted is that the M-C-M' circulation describes, among other things, a form of desire in the language of objects. It refers exclusively to objects (money and commodities) but in the exchanges between them, it outlines a form of an endless drive, a drive for indefinite expansion.

Because M and M′ are merely exchange values, there is no point in this circulation other than quantitative increase. Furthermore, having only quantitative value, as opposed to use value as its goal, there is no particular end to this increase. The £100 that turned into £110 in this circulation can enter circulation again to become £120. In Marx's words: in this circulation "the end and the beginning are the same . . . and this very fact makes the movement an endless one."[20]

The most telling point is that only at that point does Marx bring the capitalist into the picture. The capitalist appears—for the first time in the book (apart from the foreword)—immediately after his desire is outlined in terms of objects. I quote at length the paragraph where he makes his first appearance:

> As the conscious bearer of this movement, the possessor of money becomes a capitalist. His person, or rather his pocket, is the point from which the money starts, and to which it returns. The objective content of the circulation we have been discussing—the valorization of value—is his subjective purpose, and it is only in so far as the appropriation of ever more wealth in the abstract is the sole driving force behind his operations that he functions as a capitalist, i.e., as capital personified and endowed with consciousness and a will. Use values must therefore never be treated as the immediate aim of the capitalist; nor must the profit on any single transaction. His aim is rather the unceasing movement of profit making. This boundless drive for enrichment, this passionate chase after value, is common to the capitalist and the miser; but while the miser is merely a capitalist gone mad, the capitalist is a rational miser. The ceaseless augmentation of value, which the miser seeks to attain by saving his money from circulation, is achieved by the more acute capitalist by means of throwing his money again and again into circulation.[21]

When the possessor of money follows the objective form of circulation (objective in the sense that it is described in terms of objects), he becomes a capitalist. He behaves as "capital personified and endowed with consciousness and a will." His conduct is guided by a "boundless drive for enrichment" and appears as an "unceasing movement of profit making." What this means is that he embodies in his person a form of desire that is already inscribed in the sphere of objects.

This view naturally raises questions. How does an object—money—induce this type of desire on its possessor? How does it force the capitalist into this frantic, aimless activity? How does fortune give rise to an insatiable appetite for more fortune? In fact, these questions are misleading. An inert object cannot push its owner to action. Indeed, there is always the theoretical possibility that a person would stop aimlessly pursuing wealth and decide, instead, to enjoy life.

In the first, *objective* part of Marx's chapter, this possibility is acknowledged thus: if the £110 made out of the initial £100 "is now spent as money, it ceases to play its part. It is no longer capital."[22] This possibility is then echoed in the quoted paragraph, which begins with an invocation of a certain form of choice. The possessor of money need not behave according to the objective circulation of commodities. But to the extent that one does behave in this way, one is indeed a capitalist as Marx writes, "as the conscious bearer of this movement, the possessor of money becomes a capitalist." Taken together, these two qualifications seem to outline a tautology: when the possessor of money behaves according to the circulation of capital, he is a capitalist; and when he does not, he is no longer a capitalist.

The correct way to read this paragraph is not as describing a causal relation (how capital motivates the capitalist), but as an analysis of the form of action of the capitalist. In this reading, the content that rescues the paragraph from becoming an empty tautology is the crossing of the opposition between objective and subjective, which characterizes the capitalist's conduct: "the objective content of the circulation [...] is his subjective purpose." That is, simply, the capitalist is the subject who makes the objective content of the circulation into his subjective purpose.

In a sense this reading implies a choice, a decision to be a capitalist. This in itself should not deter us because what is entailed here is actually a paradigmatic example of willful submission—a moment that in many ways Marx has posed as a challenge to any critical political thought. Of course, we usually attribute willful submission to the exploited and the suppressed. We invoke ideology as an answer to the basic enigma of why do the oppressed voice the message of the oppressor.

However, evidence to the generality of this moment of willful submission is the fact that here Marx attributes it to the exploiter and not only to the exploited. Being a capitalist involves a gesture of willfully submitting oneself to the object, of surrendering one's subjectivity to the objective form of the circulation. This originary gesture of the capitalist deserves the name *submission* not simply because the capitalist follows the rules of the market, but because this choice involves an effacement of subjectivity. This is most evident in the assertion that "use values must therefore never be treated as the immediate aim of the capitalist," that is, the capitalist's conduct is defined by a negation of the immediate reality of things, of the uses and satisfaction they provide to people, and through this negation, there emerges the drive for appropriation of "wealth in the abstract." It is a gesture of renouncing all subjective whims and desires.

The conduct of the capitalist can be thus termed objective in two complementary senses, from without and from within. On the one hand, the conduct is objective in the sense of conforming to external reality—to the circulation of commodities, to the prevalent economic conduct, to the rules of the market, and so on. On the other hand what Marx eventually claims is that this sense of external objectivity necessarily implies a further one—of objectivity as a specific form of subjectivity. It entails a subject position characterized by a renunciation of subjectivity.

This relation between subjectivity and objectivity can be described from the other end of the opposition, namely, from the perspective of the object. In a sense Marx inquires here after the mode of objectivity of capital, the sense in which capital can indeed be conceived of as objective reality. Viewed from this perspective, what Marx suggests here is that the existence of capital necessarily implies a certain subjective residue marked by objectivity.

The objective existence of capital implies the subjective position of the capitalist who behaves according to objective imperatives that emanate directly from the market. In a sense what Marx analyzes here is the *condition of possibility* of capital. To conclude briefly: *the objective existence of capital implies the subjective position of the capitalist who behaves as if money itself wants to accumulate.* This formulation most fully realizes the scandalous potential of *Capital*. It should be read not as an analysis of the way people use the market to increase their wealth but rather as a work that describes how money wants to accumulate.

There is more to Marx's analysis of the objectivity of capital. Another point is that the objectivity of capital is itself a condition of its existence. Objectivity is not simply a predicate of capital. For capital to exist, it must exist objectively in the sense of annulling all subjective goals of the capitalist. In a way, from this perspective, Midas's lethal touch becomes actualized in capital. The insatiable desire for money can indeed take effect only when it is embodied in an object that confronts subjects as an external lethal force.

At this stage we can finally return to the strange inability of economics to conceptualize greed. The unthinkable nature of greed does not, obviously, result from the fact that greed is a non-economic topic, but rather that it reflects its location beyond or at the limit of the subject. For orthodox economics, greed is unthinkable because it transcends the horizon of utility-seeking individuals. It cannot be fully incorporated within the perspective of individuals. However, for Marx this is precisely what makes it an *objective* economic reality. In this sense the economic oversight of greed is not simply a theoretical mistake. It is an ideological error in the sense of an error that partakes in the social reality it observes. The unthinkable nature of greed is actually a part of its structure.

Is Greed Inherent in Money?

Marx's thought implies a conceptualization of the desire for money as embedded in the economic object of capital. The question that arises is whether this desire also is related to money and whether it is related to money in its ordinary appearance, that is, as it is used in everyday conduct—the money we use to buy a cup of coffee or a newspaper. In terms of theory, this is the question of whether capital is already implied by money or whether it is only a specific use of money. This question is also highly relevant to the discourse about the 2008 financial crisis. The prevalent narrative in this respect separates Wall Street from Main Street or the financial economy from the real economy. The crisis, according to this narrative, originates in a certain pathology that is related to the arcane economic sphere of finance but like a parasite, it spreads to contaminate the whole economy until every citizen suffers from its effects. This narrative correlates with the insistence of orthodox economics on the primacy of the real economy, but it seems to dominate even critical perspectives on the economy (even the term *money* seems somewhat quaint in the critical discourse about finance).

This conception can be traced even in Don DeLillo's literary approach to finance in *Cosmopolis*, which describes the journey of the international financier Eric Packer across Manhattan to get a haircut. During the journey in his limousine, filled with screens and computer monitors, Packer loses the assets of his clients in a bet against the yen. This literary device reflects the assumption that finance occurs in no-place, always remote from everyday experience. It is represented through double detachment, in the detached space of the limousine and in Packer's detached attitude toward his business.

Marx seems to suggest a different view, in which finance is not simply a specific use of money but is already implied by its ontology. At its beginning, the fourth chapter of *Capital* states that the conceptual transition from commodities to money is entailed with the transition from money to capital.

> If we disregard the material content of the circulation of commodities, i.e., the exchange of the various use values, and consider only the economic forms brought into being by this process, we find that its ultimate product is money. This ultimate product of commodity circulation is the first form of appearance of capital.[23]

In other words, money is to commodities what capital is to money. What are the grounds for this homology? We arrive at money by abstracting all of the *thingness* from commodities. That is a premise of Marx's concept of commodity money: money is a commodity like all others yet abstracted from use value. But this abstraction from thingness already implies capital. The unceasing movement or the boundless drive of capital derives from money's lack of thingness.

This characteristic provides us with one more opportunity to formulate the difference between Marx and the economists. Just like Marx, contemporary economics assumes that money is not a thing. That is what lies at the root of the conception of money as a tool in the administration of things. The difference, however, is that Marx considers this absence of thingness as a positive quality of money. This quality of money enables him to conceptualize the M-C-M' circulation. The drive for endless accumulation results precisely from M and M' having no thing-qualities, and its conceptualization requires that this absence of thing-qualities be considered as having real economic effects.

Later we shall see that this view of money is supported by a historical ontology: history, as the prototypical form of real absence, is the ultimate horizon that confers positive reality on other absences. In the meantime we can point out how the topology of money mirrors the topology of the desiring subject, by invoking again the Lacanian concept of extimacy. For the capitalist, money is in the extimacy of the subject, an external object that carries the deepest, disavowed drive of the subject.

Similarly, with reference to capital, money is in the extimacy of things. It is, on the one hand, an external member to the sphere of things, an additional *no-thing*. However, on the other hand, it is also the innermost secret of things. It is what remains when we abstract all the contingent properties from things. This homology points to a general possibility of weaving desire into the history of money or of conceiving of desire as the historical substance of money. Money emerges as an object abstracted of thingness, and what sustains its value through time is a formation of desire that attaches to its nothingness.

To illustrate this idea in a concrete way, consider one of the most famous, realist literary representations of greed from Frank Norris's *McTeague*. The novel tells the story of the disintegration of the marriage and lives of Trina and the brutal dentist McTeague. In the beginning of the novel, Trina wins some money in a lottery and deposits it with her uncle for a monthly interest. Despite her husband's appeals, she refrains from withdrawing the principal sum during the calamities they suffer when McTeague is forced to close down his practice.

After McTeague abandons her, Trina withdraws her money to take pleasure of it in the solitude of her room. With shaking fingers, she empties the sack of money on her bed.

> Then she opened her trunk, and taking thence the brass match-box and chamois-skin bag added their contents to the pile. Next she laid herself upon the bed and gathered the gleaming heaps of gold pieces to her with both arms, burying her face in them with long sighs of unspeakable delight.[24]

The first thought that comes to mind with reference to this scene is Marx's distinction between the irrational miser who clings to his money and the rational capitalist who knows that one has to temporarily part from it to nurture it. But the scene also highlights the connection that Marx establishes between these two figures: "while the miser is merely a capitalist gone mad, the capitalist is a rational miser." Trina's direct pleasure of money comprises an indulgence in its uselessness. It articulates the fact that uselessness is not simply an absence of use (as meant by the economic emphasis on money as neutral) but a spectacular quality of gold. Yet this irrational conduct echoes the rational capitalist one, which never aims at use values, but at "the unceasing movement of profit making."

Of course, Trina's act manifests a perverse pleasure of money and, as such, can be dismissed merely as one possible relation to money and not as a necessary condition of it. To see how the financial motive may be embedded in everyday money, we must look more closely into the financial crisis.

Shopping as Finance

The introduction to the Financial Crisis Inquiry Commission (FCIC) report includes two interesting references to science fiction. The first one refers to the situation on the eve of the crisis:

> On the surface, it looked like prosperity [. . . .] But underneath something was going wrong. Like a science fiction movie in which ordinary household objects turn hostile, familiar market mechanisms were being transformed.[25]

By now we should know that such tropes must be taken seriously, not simply as literary embellishments but as points that unearth ontological difficulty.

The science fiction metaphor captures the topology of the financial and real economies, Wall Street and Main Street. Like so many films of this genre (*Alien*, *Invasion of the Body Snatchers*, and many others), the metaphor alludes to a situation of a coincidence of the exterior and the interior, of an external faceless danger that lurks paradoxically from within, of an exterior force that annuls the very sense of the reality of the immediate surroundings. The metaphoric language is necessary because this topology is foreign to the orthodox economic view, which renders the real economy as logically preceding finance. The science fiction metaphor is required to account for the subversion of these references that surface at times of financial crisis.

In his book about the great crash of 1929, John Kenneth Galbraith pointed to this subversion as characteristic of any financial crisis. In a financial bubble, he wrote,

> [A]ll aspects of property ownership become irrelevant except the prospect for an early rise in price. Income from the property, or enjoyment of its use, or even its long-run worth [become] academic.[26]

A certain object—from tulip bulbs in seventeenth century Amsterdam to real estate lots in the 1920s Florida land boom—becomes caught in a financial bubble when it is detached from its real properties and is considered only in terms of profit making.[27]

It is here that Marx's topology of money as a no-thing, which nonetheless embodies an inner principle of all commodities, becomes crucial. In Marxian terms we can say that in being abstracted from any real quality, the object of a financial bubble becomes a form of money. In the *Grundrisse* Marx provides a perfect terminology for this topology when he refers to the "money-property" of things. Exchange value is the "immanent money-property" of commodities, and we can speak of money proper when this property "separates itself" from the commodity in the form of money.[28]

Yet what seems to be unique to the 2008 bubble was the object involved—not exotic, unknown, far-away objects like tulip bulbs, Florida lots, stocks of unknown ventures in the South Sea bubble of the 1700s, or Internet stocks in the 1990s—but nothing less than the American home, an epitome of the real economy if there ever was one. As the FCIC report states: "it involved not just another commodity but a building block of community and social life and a cornerstone of the economy: the family home."[29]

Taking this claim literally, the report seems to suggest that finance has penetrated the fundamentals of social life. Indeed, one can cling to the narrative of finance as parasite and argue that finance has simply become so vast in scope that its breakdown inevitably undermines the foundations of the real economy and social life. However, this narrative ignores the fact that the housing bubble that exploded in 2008 was entangled with everyday life to begin with.

What had driven the bubble were, to a large extent, loans taken as means to extract cash from the growing equity of American homes, a large part of which was channeled to consumption. The FCIC report notes in this respect the inflationary use of mortgage products with "strange sounding names": "Alt-A, subprime, I-O (interest-only), low-doc, no-doc, or ninja (no income, no job, no assets) loans; [...] liar loans; piggyback second mortgages; payment-option or pick-a-pay adjustable rate mortgages."[30]

Reading these arcane names one might recall Marx's caution against the tendency to compare money to language. If compared at all, money is to be compared to a *foreign* language. According to Marx, language does not dissolve the peculiarity of ideas articulated in it, as prices do to commodities.

Paraphrasing him, in the financial crisis we saw the foreign language of money dissolve real things.[31]

However, a Federal Reserve working paper, authored by Alan Greenspan and James Kennedy in 2007, spelled out the uses of cash from those loans. It estimated that in 2005 more than 500 billion dollars were extracted through loans based on home equity (compared to about 50 billion dollars in 1991). Out of the 500 billion dollars, more than 260 billion were spent on consumption and repayment of former non-mortgage debt (i.e., on past consumption). Much of the rest went to home improvement and real estate investment, which kept fueling the rising prices of homes (which in part were to be extracted, again, for consumption).[32]

It appears that a unique characteristic of the 2008 crisis was that consumption played a defined role in the bubble. The extraction of cash from rising home equity for consumer demands stimulated the mortgage market, while the cash extracted served in part to drive the rising level of real estate prices higher. This entanglement of finance with everyday consumption calls for a new conceptualization of the relations between the two. It forces us to examine the possibility that the contemporary consumer economy and finance are more intimately related than what the narrative of finance as a parasite implies. Maybe it is not simply that the financial crisis has shaken the consumer economy, but that the consumer economy, in its everyday aspect, was in some sense financial to begin with.

This is precisely the point raised by the 2009 romantic comedy *Confessions of a Shopaholic* (based on a series of novels written by Sophie Kinsella). The movie's protagonist Rebecca Morewood is a young, single woman addicted to fashion. Her entire apartment is stuffed with the clothes she buys, and her paychecks are immediately swallowed by the bills she can never fully pay. Throughout the movie she is constantly on the run from an annoying debt collector.

Rebecca works as a journalist for a small gardening magazine, but her dream is to get a job at the prestigious fashion magazine *Alette*. However, through a bizarre narrative twist, she ends up working, of all places, at the financial magazine *Successful Saving*. In a desperate attempt to attract the attention of the fashion editor of *Alette*, Rebecca had written her a letter describing how she picks the right shoes to buy. Instead, the letter arrived at the office of the editor of the financial magazine, and he interprets it as a sophisticated allegory about how to pick the right investment assets. He hires Rebecca as a columnist, and overnight her column becomes a hit for the dull magazine. Although she knows little about finance and money management, she succeeds in writing about these topics in metaphors taken from the world of shopping.

Maybe this narrative should be taken as an economic observation. It suggests that shopping is actually a type of financial activity. Of course, at first glance, shopping is the very opposite of finance, not only because it deals with the purchase of commodities—real things—rather than with money, but also because it entails spending money rather than making profits. Nevertheless, there is a logic that precisely situates a financial motive in this excessive form of consumption. Defining finance not simply in terms of profits but through its topology, its complex relations to the real economy, we can come up with a very broad definition that also includes shopping: finance is the economic activity in which things are the necessary placeholders in the movement of money.

The financier typically exchanges assets of different forms, with different levels of proximity to things: money, bonds, stocks, commodities, futures, and so on. An object may enter these transactions as a position in a process whose end is defined in money terms. That is why, from the financial point of view, things are epiphenomena of money. But in a sense this is true also for the shopaholic. If the shopaholic is the person who is interested in the purchase of things more than in the things themselves, then in the broad view his or her activity is financial. As in finance, for the shopaholic things are necessary placeholders in the movement of money. The only difference is that for the financier, things serve the purpose of increasing monetary value, whereas for the shopaholic, things serve the need to spend money. But the status of things in relation to money is similar: the shopaholic needs to buy, and things are his or her only way to do so.

Georg Simmel provides a basic insight that pertains to this parallel when he notes in *The Philosophy of Money* that "[e]xtravagance is more closely related to avarice than the opposition of these two phenomena would seem to indicate."[33] The basis for this surprising proximity is that both the miser and the spendthrift, in two different ways, prefer money to the objects it can buy. The former avoids buying and keeps his money to himself or herself, while the latter buys compulsively, which means that he or she uses things as a means to enjoy money. Simmel refers to these two extremes in psychological terms. The greedy person is one who carries to an extreme what Simmel terms "the psychological expansion of qualities," whereby a means to a valuable end acquires value in itself (to which money is the extreme example).[34]

The more interesting possibility is to conceive of these two personalities as embodying the impersonal economic and cultural phenomena of finance and shopping; to conceive of avarice and extravagance not merely in psychological terms but as embedded in the economy and inscribed on economic objects. Is this not what Marx suggested in his claim that in the monetary economy, money is "the object most worth possessing"? However, viewing finance and shopping as the objective ground of avarice and extravagance necessitates a change in the direction of the expansion that Simmel invokes: it is no longer that goods confer value on money but the opposite, that money confers value on goods.

The shopaholic indeed represents an extreme position where things lose their reality and become effects of money. The movie shows this quite well by its depiction of the difference between the status of things before and after their purchase. At one point in the movie, after Rebecca promises in vain to change her ways, all the clothes that she vacuum-packed and hid in her closet suddenly erupt from it and cover the floor of her room like debris that remains after a storm.

That is the status of the consumer object after it is bought by the shopaholic: a burdening piece of junk, a lifeless remain. In stark contrast, when things are in the shop—as we see them through Rebecca's eyes—they actually speak to her seductively. The mannequins in the display window bow to her and invite her to buy. The breath of life they lost after leaving the shop is money. In the shop they can still stand in for money. They are alive when they have money *in them* but are dead without it.

The shopaholic should not be seen as a freak but as an exaggerated symptom of modern consumer culture. The very emergence of the term *shopping*, which stresses the act of purchasing over the fact of ownership, discloses this peculiarity. The term *shopping* predates the consumer economy, and its first recorded occurrences already situate shopping beyond mere utilitarian consumption. The *Oxford English Dictionary* cites the following from the 1764 pamphlet *A Seasonable Alarm to the City of London*: "Ladies are said to go a Shoping, when, in the Forenoon, sick of themselves, they order the Coach, and driving from Shop to Shop [etc.]."

Indeed, we can conceive of the most mundane money transactions as financial in this manner. When I meet a colleague, especially not a close one, it is quite natural that we go to the cafeteria and buy a cup of coffee. However, it is not far fetched to assume that it is not simply the coffee itself that smoothes the social interaction but also the fact of buying it. In a way, we need to buy something together to relieve the awkwardness of the situation, and coffee fulfills this need.

The shopaholic, therefore, suggests a new meaning to the term *financial bubble*, not as the eruption of the effects of finance into the real economy, but the expansion of finance to subsume the economy. One of the most desirable pieces of merchandise of our time may be seen as the epitome of this expansion. Part of the irresistible allure of the iPad is that it conferred a tangible quality on ephemerality itself; that it emerged, in other words, as a concrete no-thing.

To Have and to Have More

I discuss the suggestion of associating the consumer economy and finance only partially here. I explore it more fully in Chapters 3 and 5: the former examines in detail the brand name and suggests in this context that modern symbolic money can still be considered a form of commodity-money; the latter presents Thorstein Veblen's early work as an economic theory of waste. However, at this point we already can base this suggestion in the difference between two concepts of the economy.

As an example of the orthodox concept of the economy, we can return to Keynes's paper "Economic Possibilities for Our Grandchildren." Almost a century after the writing of this essay, we cannot avoid the question of how this great thinker was so naive as to believe that in our time humanity would have freed itself from the problem of scarcity. An answer can be found in the paper itself.

Keynes distinguishes between two types of needs: absolute needs, which are unrelated to the situation of our fellow human beings, and relative needs, which drive us to feel superior to our fellows. Keynes acknowledges the fact that the latter type of needs, in contrast to the former, has no theoretical possibility of satisfaction. Yet, he claims that with reference to absolute needs "a point may soon be reached [. . .] when these needs are satisfied in the sense that we prefer to devote our further energies to non-economic purposes."[35] This conclusion rests on the commonsensical idea that absolute needs are prior to relative needs. That is to say, people toil to have what they absolutely need and, once they have it, may try to have more than others (but being rational, they will tend to give up on this goal). In other words, Keynes's prediction rests on the idea that *having* is logically prior to *having more*.

This commonsensical distinction provides a perfect first step for the introduction of the revolutionary force of Thorstein Veblen's historical overview of the economy. One way to introduce the fundamental difference of Veblen's thought from orthodox economics is that it situates "having more" as the basic form of ownership itself. From its very origin, ownership was an "invidious distinction" and had little to do with consumption or sustenance.[36]

Veblen does not renounce the idea held by some anthropologists that in primitive societies, needs are satisfied in part in a collective and, in some sense, in a communist manner (as David Graeber puts it, "from each according to their abilities, to each according to their needs").[37] Rather, precisely because of the necessarily collective manner of production in such societies, Veblen seeks the origin of ownership *outside* of the ways societies organize the satisfaction of needs.

In its origin, the social institution of ownership simply does not apply to the ordinary objects that serve the sustenance of life. Ownership enters society with things outside the circle of daily sustenance that serve to symbolize the strength of their owner (in Veblen's speculation it begins with the forceful domination of a chief over captive women and from there spreads to objects that these women produce).[38] Private property in this respect is not about the needs of an individual but rather, from its beginning, it is something directed at the gaze of others. According to Veblen this motive of ownership is not limited to its speculative historical origin but retains its primacy in every historical stage. Emulation and invidious distinction continue to be active forces in the development of the institution of ownership.

Of course, one may ask how this view can be reconciled with modern societies where sustenance and consumption seem to occupy a vast portion of economic activity. The following is one of Veblen's most radical suggestions: "in a community where nearly all goods are private property the necessity of earning a livelihood is a powerful and ever present incentive for the poorer members of the community."

That is a truly radical use of history, wherein a historical narrative turns upside-down our very basic notions of the present. We are accustomed to thinking that the economy is fundamentally related to scarcity. Through the economy we handle our always scarce resources to best gratify our needs and desires. In stark contrast, Veblen presents the economy of scarcity and sustenance as a result of the expansion of the economy of human competition and honor. It is not that people initially strive to have what they need and after that turn their efforts to acquire more than others. Rather, because the competition to have more than others has widened to encompass all goods, we must handle *even* our livelihood through the economy.

Of course, Veblen does not indulge in the fantasy that archaic societies were immune to scarcity. What he claims is that scarcity was not originally managed through private property, that is, through what today coincides with the realm of the economy. Private property had originally to do with a certain sense of affluence—it applied to the superfluous and extravagant.

The Veblenian framework might seem counterintuitive in comparison with the Keynesian one. After all, one must first have *something* in order to have more than others. But this is precisely its strength. It conceives of private property as a social institution through and through. Grounding property simply on having replicates the illusion that property is reducible to objects; that the institution of private property can somehow evolve from the direct relations of people to things. Grounding property, by contrast, on having more enables us to conceive of private property not in terms of objects, but in terms of the social relations that objects stand for.

Veblen's historical speculation seems particularly essential in the face of the unresolved tension between the insistence of economics on both the practical necessity of growth and the theoretical emphasis on scarcity. Economists are always interested in how to maintain growth, but the paradox is that theoretically there is no future horizon where this growth is expected to finally banish scarcity. This tension is most easily resolved in Veblen's conceptualization, which distributes scarcity and affluence differently. Scarcity and affluence are not measured in things, but define the economic status of a thing. Scarcity in this respect is not simply a shortage of things but is inscribed in the form of existence of the economic thing. An economic thing entangles abundance with scarcity if it is conceived primarily as something that others do not possess.[39]

Furthermore, Veblen's view suggests an alternative formula for the basic problem of the economy. It is not just the problem that some people do not have enough to satisfy their most basic needs. Rather, perhaps the problem of the economy today is that we satisfy even our most basic needs with luxury goods. An effective initial definition of brand names is that they satisfy basic needs while at the same time, they are more than a plain product that satisfies a need. But the paradox is that we can hardly avoid brands even for the most basic needs such as food and clothing.

The question "What is economy?" is in part a semantic question. One can indeed conceive of the economy as the way a society organizes the reproduction of its means of subsistence—that is what classical political economists like Adam Smith had in mind when they thought of the economy. What Veblen suggests is that the economy of private property—and by extension, of money—does not overlap with the economy of subsistence, and furthermore, that it subsumes the economy of subsistence.

In Veblen's thought we can locate a certain sense of a financial drive in the basic form of private property. The insatiable financial drive is already implied by an economy where a thing is not simply possessed but fills the need for having more. This financial drive does not appear to bear any specific relation to money, yet money may be seen as its *pure* embodiment. Recalling Marx's remark that "greed is impossible without money" because other forms of accumulation are restricted by needs, we can say that in the economy of having more, things are desired as money.

PART II: WHAT IS A SOCIAL OBJECT?

As we have seen, Marx uses the term *objective* in a manner that is very different from its usual meaning in economics. The term *objective* does not refer simply to that which is external to the subject and independent of it, but implies a subjective relation (the objective content of the circulation of capital is the capitalist's subjective purpose). A full account of this theoretical position must explore not only objectivity but also present the question of the object. What is an economic object? What is Marx's concept of a social object?

The best way to approach these questions is by comparing Marx's thought to a parallel attempt in analytic philosophy in the work of John Searle. Both Searle and Marx are concerned with the same basic riddle: How do objects partake in social reality? A comparison between their analyses clarifies what the difference is between materialism and mere physicalism. Because the latter assigns primacy to physical objects, it cannot consider objectivity as socially constituted. For that reason it cannot develop a comprehensive theory of the social object, that is, of an object that is *irreducibly* social, as materialism does.

The Constitution of Objectivity

As noted above, Friedman suggests to ground money on thought: an object is money insofar as people think it is money. This idea, which Friedman mentions only briefly, is systematically elaborated by John Searle in his book *The Construction of Social Reality*. Although money is not the topic of the book, it is one of the central examples that Searle brings of what he calls "institutional facts." Searle's argument is worth exploring in some depth because it highlights theoretical impasses that analytic philosophy shares with economics. The following are the opening sentences of the book:

> This book is about a problem that has puzzled me for a long time: there are portions of the real world, objective facts in the world, that are only facts by human agreement. In a sense there are things that exist only because we believe them to exist. I am thinking of things like money, property, governments, and marriages. Yet many facts regarding these things are "objective" facts in the sense that they are not a matter of your or my preferences, evaluations, or moral attitudes.[40]

Consider a seemingly marginal question: Why does the adjective objective occur within quotation marks and right at the beginning of the book? Without dwelling yet on the solution that Searle proposes to the problem he poses, these quotation marks suggest that he might have already taken a wrong turn in formulating the question. Searle inquires about the existence of things: How is it that money exists although its existence is entailed with a subjective relation? In such a question the quotation marks are in order because this question is not aimed at the *concept* of objectivity. Instead, objective appears here as an adjective that qualifies existence in certain, not necessarily specified, ways (it emphasizes existence—money really exists—and at the same time problematizes existence—money does not really exist, for example, not the way a stone exists).

Of course, had objectivity as a concept been the issue questioned, the quotation marks would not be in order. They would not be in order had Searle chosen to inquire not after the *existence* of money but after its *objectivity*. In what manner is money objective, considering the fact that its existence is entailed with a subjective relation?

This may seem to be a minor difference in emphasis. Nevertheless, it leads to two opposing ways of answering, which can be designated as agreement and disavowal. If one asks how money exists, one may use, like Searle, some notion of human agreement. An arbitrary object functions as money insofar as there is human agreement to treat it like money, regardless of its properties (people pay with it for goods; other people give goods in return, etc.). However, if one inquires how it is that money appears *objective*, then one is forced to insert in the answer some notion of disavowal or negation, which stands in basic contrast to the idea of agreement. If the existence of money is objective in some sense, this necessarily means that the place of the subjective relation in its constitution escapes the view of the subject itself. If there is indeed something objective in money, it is because it appears to the subject as independent of his thoughts, beliefs, and will.

The importance of this difference can be emphasized by the effort that Searle exerts to keep the possibility of negation or disavowal away from his argument. This effort is most evident in two complementary rhetorical gestures that recur throughout the text: reducing negation or disavowal from a logical necessity to a mere possibility; and invoking certain intuitive, non-conceptual versions of history and institutionalization. When Searle lists the properties of institutional facts, he starts with the claim that an institutional fact is "created by human agreement." Then he elaborates its pattern as "X counts as Y in C" (a certain object [X] is assigned a function [Y] in a certain context [C] regardless of its physical properties, that is, a certain piece of paper counts as money in commercial contexts).[41]

Only as a third property does Searle bring in the idea that such mechanisms can work unknowingly. He notes that "the process of creation of institutional facts may proceed without the participants being conscious that it is happening according to this form," and repeats that "we need not be consciously aware of its ontology" and that "the participants need not be consciously aware of the form of collective intentionality by which they are imposing functions on objects." Furthermore, Searle notes that "in extreme cases they may accept the imposition of function only because of some related theory, which may not even be true. They may believe that it is money only if it is 'backed by gold.'"[42]

The question is: What is hidden behind so many *maybes*? It is, of course, the shade of necessity—the possibility that there are objects that perform their social function *only insofar* as subjects are unaware of the manner that they participate in their constitution. And these are two completely different things: (1) to claim that a thing *can* assume a function although the subjects are unaware of it and (2) to claim that the subjects are *necessarily* unaware (or that there is a special class of objects where this is necessary). Whereas in the former, the object can indeed be seen to stand for human agreement, in the latter it stands for disavowal. It stands for what cannot, in principle, be acknowledged. To put it more concretely: it seems futile to base money on human agreement between people who have money and people who don't have money.

This reduction of the necessity of disavowal to a mere possibility is supplemented by Searle with a second rhetorical gesture, that of invoking history as a non-problematic background wherein things simply persist. In fact, one can trace this lacuna in Searle's recurrent use of the adverb *simply*, such as in "obviously, for most institutions we simply grow up in a culture where we take the institution for granted."[43] Of course, there is nothing really simple about this mode of institutions simply existing. Rather one of the fundamental theoretical questions of history is: How do things simply persist? One should not mistake here the position of a subject suffused in a historical reality with the theoretical position. That which appears to the subject as simply existing is in fact the most elaborate theoretical question.

In Searle's argument, however, this invocation of *simple* historical persistence allows him to maintain the idea of human agreement as the paradigmatic form of the institutional fact. In this framework there is a moment of real or imagined human agreement, and the rest, as they say, is history, that is, things simply persist, with or without the awareness of subjects.

Nowhere is the artificial nature of this distinction more evident than in Searle's account of the evolution of paper money. At first, he writes, people stored their gold with bankers and received in return paper certificates, verifying their entitlement to that amount of gold. Later, these certificates themselves started circulating in place of gold. But then,

a stroke of genius occurred when somebody figured out that we can increase the supply of money simply by issuing more certificates than we have gold. [. . .] The next stroke of genius came when somebody figured out—and it took a long time to figure this out—we can forget about the gold and just have the certificates."[44]

The question here is not about the accuracy of the narrative but, rather, about the peculiar use of history it entails. What the awkward image a "stroke of genius" achieves is a notion of a historical moment carried by subjects, which can sustain the idea of human agreement.

Nevertheless, Searle's misuse of history points in the right direction. It shows what is required for a full account of social objects, namely, both a social and a *historical* ontology. Once we remove the image of a stroke of genius as motivating history, we arrive at the possibility that Searle's narrative avoids. In that case, what needs to be explained are two interrelated questions, namely, how a thing carries a social role that is never fully understood by subjects, and how it persists in this role through time. What should be noted is that these are the predicates we usually attribute to objects. Objects are opaque, impenetrable to our thought, inert, and persist independently of us. Thus, what a genuine theory of social objects would explain is how their very objectivity is socially constituted, how their persistence and opaqueness are actually social characteristics.

In terms of philosophical method, Searle's error stems from his adherence to physicalism. Searle pledges allegiance to this doctrine in the first pages of the book, where he lists an ontological hierarchy, beginning with particles and forces and climbing to conscious and intentional beings:

> [W]e live in a world made up entirely of physical particles in fields of force. Some of these are organized into systems. Some of these systems are living systems and some of these living systems have evolved consciousness [. . . .] Now the question is, how can we account for the existence of social facts within that ontology?[45]

Put aside the question of how it is that a philosopher accepts a physical doctrine as a given. The more urgent question is what these particles and forces have to do in a theory that purports to explain things such as banknotes? At first glance this invocation of particles may appear as mere lip service to the physicalist world view. However, looking more closely, there appears a function for this reference to physical objects. It enables Searle to avoid the question of the objectivity of the social fact. That is to say, it enables him to bypass the need to formulate a theory proper to social objects, independent of physical law.

This becomes evident in one of the first examples of institutional facts that Searle brings—of an imagined wall that a primitive tribe builds around its territory. At an early stage, the wall fulfills its function due to its physical properties. But then, Searle adds,

> [I]magine that the wall gradually decays so that the only thing left is a line of stones. But imagine that the inhabitants and their neighbors continue to *recognize* the line of stones as marking the boundary of the territory in such a way that it affects their behavior.[46]

The physical inertia of the line of stones fills here the function of the persistence of the social fact. But obviously this does not answer the true question, which is how the social fact persists *as a social fact*.

Against this background the novelty in Marx's position becomes most visible. In the chapter on the fetishism of commodities, which explains how in capitalism social relations are mediated by commodities, Marx writes that

> the mysterious character of the commodity form consists therefore simply in the fact that the commodity reflects the social characteristics of men's own labour as objective characteristics of the products of labour themselves, as the socio-natural properties of these things.[47]

The uniqueness of Marx's position resides in the phrase "socio-natural properties of things." What he explains is not how a given physical object functions in a social context, but how the social properties of things appear in the mode of natural properties. In other words, it is the objectivity of the social object that is placed into consideration.

This general line of thought crosses the prevalent distinction between Marx's early and mature writings. It already appears in the early economic manuscripts in Marx's concept of alienation:

> [T]he object which labor produces, its product, confronts it as an alien being, as a power independent of the producer. The product of labor is labor that has solidified itself into an object, made itself into a thing, the objectification of labor.[48]

Note that the physicality of the object produced by the laborer plays no special role in this case. The object is not a given physical object. It is something that *becomes* an object as it is situated in a specific, capitalist, social mode of production. Its objective qualities—the fact that it confronts the subject, that it is alien to him and independent of him—describe the social relations of production in capitalism. It is objective because of the specific subjective relations invested in it.

A clear demonstration of this theoretical position is found in the example of the capitalist discussed above. A crucial point in this example is that the very existence of capital coincides with its objectivity. For capital to exist at all, it must acquire objective attributes in the sense of denouncing any subjectivity. It is not an existing object invested with subjective relations. It exists as an object insofar as it is invested with a specific subjectivity.

Now we can note the diametric conceptual contrast of Marx's position to Searle's. Searle inquires how physical objects fill a role in social life, and his solution rests on the metaphor of human agreement: people agree to assign a function to an existing object, regardless of its physical qualities. Marx elaborates the opposite view: things are objects because they embody a certain aspect of social life that cannot be subjectivized, that entail a denunciation of subjectivity. That is why his thought is materialistic rather than simply physicalist. It explores how social things acquire properties that we usually attribute to physical objects. It becomes a genuine theory of the social object.

One advantage of this view becomes evident against the background of the various processes of dematerialization that have characterized the economy in the last few decades. Economic things are no longer primarily physical objects because a growing share of them belongs to the wide realm of intellectual property (brand names, cultural content, and software). Yet the institution of private property has remained essentially the same throughout this shift. It sailed quite smoothly through this shift, which according to some perspectives was a major sea change.

Searle's ideas, in principle, can refer to an economy governed by the material mode of commodities: things, physical objects, function as private property because of the social arrangements in which they are bounded. The dematerialization of the economy reveals the force of the opposite view. Things, notwithstanding whether they are material, are economic *objects* because of the social arrangements that surround them. They are not objects within a given social arrangement; they *are* objects because of a social arrangement.

The Split Object of Fetishism

Another way to formulate the difference between Searle's institutional facts and Marx's social objects is to say that Marx folds the split between the subjective and the objective into the object itself. Searle outlines the split between physical, meaningless objects and the social, meaningful role they play. Since Marx's thought does not assign a particular place to the physicality of objects, it situates this split within the social object itself. As the example of the capitalist shows, capital exists through the coincidence of two allegedly contradicting meanings of objectivity: on the one hand, capital is objective in the sense that it exists independently of subjects; on the other hand, its existence entails subjects who behave *as if* capital is objective reality, *as if* money itself needs to accumulate. Capital is both an object and *as if* an object. We can notice this split in Marx's discussion of commodity fetishism that elaborates most fully his concept of the social object. The following is his famous definition of commodity fetishism:

> To the producers, therefore, the social relations between their private labours appear as what they are, i.e. they do not appear as direct social relations between persons in their work, but rather as material relations between persons and social relations between things.[49]

Note the peculiar function of appearances: things appear as what they are. As Žižek notes, this coincidence of reality and appearance is not a sort of demystification; on the contrary, it suggests that mystification is "inscribed into social reality itself."[50]

To clarify this coincidence of reality and appearance, consider the simplest example. How do relations between people appear to them as what they really are or as relations between things? Consider the concept of price. Price is a relation between things (the commodity-thing and the money-thing), yet it encodes a whole web of relations between persons (the wage that the worker is paid for his labor, the profit that the entrepreneur makes from it, etc.). This does not mean that prices are only appearances masking real relations between people. Rather, *as appearances* they constitute relations between people. Only to the extent that prices appear objective, as properties of objects, can they indeed fully embody relations between people.

The overlapping of the two senses of objectivity—*real* objectivity and *as if* objectivity—may appear at first glance as an unaccounted redundancy, a too-heavy theoretical burden on the idea of a social object. However, it is a necessary condition if we situate the social object not in the context of human agreement, but as standing for an aspect of social life that transcends conscious agreement. In such a case, social objects such as money, capital, or private property can objectively exist only when their existence is sustained by subjects who behave as if they are really objective. From this perspective, Searle's insistence on tying his example to physical objects appears as an ideological gesture: insistence on a dimension of the real, neutral objectivity of institutional facts. Indeed, his benign view of objects as representing human agreement is most easily settled with the liberal economic belief in the market as a sphere of free, human activity. To understand how Marx, by contrast, situates the economic object as embodying a fundamental antagonism, we must look further into his social ontology.

The Subject Is a Relation to an Object

According to Marx, the position of the capitalist is maintained by the relation of a person to an object. The objective existence of capital depends on the gesture of subtraction, namely, the gesture of the person who behaves as if money itself wants to accumulate. This idea can be generalized into a comprehensive social ontology if we add to the capitalist-money pair another pair that stood at the center of Marx's early work: that of the laborer and the commodity. The idea of commodity fetishism was as yet unformulated at this stage of Marx's work; however, we already can find here the basic principle of the social object. Reading the early work together with *Capital*, this principle can be formulated thus: *the subject is a relation to an object*. Both the capitalist and the laborer are defined by a relation of submission to the object: the capitalist submits his person to his money and thus maintains capital (and thus becomes a capitalist), and the laborer submits his person to his labor product to maintain private property (and thus becomes a laborer).

The first matter to note regarding the combination of the laborer and the commodity is the recurrence of the idea of a hostile object, of which capital can be seen as a later transformation (capital that annihilates the subjective ends of the capitalist). This idea stands at the center of the concept of alienation, developed in the *Economic and Philosophic Manuscripts of 1844*. In review: "the object that labour produces, its product, confronts as an alien being, as a power independent of the producer." Further on Marx adds that the realization of labor "appears as a loss of reality for the worker, objectification as a loss of the object or slavery to it."[51]

The concept of alienation had an unfortunate fate. It is identified with a humanistic phase in Marx's work, which sometimes is a code name for less rigorous thought. Allen Wood, for example, argues that alienation is not at all an explanatory concept but a descriptive notion that loosely refers to various evils of industrial capitalism.[52] Marx's early work, he writes, "could be called 'rigorous' only by someone who has little familiarity with the property that term denotes."[53] However, we should keep in mind that the heart of the chapter on alienated labor is a sharp conceptual argument. Whereas economists accept private property as a given, Marx claims that we should see alienation as logically prior to it: "although private property appears to be the ground and reason for externalized labor, it is rather the consequence of it."[54]

How can we accredit this conceptual core of Marx's text? The concept of alienation appears to lack rigor because it is commonly read with a focus on the characteristics of the conditions of capitalist production that Marx associates with this concept. Marx lists a few forms of alienation entailed with the capitalist mode of production. The laborer is alienated to the work process ("labour is exterior to the worker . . . it does not belong to his essence . . . he does not confirm himself in his work, he denies himself"); he is alienated to the essence of humankind (since nature is man's "inorganic body," alienated labor "alienates from man his own body, nature exterior to him, and his intellectual being, his human essence"); and he is alienated to his fellow human beings ("the alienation of man . . . is first realized and expressed in the relationship with which man stands to other men").[55] These senses of alienation can be read as a basis for a moral and political critique of capitalism. Yet, focusing solely on them does indeed give the impression that alienation is not a concept but an assembly of symptoms (and respectively, these make for a moralistic, rather than moral critique of capitalism).

What renders alienation a rigorous concept is the basic sense that Marx attributes to it, which precedes all others. In its basic sense, alienation does not immediately appear as a social concept and does not refer directly to social relations. It is a relation between people and things. It refers to the fact that the laborers produce everything and yet remain impoverished: "labour produces works of wonder for the rich, but nakedness to the worker. It produces palaces, but only hovels for the worker; it produces beauty, but cripples the worker."[56] The concept of alienation aims to reduce this situation to concrete relations: "the immediate relationship of labour to its products is the relationship of the worker to the objects of his production."[57] The impoverishment of the workers is eventually grounded in the immediate relation of a laborer to the thing he produces.

Thus, eventually, Marx sets as a basic reality of capitalist production a very simple relation between a person and a thing: "the worker relates to the product of his labour as to an alien object." The basic fact is that the worker produces a thing, and the thing is not his. Certainly we have some commonplace explanations why this is the case. We might say that the worker was paid in exchange for his labor or that the worker does not own the machines used in the process of production. But these explanations do not really solve the riddle because they accept as given the concepts of money, wage, and private property. These concepts belong to the language of the economic order itself—to what economists, from the days of Marx to our own, accept without any need of consideration. These are the concepts whose naturalization is a part the economic order itself. Thus, invoking private property (the laborer does not own the machine) cannot explain the basic sense of alienation. Rather, such explanations only show how alienation penetrates the most neutral economic language.

The way that the basic sense of alienation is suffused in the economic order and in the economic language can now explain the status of the further senses of alienation, those that Wood sees as vague and descriptive. These are actually the conditions of possibility of the basic sense of alienation as a relation to a thing. Marx states this explicitly: "How would the worker be able to affront the product of his work as an alien being if he did not alienate himself in the act of production itself?"[58] The ostensibly social senses of alienation—alienation to the labor process, to fellow workers, to the essence of humanity—do not belong to the conceptual core of the notion. They are conditions that enable the basic premise of capitalist production, wherein the worker produces what is not his own. They are the way Marx expands the basic abstract sense of alienation into a positive description of the nature of social production in capitalism.

Marx does not define alienation simply as the fact that workers do not own their products but rather that their products confront them as objects. But this is precisely because what he explores is a question of social ontology, of the mode of existence of economic things in capitalism. That the product becomes an object means that it confronts the worker as independent of him or her, that the social fact of ownership wears the shape of a natural quality of objects. In alienation we thus find one more occurrence of the split object: alienation means that workers behave *as if* their products are not theirs. A comparison with the Hegelian notion of property may clarify this.

Hegel already noted the social structure of ownership, where the possession of a thing involves the recognition of others.[59] Marx brings about a change in this formula. In a society where one class controls the means of production, ownership does not simply entail the recognition of others (which would amount to the absurd claim: the laborers acknowledge that the machine is the property of the capitalist and, therefore, yield their product to him). Rather, it entails a disavowal on the part of the laborers of their actual participation in maintaining the ownership of other people. The machine appears as *immediately* the possession of the capitalist (as a "socio-natural property" of it) insofar as the laborer misrecognizes his own participation in this relation of ownership.

Again, as in the case of capital, the objectivity of capitalist private property is entailed with its form of existence. It exists insofar as it exists as an object, in the sense of effacing the subjective relation entailed with it. It is not simply a given object intertwined with subjective relations, as in Searle's theory. It becomes an object—the economic object entitled private property—precisely through alienation. Furthermore, as in the case of the capitalist, alienation implies, theoretically, a choice. An inert object, the physical object that fills the place of property, cannot really exert a coercive force over the laborer. It is only through a gesture of willful submission that the product becomes private property.

The parallel between the two pairs, laborer–private property and capitalist–capital, suggests that what we encounter here is the first law of a general materialist social ontology, in which subjects and objects are mutually determined through their relations. The subject's position is determined through a submission to an object (the capitalist cancels any other wish in favor of his or her drive to accumulate money; the laborer relates to his product as not his). At the same time this relation sustains the social object (capital or private property). That the concepts of fetishism and alienation touch a basic ontological premise is evident in the fact that in both cases, Marx reverts to a religious metaphor. He writes regarding alienation: "It is just the same in religion. The more man puts into God, the less he retains in himself."[60] About fetishism, he writes: "In order, therefore, to find an analogy we must take flight into the misty realm of religion. There the products of the human brain appear as autonomous figures endowed with a life of their own."[61] In a sense, for Marx the social object is in essence a sacred object.

Another way to present Marx's concept of alienation is to read it as a formal analysis of private property as a social relation. What it suggests is that private property is founded on a relation of in-ownership or dispossession. Economics has a long tradition of ignoring the social character of ownership. It starts with the Lockean myth of the origin of property in labor invested directly in nature. A person picks apples from a tree, and this labor makes them his own:

> [I]t is the taking any part of what is common, and removing it out of the state Nature leaves it in, which begins the property [. . .]. And the taking of this or that part does not depend on the express consent of all the commoners.[62]

The crucial point here is that property is conceived of primarily as a relation consisting of a person and an object. The relations of others to one's property are only derived from this primary relation of property. A man cultivates a piece of land to make it his property and "by his labor does, as it were, enclose it from the common."[63]

Contemporary economists no longer dwell on such myths of origin. But one reason for this is that they no longer view it as necessary to inquire into ownership. The presuppositions of the Lockean myth are simply imbued in the economic world view. In the economic version of methodological individualism, a full description of an economy consists of individuals and their respective property—people and their things.

Strangely enough, the Marxist view can actually be described as the correct form of reduction of society to individuals. What it suggests is that such a reduction can be achieved only when the social is inscribed in the form of a negative, pre-conceptual, real relation on the part of the individual. The reasoning for this is quite simple. The assertion "X is the private property of A" cannot be reduced to the series "B, C, and D acknowledge that X is the private property of A." Such a reduction clearly begs the question. It posits the social notion of private property in the relations of all others to one's property. By contrast, in purely formal terms, the basic ownership assertion can be reduced to the series "B, C, and D actually relate to X as not theirs."

This is the valid form of reduction because *relating as not one's own* does not necessarily entail the acknowledgement of others and, thus, can *in principle* be viewed as the real relation of a person to an object. Marx uses this relation as the building block of social reality when he quite strangely infers the existence of the capitalist from the alienation of the laborer:

> If the product of the labor does not belong to the worker but stands over against him as an alien power this is only possible in that it belongs to another man apart from the worker. If his activity torments him it must be a joy and a pleasure to someone else. This alien power above man can be neither the gods nor nature, only man himself.[64]

The idea that in-ownership is logically prior to ownership may seem paradoxical. In-ownership appears conceptually secondary to the concept of ownership as it is but a negation of the latter. But this fact only demonstrates that our most basic economic terms partake in the ideological constitution of private property. Yet the primacy of in-ownership is now confirmed in the basic experience of consumer society. In the traditional grocery store, we could still see the shopkeeper keeping an eye on his merchandise; in modern consumer spaces, things confront us simply as *not ours* ("Don't take it, it's not yours," says the parent to a child in the supermarket. But whose is it, then?).

The Object Stands for Antagonism

In viewing the object as entailed with a disavowal on the part of the subject, we have covered only half of the picture of the Marxist social ontology. We have explored the phenomenology of the object: the manner that the social confronts subjects in the shape of objects; the manner that social things appear *as if* they are objective. But the question that remains is how social objects are at the same time *really* objective; how they persist in their existence independently of any specific subject's relation to them.

Thus, if the first question is of social phenomenology, the second refers, broadly speaking, to history. These two questions are of course interrelated. Marx provides a framework where the social object is inherently related to social antagonism. The object as entangled with a gesture of willful submission embodies an aspect of social life that cannot be agreed upon. The question of how it persists is therefore the main theoretical question of history for Marx: How does an antagonistic social order persist? How is it that laborers keep producing their impoverishment? How does the circulation of capital continue to advance even as it entails not only the exploitation of laborers but also an irrational gesture of submission on the part of capitalists?

To recall the first sentence of the *Manifesto*: "The history of all hitherto existing society is the history of class struggles." Reading this sentence as a theoretical statement, rather than as an empirical observation, raises the question of the way social antagonism is transferred through time, of antagonism as historical substance. The simplest answer to this riddle is the social object. The object both embodies social antagonism and transfers it through time. This amounts to a complete reversal of Searle's position. Searle relates the social role of things to human agreement and, for that very reason, dispenses with the possibility of meaningful history (things simply persist or persist with the inertia of physical objects, like a stone of the decaying wall). In other words, Searle's theory demonstrates the necessity of conceptualizing history as inherently related to antagonism. However, Searle also provides us with a good starting point to explain the way antagonism persists in the mediation of the social object. An important distinction he elaborates is the one between epistemic and ontological aspects of the opposition between objectivity and subjectivity.

In the ontological sense, the opposition refers to a mode of existence of things. It refers to the question of whether or not the existence of a thing depends on its being felt by a subject. Thus, pain is ontologically subjective whereas stones are ontologically objective. In the epistemic sense, the opposition refers to judgments. It refers to the question of whether a judgment depends on the attitude, feelings, or point of view of a subject. Thus, the statement *this picture is beautiful* is epistemically subjective, whereas the statement *this mountain is 1,000 meters tall* is epistemically objective. The importance of Searle's distinction is that it situates the institutional fact in the weird category of things that are epistemologically objective yet ontologically subjective. It refers to things whose existence involves a subjective relation (ontological subjectivity), yet are independent of any specific subject's relation to them (epistemic objectivity). This category suggests a topology in which beliefs or thoughts confront the subject in the shape of external objects.

However, the importance of Searle's distinction is that it is actually not as stable as it may seem. The "epistemic objectivity" of things such as money is not independent of their "ontological subjectivity." The subjectivity invested in things such as money must reflect the fact that they exist regardless of our relation to them. Epistemic objectivity thus becomes one more form of subjective relation. Instead of the simple form *I believe this object is money*, this subjectivity wears some kind of a disavowed form, such as *this object is money regardless of whether or not I believe it*.

This form of existence points to what Žižek termed as the intersubjective form of belief. A belief need not take the form of an internal subjective persuasion but can be a belief that others believe. (In Žižek's example, we celebrate holidays in order not to harm our children's supposedly naive belief.[65]) This intersubjective dimension is precisely what Searle's conceptualization lacks. His invocation of epistemic objectivity points to the need to account for plurality because it refers to a state where *everybody* believes in something (e.g., that a certain object is money).

Yet his concept of plurality is based on his idea of "collective intentionality," whose weakness is precisely that it conceives of the social as something shared. It cannot account for situations where social beliefs contrast with the actual beliefs of individual human beings. To put it in simple terms, what Searle misses is a concept to account for the situation where everybody believes, yet nobody *really* believes (but maybe believes that everybody else believes, to use Žižek's idea). And that is precisely the concept of intersubjectivity, which allows for a conception of the social not just as an amalgamation of individuals, but as opposed to every concrete individual.

What must be added to Žižek's idea of the intersubjective structure of belief is that in an economic context, this structure is necessarily mediated through an object. The object stands for the level of intersubjectivity *insofar* as it is opposed to any specific subject. The object represents for everybody the fact that everybody believes, even in a situation where nobody actually believes. In this sense, the object is essential in contexts characterized by a radical split between specific subjects and the dimension of the intersubjective.

Consider the following simple example. At a dinner party, often the last piece of cake remains untouched on the plate. It is perfectly correct to claim, from a physicalist perspective, that it remains there in accordance with Newton's first law of motion. But, naturally, this is far from answering the question of its persistence. The full answer is that in this case, the inertia of the physical object plays a role within an intersubjective web. Its inertia represents for everyone present that everyone else avoids taking the piece of cake. Indeed, we would hesitate to view the inertia of the last piece of cake as an objective social property of it. But this is so because in this case, the intersubjective can indeed be reduced to specific individuals (and, therefore, one can overcome the inhibition with a joke and take the cake after all).

The true intersubjective situation is the parallel example of the supermarket. Here, too, the inertia of the merchandise on the shelves represents to everybody the fact that everybody else avoids taking things as they please.[66] In the case of the supermarket shelf, the difference is that the intersubjective is irreducible to specific individuals. The individuals present at any moment are just representatives of the intersubjective as such. And, indeed, in the case of the supermarket, the inertia of the merchandise on the shelves represents an *objective* social property of it, namely, its being a form of private property. The lesson to be learned from conjoining these two examples is that the social object represents the intersubjective *insofar* as it is not reducible to any group of subjects.[67]

These examples are narrow in scope, yet they may be read as a model for a possible social and historical ontology found in Marx that will be developed throughout this book. In this model the object is seen as the outer limit of the subject. The object is what captures something of the subject that escapes the subject's own perspective. It is a part of the subject that transcends *mere* subjectivity. In this sense, it is the object that confers ontological consistency on the subject; it is the arena in which the subject's persistence is inscribed. It is the answer to the question of how this flimsy entity, the subject, can have a history in the first place.

How Is There History?

In Marx, the object is an answer to a two-part question: How is there society, and how is there history? In broad terms, society is a meaningful context to the extent that there is something else apart from individuals. But this is true also for history if the reality of history entails that something blindly inherited from the past still shapes our present. This is more or less that dimension of history that the Annales school termed *longue durée*.

Orthodox economics, which reduces everything to individuals, theoretically makes no room for both a concept of society and a concept of history.

It seems that its world view owes some part of its public force today to the commonsensical nature of the idea that every human phenomenon can be boiled down to individuals. Today, it is those who argue for the reality of society or history that must prove what there is besides individuals. A common response to that challenge invokes notions such as shared norms, beliefs, or values that define society. This may be an apt response, yet its scope is limited to begin with to the explanation of that aspect of society that is marked as being shared.

Marx, by contrast, provides an answer that is both more concrete and allows for a fundamental explanation of the antagonistic aspect of society. Margaret Thatcher, a champion of neo-liberalism, famously exclaimed "Who is society? There is no such thing! There are individual men and women."[68] Paraphrasing her words, we can say that according to Marx, there is society precisely because it is a thing—besides individual men and women society exists because it is historically imbued in things.

This theoretical perspective lies at the heart of Žižek's argument that commodity fetishism should be understood in terms of repression: the direct relations of feudal domination and servitude are abolished in modern capitalism where everyone is equal before the law; yet, commodity fetishism explains how these power relations persist as mediated through commodities.

We see the persistence of domination when we look not only at people, but consider society as consisting of objects as well. However, a small but important correction is required here. It is incorrect to argue that in feudalism, in contrast to capitalism, the political takes the form of direct relations between people (lords and serfs). These relations are also mediated through things and very much in the model of Marx's social object. A feudal lord is not simply defined as the owner of land but by the additional feature that he cannot sell his land (had he been able to sell it, he would have gone halfway toward being a capitalist). It is this constraint—which we can formulate only in retrospect—that confers a natural quality on the lord's relation to his land, almost as an extension of his person (a socio-natural property of the land, to paraphrase Marx again). So just like the capitalist and the laborer, the subject lord is defined by a gesture of contraction in relation to an object.

The idea of fetishism as a form of repression carries vast theoretical implications for the concept of history. It points to a concept of history as insistence, or as persistence, through change. Repression turns our attention to what refuses to go away. In terms of history, it directs us to seek what remains the same beyond the semblance of change. This notion goes against the current tendency to conflate history with change and contingency. This tendency is no doubt related to a certain emancipatory quality that we have come to expect from historical knowledge. In a somewhat simplified manner, by showing that capitalism has a history (that it is not natural), we seem to prove to ourselves that it can also disappear or radically change. An immediate doubt arises in reference to this use of history. Even when focusing on change, don't we first have to ask: *What is it that changes*? Shouldn't a genuine historical approach seek that thing whose identity is most fully revealed through its change?

This theoretical approach finds a clear echo in the work of one of the great scholars of the history of capitalism. Reflecting on his seminal studies of the history of capitalism, Fernand Braudel presents the notion of inertia as a key for developing "historical economics." This notion directs our attention from change and progress to impediments and to what inhibits change. Braudel writes:

> For one possibility which was fulfilled, there were tens, hundreds, thousands, which disappeared, and there are even some which, numberless, never even appear to us at all, too lowly and hidden to impose themselves directly on history. We must nonetheless somehow try to reintroduce them, because these vanishing movements are the multiple material and immaterial forces which have at every moment put the brakes on the great forward impetuses of evolution, slowed down their development, and sometimes put an early end to their existence.[69]

We can recall Searle's shorthand account of the history of money to understand the necessity of this concept of inertia:

> [A] stroke of genius occurred when somebody figured out that we can increase the supply of money simply by issuing more certificates than we have gold. [. . .] The next stroke of genius came when somebody figured out—and it took a long time to figure this out—we can forget about the gold and just have the certificates. (See note 44.)

This fictitious narrative points to a real difficulty of writing a history of money.

The problem is that it is too easy to tell the story of money in a logical form. Taking this form literally, as Searle does, the history of money should have occurred in no time. But this only underlines the importance of a notion such as inertia. The subject matter of this history is not just what happened, but why it happened so slowly—a subject matter that necessitates a philosophy of history since it addresses also what did not happen. Using Searle's own terms, history is folded in the clause: "and it took a long time to figure this out." Accounting for this interim period invokes some basic questions of a philosophy of history: What is the status of the object that is not yet figured out? How does it function without being fully understood? How can we account for it as not yet something else?

These are some of the questions that this book confronts. It does not deal much with the grand scale of the history of money and its origin (though it presents a new thesis about the dissolution of the gold standard). But it deals at length with the question of the historicity of money—with money being a historical object, with its being *in* history. It is the question of money as a medium of history, of the manner social relations are transparently embedded in it, and the manner in which they are carried with it through time. This is the two-part question with which a notion of historical materialism confronts us if we take it seriously. On the one hand, it is the question of what is the material substance of history and on the other hand, it is the question of how can matter have history.

Critical perspectives on the economy have always tried to rebuke mainstream narratives of the origin of money (mainly the story of its evolution from a barter economy). From Karl Polanyi to David Graeber, critical scholars provided evidence to the contrary or suggested alternative narratives. This book addresses a more fundamental question, namely, what difference does a story make? What difference does it make whether the origin of money was in barter, in the state, in marriage settlements, or in penalty law? Obviously, the answer to that question cannot be gained by a narrative. It should lead us to wonder about the form of the presence of history, to inquire about the form of the presence of an origin in its later effects.

Materialism

The notion of materialism poses an obstacle in the reading of Marx. The problem is that physical materiality plays no special role in his social, economic, and political thought. If materialism is a doctrine that holds that material reality determines or shapes social reality, then Marx is *not* a materialist. For

Marx, materialism is the idea that social reality assumes the form of material substance, which is quite a different idea. That is why capital is the most typical social object in Marx's thought although it is not a material object at all. It is typical because it lacks materiality and, therefore, demonstrates most clearly how something assumes the role of a social object. In a way, focusing our attention on physical objects that play the role of social objects may mislead us because they conflate physical with social objectivity. Doing so hides the crucial question of how something assumes the place of a social object regardless of its materiality.

This paradox becomes clearer when we explore the difference between Marx and the renewed interest in the material aspects of the social—in new schools of philosophy and social thought, such as object-oriented ontology and actor-network theory.

Actor-network theory, as developed by Bruno Latour and others, is also interested in the way objects partake in social reality. Further more, in his famous lecture "Where Are the Missing Masses? The Sociology of a Few Mundane Artifacts," Latour explicitly argues that we must turn our attention to objects to account for the very existence of society. Sociologists are looking for "social links sturdy enough to tie all of us together or for moral laws that would be inflexible enough to make us behave properly" but since they are focused on humans with their "weak moralities," the society they try to conceptualize "constantly crumbles." The "missing masses" that tie society together and escape the eye of sociologists are artifacts.

Latour examines the ways artifacts assume some roles of humans and, in turn, shape human behavior. His beautiful example is a simple spring-door mechanism in a public place. It carries a function related to everyday morality, of closing the door after someone comes in and keeping the cold out for the comfort of all present. It takes the place of a basic human courtesy to others (or the place of a porter who previously performed this role). And, in turn, it forces humans to adapt to it (e.g., avoid the slam of the door in their faces).

This focus on a mechanism makes clear the difference between the two versions of materialism discussed above. Latour grounds the social function of the object in its physical properties. But for that reason his objects are neither irreducibly social nor genuinely historical. These features follow from the very form of his argumentation. To arrive at the agency of artifacts, Latour imagines what it would be like if they were gone. But this means first, that their social role is equivalent to human agency, and second, that they can in theory disappear just as they emerge (absent the door mechanism, people can learn again to close the door after they come in).

The uniqueness of Marx is clearly evident in this respect. The objects he refers to—money, capital—do not perform an action that could otherwise be done by humans. They perform a role that can only be done when transferred to an object. They are not given objects that perform a role; they *are* objects because of the role they perform. We should note the exact symmetry between these two positions. An artifact can perform a moral role and make people behave properly due to its physical properties. But in the more mysterious case, where an object emerges regardless of its physical properties, it can perform an immoral role. The object can perform a role that for normative reasons cannot be performed directly by humans. To put it concretely: it is not easy for a person to say to another *I will pay you as little as possible in order to maximize profits*, but that is exactly what capital does as an object.

A further insight into the historical dimension of Marx's materialism can be gained through Jane Bennett's *Vibrant Matter*. Bennett begins her journey into the life of inanimate things with a step that is the exact opposite of one Marx takes, by stressing the need to go beyond objects into things: to obliterate the more or less fixed social form that characterizes the way things appear to subjects—"with a name, an identity, a gestalt or stereotypical template"—and go back to the level of pre-conceptual materiality.[70] For that reason her gaze is directed, to begin with, to debris, to an assemblage of waste and dead matter she stumbles upon one day (a plastic glove, a dead rat, a dense mat of oak pollen, a bottle cap, and a smooth stick of wood).

This meditative look at waste serves as a first step for approaching the life of inanimate things, the shared material substance of human beings and matter. This material substratum is concealed in everyday social life. Bennett writes:

> It hit me then in a visceral way how American materialism, which requires buying ever-increasing numbers of products purchased in ever-shorter cycles, is *anti*materiality. The sheer volume of commodities, and the hyperconsumptive necessity of junking them to make room for new ones, conceals the vitality of matter.[71]

Bennett actually pinpoints here the difference between historical and physical materialism. In part, this is a question of terminology, of what we call materialism—if by the term we refer to objects in their social role or to things beyond their social role. But we can see that the decision between the two possibilities determines which story we tell. One can indeed call contemporary American society anti-materialist, but the point is that in doing so one loses an important historical dimension—the dimension of continuity that runs from early, and explicitly, materialist capitalism to late, ostensibly anti-materialist, capitalism. In a way, what escapes from this view is capitalism itself: the unchanging kernel of the organization of production to extract profit to capital, regardless of the question of what is produced.

This blindness to history results from Bennett's notion of materialism as related to dead matter. Her drive is to go beyond the object to the thing; to go beyond objects in their social role, with their names, the identity that we give them, and reach the uncanny effect of the thing. Thus, quoting W. J. T. Mitchell, she seeks

> the moment the object becomes the Other, . . . when the mute idol speaks, when the subject experiences the object as uncanny and feels the need for a . . . metaphysics of that never objectifiable depth from which objects rise up toward our superficial knowledge. (Bennett 2010, p. 2)

Can dead matter have history? Maybe because such history is essentially impossible, it can only take the form of a catastrophe in the image of an ecological disaster.

In any case, Marx's materialist history is characterized by a drive opposite to Bennett's. Instead of going beyond the object to reach the mysterious thing, Marx finds the mystery on the side of the object. That is what he writes at the beginning of the chapter on fetishism:

> The form of wood, for instance, is altered if a table is made out of it. Nevertheless the table continues to be wood, an ordinary, sensuous thing. But as soon as it emerges as a commodity, it changes into a thing which transcends sensuousness.[72]

That is why Marx's materialism can be historical. A thing, for him, assumes a social role precisely insofar as there is a mystery in it that marks that aspect of the social that is not reducible to the perception of individual subjects. It assumes an irreducibly social and historical role precisely to the extent that it is uncanny, that there is something in it that transcends our knowledge of it. Bennett points to a split between the social role of an object and its pre-conceptual thingness. Marx folds this split into the social object itself. The social is that which is in the object beyond its thingness. Desire for money can mark this split: desire signals that dimension in gold that is beyond its meaningless material qualities.

Returning to Žižek, we find that his interpretation of commodity fetishism provides a good formulation for the way objects carry a residue that transcends the individual, utilitarian framework. The object, in his view, is not simply external to the subject, but carries an innermost kernel of the subject. Things such as beliefs or emotions have external existence in objects:

> The point of Marx's analysis, however, is that *the things (commodities) themselves believe in their place*, instead of the subjects; it is as if all their beliefs, superstitions and metaphysical mystifications, supposedly surmounted by the rational, utilitarian personality, are embodied in the *social relations between things*. They no longer believe, but *the things themselves believe for them.*[73]

Žižek applies this view to the gap between thought and practice. For example, people may know very well that in itself money has no value, but in their conduct they behave as if they believe that it is the pure embodiment of value. An important point here is that the object does not stand only for social beliefs but in this case, also for irrationality. The object stands for irrationality at a historical epoch governed by the image of the rational, utilitarian individual.

A concrete example of the irrational object can be found in the discipline of behavioral economics.

Behavioral Economics and the Irrationality of Objects

Since the 1980s we have witnessed a growing interest in the relatively new discipline of behavioral economics, with titles such as Dan Ariely's *Predictably Irrational* becoming national best sellers. As the title of this book suggests, this discipline is occupied with proving that people are not as rational as economic theory supposes them to be. This was allegedly demonstrated by a vast body of amusing experiments beginning with Tversky and Kahneman who showed, for example, that people would drive 20 minutes to save $5 off of a $15 calculator but would not do the same to save $5 when the price of the calculator was $125.[74] The main deception in this discipline lies in the word choice, namely, the eminent notion of rationality. It certainly would be true to say that such experiments show that people are not utility-maximizing animals. But such a formulation would relate the findings to a fundamental theoretical error of economics. It might suggest, alas, that there is something fundamentally wrong with the concept of utility.[75]

By formulating the claims of behavioral economics in terms of rationality—an enormously wider concept than utility maximization—it somehow shifts the blame to people: it is *people* who are not rational. (This is the oldest trick in the book of outdated science: if reality does not conform to theory, then reality must be mistaken.[76]) But this is a preposterously ridiculous claim. It boils down to the meaningless statement that the economic subject, this figment of imagination that has informed economic philosophy for more than one hundred years now, is rational, while people are not. There may be valid ways to argue that people are not rational, but certainly not when this imaginary figure is the standard of rationality.

To take the argument one step further, it would not be far reaching to say that the message of behavioral economics is that economic *objects* are rational whereas people are not. That is to say, what behavioral economics shows is that people's behavior does not conform to the manner of conduct derived from a basic assumption of economics about objects, namely, that money is a neutral means for purchasing objects of utility and for measuring and comparing utilities of different objects.

Our discussion suggests considering the opposite view, namely, that it is the object rather than the subject that is irrational. Economic objects confront people with crystallized patterns of irrationality regardless of how rational or irrational these people are. (But how can an object be irrational? Well, this is certainly less strange than the idea that imaginary, theoretical constructs are rational, keeping in mind that rationality is primarily a predicate of human beings.)

A direct demonstration of how an allegedly irrational behavior is actually inscribed in economic objects is found in Ariely's work. Ariely wonders why ordinary people might steal small items in certain circumstances—a can of Coke from a refrigerator in a common area, office supplies from their work place, and so on—but would not steal an equivalent sum of money. Ariely conducted a series of experiments to verify that this is indeed the case and to explain "how does this irrational impulse work?"[77]

Regardless of the explanation Ariely eventually formulates, a simple answer already lies in the question, obscured only by the economic tenets of utility and equivalence. The simple explanation is that people are basically honest, and they would not steal an object of value. Of course, in strict economic terms a $1-pencil is equivalent in its value to a $1-bill. Yet this equivalence is in contrast to the reality of the contemporary consumer economy where a $1-pencil is in fact a type of rubbish. The pencil has no economic value whatsoever once it is purchased. It ceases to be an economic thing (i.e., something that can be sold and bought) and enters the untraceable sphere of objects that the consumer economy places at our disposal—some of them more useful, some less, but as whole comprising a burdening mass we constantly take care of. (Every citizen in a consumer economy gets a sickening feeling from time to time; we simply have far too many *things*—something we never say of money.[78]) In other words, what Ariely's question fails to notice is Marx's insight about the monetary economy—money is more valuable than any specific thing that money can buy. Ariely's experiments confirm the status of money as an irrational object: a thing that surpasses its equivalents.

An interesting historical view arises from this coincidence. Marx formulated his interpretation of money in an age of industrial capitalism and gold-based money, but it has become specifically valid for late capitalism with its fiat money. Indeed, even in industrial capitalism, most things lost economic value once they were purchased. But this feature is overwhelmingly underlined in late capitalism with its culture of disposable objects and frantic consumption.

The intriguing point is that precisely through the process of dematerialization, money assumes to the fullest a place allotted to it already in the time of gold-based money. At first glance, the dematerialization of money seems to conform to the economic conception of it. It suggests that money sheds the irrational aura of gold to become a perfect means—a thing of *lesser* importance than the commodities it can buy. But reality proves otherwise; as with the parallel processes of dematerialization of commodities, money becomes even more important in comparison to them. It is the irrational stain of money that governs its historical process of dematerialization.

Perhaps we should look at Ariely's explanation of the peculiarity of money after all. He presents various experiments and observations that confirm the basic insight in various contexts. People steal or tell lies a little in reference to non-monetary things, much more so than with cash. But his explanation only reiterates the findings in more general terms:

> When we deal with money, we are primed to think about our actions as if we had just signed an honor code. If you look at a dollar bill, in fact, it seems to have been designed to conjure up a contract: THE UNITED STATES OF AMERICA, it says in prominent type, with a shadow beneath that makes it seem three-dimensional. And there is George Washington himself (and we all know that he could never tell a lie). And then, on the back, it gets even more serious: IN GOD WE TRUST, it says. And then we've got that weird pyramid, and on top, that unblinking eye! And it's looking right at us! (p. 229)

The grain of truth in this strange account is that money is a mysterious thing. But the wrong path is to ground this mysteriousness in the actual properties of a banknote. The true philosophical question is: How can a thing be mysterious in any real sense of the term? Basically, a thing is mysterious when we do not understand it. But in the usual sense of the word, the mystery refers only to our knowledge of the thing. A thing can be really mysterious when our mystification of it is a part of what constitutes it as an object. That is why the moon cannot be really mysterious, but money can.

The mysteriousness of money, however, can also be considered a basic form of associating desire and history. On the one hand, mystery may mark the historicity of money, the way it carries a vestige that transcends the subject's knowledge. On the other hand, mystery is the way money is desired against its formal properties. It is useless in itself but still desired more than the useful things it can buy. Mystery is indeed often related to desire—think of the way a certain mysterious quality turns our desire to a man or a woman. But in the case of money, we are faced by a coincidence of mystery and desire: there is no mysterious quality of money that attracts our desire. It is mysterious insofar as it is desired.

Desire and History

To see why desire is indeed a plausible ontological basis for money, we can recall Arjun Appadurai's idea of *methodological fetishism*. An interpretation of the social meaning of things requires the counterintuitive assumption that things do have meaning. The commonsensical assumption that inanimate things are devoid of meaning in themselves and that meaning is bestowed on them only by humans does not take the anthropologist very far regarding the illumination of the "concrete, historical circulation of things." This task requires the assumption that the meaning of things is somehow inscribed in them. To decipher their meaning, Appadurai writes that "we have to follow the things themselves, for their meanings are inscribed in their forms, their uses, their trajectories."[79] That Appadurai stresses the fact of circulation is essential in this respect. It allows us to postulate that the meaning of an inanimate thing does not indeed reside *in* it, yet because it is related to its relations to other things, it also transcends the meaning that an individual bestows on it. Money, in that case, represents the pure form of methodological fetishism because it is constituted only by its relations to other things.

This assumption of methodological fetishism can be rendered into a phenomenological requirement of the subjective relation associated with money. Granted that it must be entailed with some kind of a subjective relation, we have come across different options: thought, belief, and desire, to mention the most obvious ones. The choice between them should be guided by the fetishistic reversal that characterizes the form of this subjective relation. With money, perhaps more than with any other economic object, this relation appears to emanate from the object itself, regardless of our real relation to it. This reversal cannot be easily reckoned with regard to thought. It requires a certain agility to claim that we think that the money is valuable even if in actuality we think otherwise.

In reference to belief, the question is what we mean by the term. If we use belief in the sense of expectation (I believe that the sun will rise tomorrow; I believe that other people will accept this banknote), then the same problem of grounding money on thought applies here also. However, in reference to religious beliefs, the reversal is very common as evident with regard to sacred objects. The sacredness of objects is maintained by our relation to them, yet sacredness is predicated on its appearance as the object's own quality, independent of our belief. Indeed, it makes a lot of sense to theorize money as a sacred object. However, this reversal also seems a basic feature of desire.

In the case of desire, it seems almost necessary that the subjective relation appears as emanating from the object—as if the object is desirable and not that it is we who desire it. In a sexual context, for example, Freud emphasized such a reversal as distinguishing the erotic life of modern times in relation to antiquity:

> The ancients glorified the instinct and were prepared on its account to honor even an inferior object; while we despise the instinctual activity itself, and find excuses for it only in the merits of the object.[80]

Understanding the fetishistic reversal as characterizing, in some form or another, desire as such—and not just as one specific historical formation of it— paves the way to positing it as a historical substance or as the mark of historicity upon things. Naturally, we tend to conceive of desire as a deep and very personal affect, which is the very opposite of historical substance. But considering that the object of desire is by definition not fully intelligible for the subject, it can be the medium where history confronts the subject as impenetrable.

Marx's idea that money is worth more than its equivalents demonstrates precisely such articulation of desire and history. It refers on the one hand to a basic, objective historical reality, namely, to the situation where money can be exchanged for any economic object. But it also traces on this basic economic reality a form of perverse desire, inconceivable in terms of the rational individual. In other words, it is precisely this view from the vantage point of desire that allows us to conceive of money as a historical object and not just as a-historical, rational means.

In Judith Butler's reading of the function of desire in Hegel's *The Phenomenology of Spirit*, we can find a more radical way to weave desire into history.

> Desire in its articulation always thematizes the conditions of its own existence. When we ask, what is desire "after," we can always give a partial answer: the illumination of its own opacity, the expression of that aspect of the world that brought it into being.[81]

Here desire is understood not only as a historical condition of a subject's confrontation with the world but also as conferring a certain shape on history.

If we put aside the Hegelian notion of history as the unfolding of reason in the world, we can find in Butler's formulation a framework for an overarching history of money as an object of desire. It suggests a narrative of the thematization of an irrational kernel of money that emerges precisely through its growing rationality. Paraphrasing Butler, we could say that money develops through the illumination of the opacity of the desire for money. But what is illuminated through this course of history is never a substantial aim of the desire for money, but the empty negativity of this desire, the fact that it cannot have a substantial aim or even that it annuls substantial aims.

The notion of desire illuminating its conditions of existence can be read as the key to processes of financialization that characterize late capitalism. With these processes, production aimed at profits gives way to financial profits. In Marx's words:

> [T]he circulation M-C-M' presents itself in abridged form, in its final result without any intermediate stage, in a concise style, so to speak, as M-M', i.e., money which is worth more money, value which is greater than itself.[82]

The point is that the final result M-M' is not an aberration of the circulation of capital but its true aim. Production was organized to begin with as the aim of profit. The devastating effects of the shift to a financial economy—the degradation and emptying of urban industrial areas—can be seen as money illuminating its empty negative desire. Setting aside this grand narrative, this book shows the shape of the historical process to be conducive to the understanding of more local histories.

Chapter 3 presents the dissolution of the gold standard, not as an overcoming of the pathological desire for money but, as the desire spilling over to the sphere of commodities in the consumer economy where brand names are the effects of desire for money in the sphere of things. Chapter 4 deals with Weber's thesis about the emergence of the capitalist spirit from a religious ethos and presents the movement of secularization as an explication of the empty kernel of desire for money. Chapter 5 deals, from a Veblenian perspective, with the shift from an old money culture to a new money culture and presents the shift not as a process of vulgarization but as the hidden logic of the economy of display becoming explicit.

Revolution

This general sketch of a concept of history should be complemented with a note on its mirror image, namely, revolution. In the Marxist tradition we find discussions of the objective conditions for a revolution (e.g., when objective economic conditions become unbearable so that only a revolution would provide a solution). In light of Marx's concept of the social object, these discussions appear partial. There can be no objective conditions for a revolution because a revolution must include an element of overcoming the object. A revolution is not brought about simply by objective conditions but entails unmasking objectivity, overcoming those elements of social life that are disguised as objective.

With reference to Marx, the overcoming of the object has a concrete and radical sense—the abolition of private property. This abolition is not just a brute political act—a redistribution of the things in the world. It is an abolition of the institution of private property, of the way we own things in a capitalist society. It thus entails a cognitive change. What would be abolished in a revolution is the way private property appears as an objective reality and as socio-natural properties of things. But the idea of revolution as an overcoming of the object also informs less radical demands for change. It is relevant for the critique of neo-liberalism because various aspects of neo-liberalism—deregulation of markets, opening economies to the influence of global finance, and so on—are typically promoted in the guise of objectivity, as a reply to an objective necessity. The first step of resisting is unmasking this guise of objectivity.

A crystallized formulation of this notion of revolution already appears in Marx's "Theses on Feuerbach." Consider the famous eleventh thesis: "The philosophers have only *interpreted* the world, in various ways; the point is to *change* it."[83] This thesis already implies the notion that revolution must include a cognitive aspect. It is not a call to forsake philosophy and take direct political action, but a demand from philosophy to partake in changing the world. This thesis is about thought no less than about revolution. It suggests that thought is in essence anarchic because thought is not committed in any way to the given order of things.

But what is this revolutionary thought? The second thesis elaborates the answer:

> The question whether objective truth can be attributed to human thinking is not a question of theory but is a *practical* question. Man must prove the truth—i.e., the reality and power, the this-sidedness of his thinking in practice. The dispute over the reality or non-reality of thinking that is isolated from practice is a purely *scholastic* question.[84]

The point that must be stressed is that this invocation of practice is not just a call for action, a demand that people act upon their views and knowledge. It is more important to read this thesis as an epistemological statement. In this reading, Marx rejects the notion of truth as correspondence. In the social world, with reference to social objects, correspondence is not truth but an ideological image. Thought that conceives of the social world in this world's own terms corresponds to reality but is not true thought. It is simply a part of the order of things, and it takes part in reduplicating this order.

Thought is real insofar as it changes something fundamental in the order of things. In this conception of thought, truth is inherently related to practice: the truth value of thought, *as thought*, is determined by activity. Truth is tested not by correspondence to the object but by its ability to intervene with the object. To give a concrete example—when we stroll in the supermarket, we may very well think that we are entitled to take whatever we please. After all, someone nicely arranged the goods on the shelves for our desire. But the nature of this thought is ultimately determined by action: thinking like this and taking whatever we please is not the same as thinking and nonetheless paying for what we take.

This notion of revolution positions it as the opposite of material history. If the history of social antagonism is the history embedded in objects, then revolution is its opposite in the sense that it entails overcoming the object. Revolution in this sense is extra-historical, which does not mean simply that it never happens. Revolution is that which does not happen in each and every moment. And history is the story of how revolution never occurs.

Literary Excursus: Two Ways of Not Having One's Money

Why should economists read Charles Dickens? His genius in monetary affairs is found in his insight into the traumatic nature of possessing money. Like Marx's capitalist, and like Midas, the monetary characters in Dickens's novels do not simply possess money but strictly speaking are possessed by it. They are possessed by their possessions, experiencing them as a source of an overwhelming influence over them. This insight should not be read in psychological terms but as a genuine insight into economic ontology. In this respect, Dickens can be read as complementary to the Marxian ontology. As a matter of fact, we can find in Dickens a link between the different social objects found in Marx: private property and money. What Dickens suggests is that money is the pure form of property precisely because it carries to an extreme the element of in-ownership that is essential to property.

One of the best portrayals of this aspect is found in *David Copperfield* in the coupling of Mr. And Mrs. Micawber, on one side, and Barkis, the cart driver, on the other. The Micawbers lavishly spend money that they don't have. They extravagantly spend the money that they expect to receive after the success of their latest economic initiative, which eventually and invariably fails. Barkis, on the other hand, has gathered a "heap of money" without such colorful schemes but simply through years of thrift, and he keeps it under his bed in a closed box that he pretends is full of coats and trousers.

These two approaches to money should not be seen simply as opposites. Recalling again how Simmel brings together avarice and extravagance, we should see these approaches as mirror images, two complementary positions in reference to money: not spending the money one has and spending the money one does not have. These two positions can be seen as the two extreme forms of the enjoyment of money. Naturally, one can also buy pleasurable things with the money one has but, strictly speaking, this would not be an enjoyment of money. To use Keynes's words, in this case money is only "a means to the enjoyments and realities of life."

Following Simmel we can also understand why, in his strange way, Barkis, in contrast to Dickens's portrayals of capitalists, is an affectionate figure. He is the true generous character in the plot, not only because he goes against his nature and, with the aid of ridiculous masquerades and presumably through immense spiritual efforts, takes money out of the box to give to Copperfield but also because it is his will that resolves the plot, including the Micawbers' ongoing predicaments. It is, paradoxically, a generous will, an act of generosity beyond death.

However, the symmetry between Barkis and the Micawbers should also be described in terms of the ontology of money. Rephrasing this ontology in terms of everyday experience, we can speculate that the fantasies about things we can do with money are related more to the reality of money than to the actual things we do with money (which is another way of explaining how money is worth more than anything money can buy).[85] But maybe we can notice this peculiarity also in a plea that Marx sends to Friedrich Engels during his exile in London: "Never has anyone written about 'money in general' amidst such total lack of money in particular."[86] In ontological terms, these inversions call for conceiving of the reality of money as intertwining presence and absence. The money that is absent (as is the money the Micawbers spend) is somehow much more vivid and visible, much more *present*, than is the dull money that actually exists (Barkis's money).

A form of absence informs Barkis's relation to his money. To enjoy it, Barkis imagines it gone. Thus, when Copperfield visits him during his illness as he lays half paralyzed by his severe rheumatics, Barkis raises with great effort a stick attached to the side of his bed and pokes at the money box:

> "Old clothes," said Mr. Barkis.
>
> "Oh!" said I.
>
> "I wish it was Money, sir," said Mr. Barkis.
>
> "I wish it was, indeed," said I.
>
> "But it AIN'T," said Mr. Barkis, opening both his eyes as wide as he possibly could.[87]

This should not be read simply as a decoy. Copperfield is very well aware of the contents of the box. And if he doesn't yet know, Barkis has surely drawn his attention to it. The gesture should rather be read literally as Barkis's true relation to his own money: he wishes it was money. It is a manifestation of the manner his own money is somehow placed beyond his reach.

It is this element of grotesque display that gradually, through his illness, takes hold of Barkis's whole being. When he is no longer fully aware of the presence of other people around him, he clings to this one gesture. That is how we see him, in the sentimental scene of his deathbed, as he is surrounded by the people he loved:

> He was lying with his head and shoulders out of bed, in an uncomfortable attitude, half resting on the box which had cost him so much pain and trouble. I learned, that, when he was past creeping out of bed to open it, and past assuring himself of its safety by means of the divining rod I had seen him use, he had required to have it placed on the chair at the bedside, where he had ever since embraced it, night and day. His arm lay on it now. Time and the world were slipping from beneath him, but the box was there; and the last words he had uttered were (in an explanatory tone) "Old clothes!"[88]

In standard economic terms, this as an extremely pathological relation to money. Yet there is a certain logic to it that can be described in simple formal terms: money that is not recognized by others is not money; therefore, Barkis's efforts to hide his money from others turn it into a worthless object, no more valuable than old clothes. His obsession of hiding his money puts his money beyond his own reach.

A richer formulation of this is found in Marx's "Comments on James Mill." In this short piece, Marx introduces a conceptual analysis of money as an extreme form of private property. He concludes in a statement that fully recapitulates Barkis's position: "We ourselves are excluded from true property because our property excludes other men."[89] Why does private property exclude its proprietor? In a society of private property, Marx writes, what a man produces is aimed at other men. It is produced to be exchanged with other men's products—what a man produces is actually his other's desire.

As a comment on a classical economic text, here one can clearly see the vestiges of the economic myth of barter (the butcher that exchanges his surplus meat with the baker). However, setting aside these vestiges, this statement can be seen as a basic condition of private property when it is conceived as a social relation. If we theoretically distinguish between possession, *true property*, as the direct relation to a thing—the enjoyments and direct uses afforded by it—and ownership as social institution, then what Marx notes is that ownership must include an element that is alien to possession, an element that is alien to the direct experience of the thing.

Thus, while the concept of alienation sets exclusion or dispossession as a condition of capitalist production, here it is set as a condition of the very institution of private property. It is in this sense that money can be seen as the pinnacle of private property. What it carries to an extreme is precisely this element of exclusion, of *not yours*, that is essential to private property. Money is the extreme form of ownership because it has no other quality but ownership—it has no sense outside the context of ownership. Yet, precisely as an extreme form of private property, it has nothing truly private in it: it is completely meaningless as a private object.

Money, therefore, embodies the element of dispossession inherent in private property. This observation proves useful for outlining how desire for money is inscribed back on things, how things can be seen as embodiments of desire for money. Consider again the watchmaker Patek Philippe. Its famous advertising slogan pronounces this quite explicitly: *You never actually own a Patek Philippe. You merely look after it for the next generation.* Notice that this slogan is not addressed to the masses, who will never be able to afford a $20,000 watch, but at the people who might actually buy it. Strangely enough, what it tells them is *even if you buy it, it will not be actually yours.*

One can think of some practical justifications for the invocation of in-ownership as an incentive for purchasing. For example, it is impossible to attribute the scandalous price to any real or imagined gratifications related to the watch or to justify it by the properties of the watch. Think how lame an advertisement would be that invokes the standard commonsensical explanations for luxury as social status: *buy the watch and people will admire you* or even the ultimate chauvinistic insinuation: *buy it and you will get any woman you want.*

Furthermore, it may well be that even an owner of such a watch relates to this fragile concentration of wealth with some awe, precisely as the slogan states. But these explanations can be seen as manifestations of an underlying logic that allows us to conceive of the watch as an object carrying the mark of money, an object that embodies wealth. If money embodies the element of in-ownership essential to private property, then an object is entangled with money to the extent that it cannot be had.

Chapter 2

HISTORY
Fantasies of a Capitalist

Literature as Heterodox Economics

Marx's notion of personification explains why economists should turn to literary fiction in search of real knowledge of money. As argued in the previous chapter, this notion should be taken seriously, not simply as a metaphor but as the mode of existence of economic objects. Capital exists only through this displacement, through the interchange between the thing and the person. Capital can exist as an object insofar as it embodies a drive that confronts the subject as an alien force.

The great literature about money can thus provide us with a phenomenological supplement to Marx's theoretical position. This is particularly true of Dickens's novels, which typically present us with characters, whether capitalists or lay people, who are overwhelmed by the fact of money. These characters can be seen as a direct echo of the Marxian economic ontology implied by the notion of personification. They experience their property as commanding an injunction. They let their property color the whole of their relations with their surroundings. They encircle it with fears, suspicions, and threats. In short they are, strictly speaking, possessed by their possessions.

The path breaking works of Marc Shell and Walter Benn Michaels have shown how money provides a fertile interpretative key to literary texts. This chapter takes this idea one step further in a reading that proceeds from literature to economics. It suggests that literature can provide real economic knowledge, which is, however, constitutively ignored by orthodox economics. To take advantage of this possibility, this chapter inserts a reading of Dickens into an imaginary debate between orthodox and heterodox economics that concerns the social and historical ontology of money. It shows how the debate between heterodox and orthodox economics can be reduced to concrete questions about the ontology of money.

The Violence of Fact

Marx's concept of objectivity as it is elaborated in relation to fetishism is distinguished by the unique form of mystification where *things appear as what they are*, which situates the social object in a tension-ridden coincidence of reality and appearance. The existence of the social object—whether private property, money, a commodity, or capital—depends on it being both *really* objective (i.e., external, inert, independent of any subject) and *as if* it is objective (i.e., entangled with a subjective relation that posits it *as if* it is external and independent of the subject).

A perfect literary parallel to this theoretical position is to be found in Dickens's *Hard Times*. We first encounter it in the opening lines of the novel, which present us with Thomas Gradgrind's obsession with facts. Gradgrind, a retired and wealthy merchant, has established a school to perpetrate his commitment to facts. In the beginning of the novel, we meet him as he shows the school to a friend:

> "Now, what I want is, Facts. Teach these boys and girls nothing but Facts. Facts alone are wanted in life. Plant nothing else, and root out everything else. You can only form the minds of reasoning animals upon Facts: nothing else will ever be of any service to them. This is the principle on which I bring up my own children, and this is the principle on which I bring up these children. Stick to Facts, sir!"[1]

Martha Nussbaum sees in the portrayal of this obsession for facts a critique of the utilitarian view, which demonstrates how the fanatic adherence to measurable facts necessarily omits the essential dimensions of human existence with its rich complexity.[2] These dimensions are scornfully marked by the factual view as fancies and are associated in the novel with the figure of Sissy Jupe, the daughter of a traveling circus man, who has just joined the school. In her first appearance in the novel, Sissy fails to provide a definition of a horse and is immediately corrected by Bitzer, the perfect pupil in Gradgrind's school, who eventually turns out to be a scoundrel. In a demonstration of the robot-like factual ideal set by Gradgrind, Bitzer recites:

> "Quadruped. Graminivorous. Forty teeth, namely, twenty-four grinders, four eye-teeth, and twelve incisive. Sheds coat in the spring; in marshy countries, sheds hoofs, too."

Adopting Nussbaum's argument we could say that though accurate, Bitzer's definition leaves out important aspects like the beauty of horses or the way we see them as noble animals.

Although Nussbaum's interpretation is valid in certain respects, it clearly misses an essential dimension, as is evident in the fact that it spoils Dickens's joke completely. It underlines what the quantifiable fact omits from the account but thus misses the point that Dickens's irony is addressed to the idea of fact itself. His critique is more radical than what Nussbaum suggests because it puts fact itself in question. By directing our gaze not simply to the factual worldview but to the *persona*, to the person obsessed with facts, Dickens situates fancy, this despised double, at the heart of fact. Thus, we should notice the switch of the roles between fancy and factuality when Sissy Jupe defends, quite commonsensically, her theoretical willingness to decorate a room with a carpet of flowery patterns:

> "So you would carpet your room—or your husband's room, if you were a grown woman, and had a husband—with representations of flowers, would you?" said the gentleman. "Why would you?"
>
> "If you please, sir, I am very fond of flowers," returned the girl.
>
> "And is that why you would put tables and chairs upon them, and have people walking over them with heavy boots?"
>
> "It wouldn't hurt them, sir. They wouldn't crush and wither, if you please, sir. They would be the pictures of what was very pretty and pleasant, and I would fancy—"
>
> "Ay, ay, ay! But you mustn't fancy," cried the gentleman, quite elated by coming so happily to his point. "That's it! You are never to fancy."
>
> "You are not, Cecilia Jupe," Thomas Gradgrind solemnly repeated, "to do anything of that kind."
>
> "Fact, fact, fact!" said the gentleman. And "Fact, fact, fact!" repeated Thomas Gradgrind.[3]

The irony, clearly, is that it is the factual attitude that manifests a deranged sensitivity to figments of imagination, unable to distinguish between representations and reality. We are not speaking of economy yet, but already we can see that we are in the general realm of Marx's fetishism, where the objectivity of facts entails a vestige of disavowed subjectivity. This shadow of subjectivity can be noticed in Dickens in the manner objectivity becomes a puritan ethics and aesthetics.

> "You are to be in all things regulated and governed," said the gentleman, "by fact. We hope to have, before long, a board of fact, composed of commissioners of fact, who will force the people to be a people of fact, and of nothing but fact. You must discard the word Fancy altogether. You have nothing to do with it. You are not to have, in any object of use or ornament, what would be a contradiction in fact. You don't walk upon flowers in fact; you cannot be allowed to walk upon flowers in carpets. You don't find that foreign birds and butterflies come and perch upon your crockery; you cannot be permitted to paint foreign birds and butterflies upon your crockery. You never meet with quadrupeds going up and down walls; you must not have quadrupeds represented upon walls. You must use," said the gentleman, "for all these purposes, combinations and modifications (in primary colours) of mathematical figures which are susceptible of proof and demonstration. This is the new discovery. This is fact. This is taste."[4]

This critique of utilitarian philosophy goes much deeper than what Nussbaum points to. Although utilitarianism presents itself as striving to establish impersonal moral judgments on facts, in Dickens, by contrast, we see how fact itself becomes a moral imperative. It is not a moral imperative deduced from a factual basis but factuality, which somehow by itself becomes an all-encompassing ethics and aesthetics. How can factuality occupy this position? In a formal sense it cannot. Fact alone cannot be a source of aesthetics and ethics. But in Dickens we see how this impossibility turns out to be a key to the *form* of an ethics and aesthetics of fact. It confers on this ethics the form of an external, incomprehensible imperative.

A similar reversal is evident in Marx's concept of capital: the possession of money cannot make one a capitalist; it cannot force one into an endless race for profit. But this gap between objective position and subjective behavior is itself the *form* of the conduct of the capitalist, as submission to an external imperative, foreign to subjectivity that allegedly emanates from the object itself. However, the obsession of fact does not involve only an ascetic ethic on the side of its followers. It is also involved with violence toward others. That is another dimension in which Dickens's critique of utilitarianism goes deeper than Nussbaum's interpretation of it.

Factuality, in Dickens, is intimately associated with violence. In this chapter, bluntly titled "Murdering the Innocents," the violence of fact is represented in the public humiliation of Sissy Jupe for her lack of adherence to the factual approach. This violence of fact suggests that although we have not yet touched economic subject matter, we are already within the economic worldview. This is how Marx characterizes economic knowledge in his early writings: it is inherently hostile to humankind. In its progress from Adam Smith to David Ricardo and Mill, economic knowledge becomes more cynical. These latter economists, he writes, advance in their "estrangement from man"; however, they do so "*only* because their science develops more consistently and truthfully."5 The strange point is that economic knowledge is cynical and hostile, not despite its objectivity, but precisely because of it: the more objective economic knowledge is, the more violent it becomes.

The question of how objectivity can be cynical or hostile rather than simply neutral is a deeply theoretical one. Yet before answering it on the theoretical level, we should note that the evolution of economic discourse seems to affirm Marx's observation. This is demonstrated by the contemporary economic trend known as *economic imperialism*, which applies an economic perspective to allegedly non-economic phenomena such as crime, the family, addictions, and others. The point is that by breaking into new ground, economic knowledge invariably manifests a cynical, misanthropic overtone.

When Gary Becker, the pioneer of this new approach, demonstrated it in his Nobel Prize lecture, he chose to analyze at length the trade-off parents may make between leaving an inheritance for their children and nurturing their feelings of guilt as alternative strategies to ensure they will look after them in old age. ("Parents who do not leave bequests may be willing to make their children feel guiltier precisely because they gain more utility from greater old-age consumption than they lose from an equal reduction in children's consumption."6)

An imperialistic economist would dismiss the accusations of cynicism that such a statement may raise by explaining that this is simply the way people are.7 Regardless of the question of whether and how this statement is true (maybe sometimes people are indeed like that), what's certain is that this is how economics thinks. Moreover, economics cannot think otherwise once it accepts utility maximization as the basic principle of human behavior. The impression of cynicism, not to say misanthropy, results simply from taking "the economic way of looking at life," to borrow Becker's own title, to its extreme and by applying it to every sphere of human behavior (an expansion that is a logical consequence of the concept of utility, since utility is meaningful only if it relates to all possible actions of a person.)

The misanthropic tone is emphasized against the background of family matters. But this shows only that the real question is how to refer cynicism to ordinary economic thought, that is to say, to economic thought directed at explicitly economic subject matter. Is ordinary economic thought also cynical? In what way? How is cynicism masked there? A possible answer is that it is hidden within economic objects. The idea that cynicism is overlooked when it is applied to economic objects may mean that it is embedded in them. But that is also the answer to our basic question: How can objectivity be not neutral, but hostile, to humanity? Objectivity can be misanthropic because of the object at stake. The *pure* economic object, namely, money is not neutral but in itself involved in hostile social relations.

First Fantasy: Desiring through the Other

In *Hard Times*, Gradgrind stands for utilitarian ideology, for its explicit self-perception (which reveals precisely through its consistency its perverse shadow). To realize the novel's full economic potential, we must move from theory to practice and from objectivity and factuality to objects. In relation to the novel, we must shift our attention from Gradgrind to his practical double and soul mate, the industrial capitalist Josiah Bounderby. The former, as a theorist, is basically a good guy, unaware of the implications of his views and, for that reason, by the end of the plot, he can repent. His practical friend, by contrast, is the main villain in the novel: a self-made man—crude, rude, and vulgar in his conduct—who cruelly oppresses his workers. In being a practical double, Bounderby has no prospect of redemption—one more demonstration of the idea that it is the object that marks the final closure of the subject, its un-freedom.

Gradgrind's obsession with facts is echoed in his friend's straightforward manner, as well as in his contempt of fancies and luxury and his repeated (false) claims to knowledge of hard reality, acquired during his childhood in the gutters. But just as Gradgrind's factuality turns our gaze toward his specific subjectivity, so does Bounderby's practical manner attract our attention to two fantasies that are central to his character. Both fantasies concern his money—his relation to his money, as well as his relations to other people mediated through his money. The first fantasy is that his workers desire some corrupt and luxurious pleasure at his expense. The second is his fictional life story of a self-made man, a story of ascension from a state of total deprivation to his present wealth. A careful reading reveals in his fantasies a deep insight into the social and historical ontology of money.

Bounderby's first fantasy springs up whenever someone appears to hint at a demand on him in relation to the workers in his factory. Whether these demands are totally imaginary or half-real, and whether they are pronounced by the workers themselves or by someone else, Bounderby's reaction is the same. He points to a corrupt wish that lies behind any hint of demand that is expressed by the workers. What they *really* want is "to be set up in a coach and six, and to be fed on turtle soup and venison, with a gold spoon."[8] This, in Bounderby's eyes, is "the sole, immediate, and direct object of any Hand who was not entirely satisfied."[9] When Stephan Blackpool, a worker who has come to seek his advice, expresses some general discontent at the legal situation that prevents him from divorcing his wife who deserted him, Bounderby warns him that he finds in his attitude "traces of the turtle soup, and venison, and gold spoon."

This imaginative phrase should not be read as mere fancy. Rather, as a fantasy it is entangled in two ways with the micro-social reality of money. First, through this fantasy, money mediates Bounderby's real relations to his workers. The fantasy of an excessive desire is part of a real relation of brutal and excessive exploitation. It is by means of this imagined excessive desire of the workers that Bounderby refuses to accede to any of their demands. Modest as it may be, every demand is interpreted as a first sign of the corrupt desire for "turtle soup and venison."

But second, and more importantly, the fantasy of other people's hidden intentions mediates Bounderby's relation to his own money: he conceives of his money through imagining how other people desire it. Here lies the more radical aspect of the fantasy. It situates a social formation in the most basic situation of possessing money and for that reason underscores the social nature of the object itself. What is this social formation? Bounderby imagines that his workers desire excessive pleasures that he himself conspicuously avoids. His earthly, vulgar attitude is often manifested in his contempt of such pleasures, his declared inability to understand them, and his preference for *simple* things.

This direction of the critique is underlined by a third category of people that surround the delicate pleasures of luxury: those who are fit to enjoy such pleasures. This category is represented by a typical old money character, namely, Bounderby's housekeeper Mrs. Sparsit, a widow who has lost her fortune but retained the delicate manners that only fortune can bestow. Surely, she does not enjoy "venison and turtle soup"—she is never actually seen eating in the novel as her manners prevent her from dining in the presence of others. Yet Bounderby enjoys lingering on the "Italian Opera" she frequented in her youth when he himself was a "tumbler in the mud of the streets." Furthermore, it is precisely because of this refined taste that Bounderby depicts himself as unworthy of Sparsit (though the truth is that he simply prefers a younger wife, the daughter of Gradgrind).

Thus, these two categories of other people put Bounderby's money beyond his own reach. His workers want to enjoy it but are prohibited, while Mrs. Sparsit is theoretically able to enjoy money, but she herself is put beyond Bounderby's reach. Keeping in mind the indigestible, traumatic kernel of desire for money, we could say that Bounderby desires through others. He transfers to others that kernel of desire for money that transcends the individual's perspective.

Economic Counterpart: The Story of Barter

Using Ingham's terms, the figure of Bounderby suggests a way to see money as a social relation. Ingham argues that money should be seen not only as socially produced, but also that in itself it should be seen as a social relation: "'money' can only be seen as constituted by social relations."[10] What the figure of Bounderby adds to this view is the idea that the social relations embedded in money are "thicker" than the formal relations that seem to account for its value (everybody accepts it and, therefore, it has value, etc.); these might include elements such as hostility, suspicion, aggression, and others.

Surprisingly, this possibility finds implicit support in classical economic thought. The structure, which puts the reality of money in relation to the imaginings of other people, has a direct echo in the age-old narrative that explains how money developed from a stage of barter exchange. This story begins with people directly exchanging with each other the fruits of their labor. The problem in this situation, as classical economics noted, is that the direct exchange of goods slows down commerce. The butcher who wants beer must find a brewer who needs meat. The following is Adam Smith's version of the key moment in this story when the market finally settles on one specific commodity that serves as a means of exchange:

> The butcher has more meat in his shop than he himself can consume, and the brewer and the baker would each of them be willing to purchase a part of it. But they have nothing to offer in exchange, except the different productions of their respective trades, and the butcher is already provided with all the bread and beer which he has immediate occasion for. In order to avoid the inconveniency of such situations, every prudent man in every period of society, after the first establishment of the division of labour, must naturally have endeavored to manage his affairs in such a manner, as to have at all times by him, besides the peculiar produce of his own industry, a certain quantity of some one commodity or other, such as he imagined few people would be likely to refuse in exchange for the produce of their industry.[11]

In this key moment of the story, a certain commodity becomes a general means of exchange. It functions, for the first time in the narrative, outside a relation of any specific person to it. In this sense it becomes social.

It is important to note Smith's careful formulation of this moment. In contrast with less attentive versions of this familiar story, the commodity becoming a means of exchange is not described simply as *something that everybody wants* or as a commodity in constant demand. Smith adds to this notion the dimension of *imagined* others. The commodity becoming a means of exchange is that which a prudent man "imagined few people would be likely to refuse in exchange for the produce of their industry." Here we have a direct echo of Bounderby. A primitive form of money is entangled here in fantasies of others and their desires. An object becoming money is dependent on imagining other people's relation to it. This is almost an exact replica of Bounderby's relation to his money: he imagines that other people want it.

There is an inner logic in Smith's formulation. The reason for invoking the *imagining* of other people and their desires rather than real people and their wants is that the story recounts nothing less than the birth of the social itself. Before the emergence of the first money-object, the story refers to a reality governed by the direct relations of people to objects. It is an economy of immediacy, of direct wants and satisfactions, where people produce in order to consume and exchange the surplus of their production with other people who want to consume it. This is a reality in which the butcher would not exchange meat for bread and beer if he was "provided with all the bread and beer which he has immediate occasion for." The problem is that in such a reality, an object that everybody wants would be immediately consumed and for that very reason will not be appropriate to serve as a means of exchange.

The insertion of imagined other people amounts to the insertion of the social itself, in the form of an object that stands for other people. Clearly, for that reason the story should not be taken literally as an account of a historical moment. It is doubtful whether there can be a narrative of the emergence of the social, and certainly this one is an absurd example of it. Indeed, critical perspectives on economy, from Polanyi to Graeber, have refuted the story, which keeps emerging in various forms across economic thought.[12] However, precisely because the story posits a possible social form embedded in money, such refutations seem too hasty. The story deserves the careful attention that we can award it if we suspend its truth judgment.

The story of barter, then, can be read as elaborating a possible manner in which the social is embedded in the money-object. It suggests that the social is embedded in the object in the form of a split: the fact that everybody avoids using the object articulates the fact that everybody wants it. We find here a perfect illustration of the idea that the social object stands for radical antagonism, that is to say, that it embodies the dimension of the intersubjective insofar as it is irreducible to concrete subjects.

Accepting, even as a type of thought experiment, the terms of the story, we can ask: When exactly does the object become money? When does it cease to be an object of use that also carries a social function and become a genuine social object, whose objective social function is detached from its physical qualities? The answer is that it becomes this when the two categories of people completely overlap, when we can no longer distinguish between the prudent, who keep the object for future exchange, and the careless, who joyfully consume it. It is a social object when everyone is both the prudent, who keeps the object, and the careless, who desires it. In this situation, the persistence of the role of the object is predicated on its social nature and not on its substantial qualities. It persists not as a physical object but as an object embodying a social structure of desire implicated with endless deference.

The money-object marks the presence of the social as a split within the individual. One avoids using the thing as a reflection of the way one desires it. In Marx, this formation is characteristic of the unique social reality of economy. Its most explicit articulation is the "three peculiarities of the equivalent form" in the first chapter of *Capital*, which refer to the same stage in the story of money we have dealt with: the moment when a common useful commodity functions as a general means of exchange.

In these peculiarities the economic aspect of things emerges through an internal opposition. Value is indifferent to use value, yet it cannot be embodied other than in a thing of use value. Value, therefore, is not simply something foreign to the specificity of the thing: to its qualities, uses, and the specific way it was made. Rather, value is what remains when we deduct any specific quality from it. This relation then expands into a set of relations between private, concrete labor and its social, abstract economic aspect:

- Use-value becomes the form of appearance of its opposite, namely, value.
- Concrete labor becomes the form of manifestation of its opposite, that is, abstract human labor.
- Private labor takes the form of its opposite, namely, labor in its directly social form.[13]

What should be noted is that these peculiarities outline economy as a specific form of the social, where the social is inscribed in a negative way on the private, concrete context. One can think of social contexts that are positively inscribed on the acts, thoughts, and wills of individuals, for example, when a group of people builds something together. That is what Searle calls *collective intentionality*: an individual's activity and intentionality that already implies the group and has no meaning outside its context (one cannot be a goalkeeper outside the context of team play).[14]

Marx's *peculiarities* mark the economy as a diametrically opposite social sphere, where the social aspect is defined by its foreignness to anything individual, concrete, and local. In the economic context, the social nature of a carpenter's labor has nothing to do with either his individuality or his positive sociability—with his specific skills, taste, and education, as well as his interactions with his fellow workers. It is what remains when we abstract all this to view his labor as an embodiment of universal, abstract, social labor.

It is this formation of the social that lies at the heart of Smith's account of the way money is entangled with the imaginings of other people. Its social nature is marked by desiring others, while it is experienced in the form of avoidance. To paraphrase the Marxian formula, we can add a further peculiarity:

- Personal avoidance becomes the form of appearance of its opposite, that is, desire as a social form.

Of course, at first glance such a formulation seems valid only in relation to a speculated, primitive money that is a certain useful commodity, such as salt or goats, which comes to assume the position of a general equivalent. In relation to modern money, and actually in relation to most forms of money known to us, there seems to be little sense in the idea that people avoid using it for the simple reason that it has no use.

However, Smith's narrative suggests a different reading. The uselessness of money can be understood as the *objectification* of the social form that entangles desire and avoidance—the manner in which it becomes fully embedded in objects. We can speculate that by being or becoming useless, money fully assumes its place as an object embodying indefinitely deferred desire. Perhaps the social formation of desire should be considered as the historical substance of money that is carried over with it through time. That is precisely the possibility suggested by Dickens's novel, where money is not simply useless but embodies an impossible pleasure.

The Impossible Pleasure of Money

To continue our thought experiment, in both Dickens and Adam Smith, money is set in a formation that associates avoidance with the imagining of other people and their desires. But clearly, there are some basic differences between Smith and Dickens, which result from the difference in the moments to which they refer: whereas Smith refers to the speculative moment of the emergence of money, Dickens refers to money that is already established. In the following, I note these differences in detail.

Smith imagines one useful commodity that assumes the function of a means of exchange. Its direct use becomes systematically avoided and that is how it enables better access to all other commodities (the butcher who wants beer does not have to find precisely that brewer who wants meat).

Let us look at Bounderby as he enjoys the estate he has bought from one of the Coketown magnates who went bankrupt due to reckless speculation:

> It afforded Mr. Bounderby supreme satisfaction to install himself in this snug little estate, and with demonstrative humility to grow cabbages in the flower-garden. He delighted to live, barrack-fashion, among the elegant furniture, and he bullied the very pictures with his origin.[15]

In certain senses, this description is the opposite of Smith's tale. What Bounderby avoids is a plethora of habits, some real, some imaginary (growing flowers, enjoying paintings, but also being fed turtle soup with a golden spoon), but not one specific object.

Furthermore, his own enjoyment, in this context, seems to belong to what in Smith's tale is the moment before economy: the immediate, practical enjoyment of things, like that of the butcher who would not exchange for more than he has immediate occasion for. In his fantasy, Bounderby avoids mediated pleasure (pleasures that require refined taste and nurturing), to get access to immediate ones (growing cabbages in the flower garden)—a mirror image of Smith's tale where the baker, the butcher, and the brewer forgo the direct use of one particular item to mediate access to all others. However, underlying these inversions, a deep affinity resides between these two moments.

What Bounderby avoids can be termed *the phantasmic, direct pleasures of money in a reality where money can no longer be directly enjoyed.* The enjoyments he avoids are all colored by money. They can easily be classified under Veblen's term of *conspicuous consumption*, which refers to things that display waste and expensiveness. Consider the example of the workers aspiration of being fed turtle soup with a golden spoon. It is not simply that it is expensive and exotic. It gives away its underlying monetary logic in its additive nature, in the dynamic of increase beyond limits: not only turtle soup, but being fed it, and not only being fed, but being fed with a golden spoon (in contrast to things, as Marx notes, money can be desired beyond any limit).

At the same time, this dynamic that inscribes money on the imaginary pleasures also makes it an impossible, unreachable one. At its peak it is a pleasure of the medium, of the tool: the golden spoon. Again, as noted, the desire for things-as-money robs them of their very thingness. How can one enjoy a golden spoon? What can it add to the enjoyment of the turtle soup? With this we can point to the final affinity to Smith's tale: for Bounderby, just as in Smith, the avoidance of the pleasure of money allows access to things. Allegedly, his enjoyments are of the direct, immediate kind. But in truth they are mediated through the negation of the desires and pleasures that Bounderby relegates to others. To be precise: his enjoyments appear immediate only in comparison with the sophisticated, mediated pleasures. He does not simply enjoy the practical habit of growing cabbage, but of growing it in the flower garden.

Thus, we have come full circle back to Smith's story. A certain structure persists beyond the changes between Smith's and Dickens's versions of the story: *the avoidance of the direct enjoyment of money mediates access to other objects.* In other words, Dickens provides us with nothing less than a key to an alternative understanding of the history of money. The classical narrative of the origin of money from barter usually carries an ideological weight. It serves to illustrate money's benign effect: money lubricates exchanges and enables easier access to commodities. In the classical use of the story, money begins as one commodity among others and gradually becomes external to the sphere of commodities, a pure means for their administration. This presentation of the narrative supports the economic idea of the neutrality of money.

Dickens's novel suggests a way to not simply reject the myth of barter but to turn it upside down. It suggests that an object assumes the function of money as it embodies a social formation of desire and avoidance and that it keeps this position only due to the persistence of this social formation. In this interpretation, the money-object does not become useless and, thus, devoid of desire. Rather, it embodies an impossible pleasure and, thus, becomes the object of desire par excellence. This latter alternative is marked in Dickens by the resurgence of an excessive phantasmic form of the pleasure of the money-object, extinguished in reality.

We can speak about money not simply as a useless object but as an object of an impossible use insofar as its factual existence is accompanied by fantasies of its direct pleasure. Bounderby demonstrates how these fantasies are not just imaginary effects. They are intertwined with the real social existence of money, that is, with the manner money mediates his real and imaginary relations to different categories of people in his social surrounding.

But it does not end here. What eventually anchors these fantasies in objective reality is that they also mediate Bounderby's relations to his own private property, both financial and real. Consider the way he examines the pictures on the walls of his estate:

> "Why, sir," he would say to a visitor, "I am told that Nickits [the previous owner] gave seven hundred pound for that Seabeach. Now, to be plain with you, if I ever, in the whole course of my life, take seven looks at it, at a hundred pound a look, it will be as much as I shall do."[16]

Money mediates his relation to his property—the picture literally stands in for the price—but it renders the enjoyment from the thing impossible (notice that Bounderby confides Marx's idea that money is worth more than the commodities it buys). But this is true also of the other, allegedly more crude enjoyments of Bounderby. These can appear as direct enjoyments of things only as embodying a negation of the possibility of refined pleasures: "growing cabbages in the flower garden." They do not embody direct enjoyments of things, like those of the speculative butcher and baker before economy, but rather the loss of this possibility. They are already contaminated with money. Their relations to the refined pleasures make them an embodiment of the impossibility of a return to direct enjoyment. In other words, they appear as direct enjoyments only by being partial to the impossible pleasure of money.

At this point, Dickens's suggestion for a grand narrative of money shows its most radical aspect. The economic view is that one object is excluded from the circle of goods to mediate an easier access to all other objects. Dickens, by contrast, suggests that the exclusion of an element from the field changes the field itself. The exclusion of the money-object taints all other commodities, making them, in part, moneyed, partial embodiments of the impossible pleasure of money. To put it in the bluntest form: instead of smoothing the access to other objects, the exclusion of money empties these objects of the possibility of satisfaction. Let us see how this speculation is sketched in the margins of the orthodox imagination.

Two Economic Examples

A classical article on economics presents an eye witness report of a modern recapitulation of the moment of the emergence of money. In an article published right after the Second World War, R. A. Radford described the workings of the limited-exchange economy in a prisoner-of-war camp. As one can easily guess, the object that quickly came to assume the function of the means of exchange was cigarettes, and they supported an extensive commerce in other items, most of them provided by the Red Cross.[17]

This story can demonstrate various things to the satisfaction of economists: the natural evolution of money, its automatic emergence in the market (just as Adam Smith writes of "irresistible reasons" that lead to the use of metals and then coins as means of exchange),[18] or the way money speeds up commerce and rationalizes the market. However, what is more important in this story is what systematically escapes economic attention, namely, the addictive nature of cigarettes. Keeping that in mind, the story seems to be asking for a different reading, alien to the benign narrative of rationalization and increased efficiency.

It is, rather, a story of the emergence of money as a traumatic social event, where a group of addicted smokers goes through a collective and sudden effort to quit. Furthermore, the notions of addiction and trauma are also foreign to the idea of a complete, closed event. Instead they refer to that which leaves traces, to that which keeps recurring, and to that which colors what follows in its wake. As every ex-smoker will attest, the difficult act of quitting is never really complete—rather, it is ever present, manifesting itself, for example, in an expanding series of replacements, habits, attitudes, and so forth.

More modern economic approaches to money tend to be skeptical of speculative narratives of origin. Yet, for that reason their elusive presence may prove more symptomatic. A basic textbook on monetary economics by Bennett T. McCallum begins its explanation of money by comparing two different economies: one where people exchange directly the things of use and another where a special object serves as a means of exchange. McCallum does not claim any historical continuity between the two nor even the historical existence of a barter economy. However, there is clearly a shade of that myth in the comparison, and it underlines the function it once had as a justification of a monetary economy. The following is how McCallum concludes the comparison:

> In this second economy, because of the existence of a generally acceptable medium of exchange, individuals are able to spend a much smaller fraction of their time and energy in shopping about. Consequently, they are able to use the released time and energy to produce greater quantities of goods and/or (as they choose) to enjoy increased quantities of leisure.[19]

McCallum's argument is the typical lesson of the barter story: with money, people most easily can get the things that they want. The important point is the typical economic fallacy the story demonstrates: although in abstract terms things could have worked that way, economic reality is actually the complete opposite.

Contemporary economies have the most sophisticated monetary system and the most efficient ways to buy, yet there was never an era in which so much time and energy were spent on shopping as there is today. Money gives people the most efficient way to buy things, yet what people in sophisticated monetary economies want most is shopping—the impossible enjoyment of money itself. In other words, money has certainly become the most efficient means of exchange, and allegedly, the most distant than ever from the sphere of commodities, yet we have to consider the possibility that our commercial spaces are more moneyed, more colored by the presence of money than ever.

Second Fantasy: The Substance of History

Reading Dickens alongside Adam Smith raises what can be termed as a double, fundamental question of historical materialism. On the one hand, it raises the question of history: What can be conceived of as the material substance of history, its medium; what is the substance that carries historical persistence and registers historical change? However, at the same time, this is a question of substance: How can material substance have history? These questions emerge in relation to the story of the money-object. Is it a story about objects (beer, bread, and meat; then, some kind of a common commodity serving as a means of exchange; and finally, metals and coins), or is it a story about a social formation of desire that confers on objects an economic function? And if it is really the story of this social formation, how is it embedded in objects? How do objects carry this social formation through time?

These questions can be addressed through Bounderby's second fantasy, which puts money in the dimension of time, through his story of a self-made man. Although it refers to a (half-fabricated) personal history, it can be read as a key to the temporality of money; and for that reason, it also can be related to fundamental questions of money and history.

Bounderby repeatedly recounts his tale of climbing to his present affluent state from the depth of the gutters. The gradual recognition of the fabricated nature of this tale is one of the central plot lines of the novel. This tale often takes the shape of animated speeches that Bounderby carries as a reproach toward his listeners. The following is such a speech directed at Mrs. Gradgrind:

"Josiah Bounderby of Coketown learnt his letters from the outsides of the shops, Mrs. Gradgrind, and was first able to tell the time upon a dial-plate, from studying the steeple clock of St. Giles's Church, London, under the direction of a drunken cripple, who was a convicted thief, and an incorrigible vagrant. Tell Josiah Bounderby of Coketown, of your district schools and your model schools, and your training schools, and your whole kettle-of-fish of schools; and Josiah Bounderby of Coketown, tells you plainly, all right, all correct—he hadn't such advantages—but let us have hard-headed, solid-fisted people—the education that made him won't do for everybody, he knows well—such and such his education was, however, and you may force him to swallow boiling fat, but you shall never force him to suppress the facts of his life."[20]

These tales underscore Bounderby's financial achievements. However, as in the case of the first fantasy, what is important in the tales is the manner in which they are intertwined in his relations with his social surroundings. This practical use of the tale is most evident in his relations with his housekeeper, the widow Mrs. Sparsit.

Bounderby exalts the noble origin of Mrs. Sparsit, in contrast to his own deprived past, to effect an ambivalent play of humility and humiliation. Bounderby allegedly manifests his reverence toward the lady's noble being, but the bossy manner in which he repeats the comparison turns it into a hostile ritual of her humiliation.

At one point in the novel, this ritual wears a semi-erotic, sado-masochistic form in a long dialogue that suggests an obscene, perverse pleasure of Bounderby. As she serves his breakfast, Bounderby harangues her with his preferred subject of her indulgent youth contrasted with his own deprived childhood. "You were coming out of the Italian Opera, ma'am, in white satin and jewels, a blaze of splendour, when I hadn't a penny to buy a link to light you," he says, and Mrs. Sparsit cannot but humbly approve, "I certainly, sir, [. . .] was familiar with the Italian Opera at a very early age."

The dialogue goes on and accelerates in shortening phrases, in which Bounderby enthusiastically elaborates Mrs. Sparsit's extravagant past, and she confirms his descriptions in a servile manner. His lustful images of her youth run from "Italian Opera" to "lap of luxury," "devilish high society," and reach a climax in her being in "the tiptop fashion," after which Bounderby "bending himself at the knees, literally embraced his legs in his great satisfaction and laughed aloud."[21] This ambivalent play of humility and humiliation delineates the framework of the relationship of this couple. By depicting himself as undeserving of her, Bounderby keeps Mrs. Sparsit at bay and prevents the possibility of marrying her.

A more extreme form of the intertwining of the tale with real relations occurs in Bounderby's relation to his mother. According to his tale, Bounderby was abandoned by his mother in his infancy. As he repeatedly tells, she left him with his grandmother, "the wickedest and the worst old woman that ever lived," a drunkard who sold his shoes for liquor, who let him sleep in an egg box, and who was the source of many more imaginative descriptions of the inhuman deprivation he suffered.

However, throughout the novel we get more and more clues that this story is somehow false until the eventual exposure of Bounderby's mother in the figure of Mrs. Pegler. Then we learn that Bounderby is indeed a self-made man, who was born to a poor family, yet his tales of emotional deprivation are but cruel inventions. His was a loving family. His poor parents saved with effort so that he could study and when his father died, his widowed mother sacrificed her comfort to find him a place as an apprentice. At this point we see how reality itself is shaped to match the fantasy: to sustain his false story, Bounderby keeps his mother away from Coketown. He supports her on the condition that she will never contact him, and she lovingly abides. Once a year she comes to Coketown clandestinely to admire her son's success from a distance.

The irony is that Dickens does not use the prototypical story of a self-made man who avoids his relatives due to being ashamed of his humble origins but in a fundamental way inverts it. Bounderby is proud of his humble origins, so much so that he practically renounces his poor but decent mother. But this ironic twist is what opens the way to an insight into the social function of this prototypical story itself.

The story relates money to different themes: time, estrangement-alienation, material and emotional deprivation, social classes and customs, and more. However, as a fantasy, it stands between two different ways to interrelate these themes. In its overt text, Bounderby's tale explains his manners and attitudes: his past deprivation accounts for his coarse, factual manner and keeps him away from the delicacies of high society. His materially deprived childhood withheld from him the possibility of acquiring refined tastes and instilled in him a straightforward yet crude attitude to the realities of life. However, if we consider the tale as a fantasy, that is to say, as it is intertwined in Bounderby's conduct and his relations with his social surroundings, then the picture is inverted.

From this perspective, it is the act of telling the tale that enacts Bounderby's rudeness and vulgar attitude. The recounting of the tale actually constitutes that very same attitude that it purports to causally explain. Bounderby's rudeness and aggressive conduct consist, among other things, of his endless retelling of his story. To borrow one of his beloved terms: in his stories the gutters of the past explain causally his current attitude; but, in point of fact, his stories bring the gutters into the present. The important point here is: the fantasy of a past of total deprivation is somehow a part of money's presence, of its synchronous existence, and of the *real* conduct surrounding it. In this sense, this fable functions in the manner of what Žižek terms social fantasy or ideological fantasy, which is not opposed to reality but serves as a support of reality.[22]

Bounderby's fantasy suggests two different ways to relate money to lack and time. Bounderby refers to lack in factual terms: the past, factual lack of money is the root cause of his present conduct and personality (his suspicion of people, straightforward rough manners, inability to appreciate the luxuries of high society). By contrast, conceiving of fantasy as a support of reality, we can see a wholly different meaning of lack. The fantasy itself effectuates a sense of lack as part of the present reality of money. Most literally, Bounderby relates to his money through imagining it absent. But it does not stop there.

The imaginings of lack colors Bounderby's relations with the whole of his social surroundings. His social relations can be said to be contaminated with these imaginings of deprivation, as various derivatives of them: hostility, suspicion, estrangement, epitomized by his disavowal of maternal love. This last point underlines the theoretical dilemma. In the false narrative, the deprivation of maternal love represents the state of total lack from which Bounderby redeemed himself to wealth. By contrast, viewing the narrative as a fantasy that takes effect in reality, the narrative is part of the way wealth is linked to the renunciation of human relations even to the point of denying maternal love.

It is here that the fantasy reveals its potential as a theoretical perspective on the fundamental questions of money, temporality, and history. The fantasy suggests that the social nature of money is related to oblivion: the way money can efface or rewrite the past.[23] The temporality of money can be related both to its local social nature and to its historical mode of existence. In the local context, Bounderby conflates the misanthropic nature of money with its ability to efface the past. He becomes the rude, oppressive person he is precisely through his fabricated stories of his past. The point, however, is to read the figure of Bounderby as demonstrating real social properties of money and its temporality.

Money Has No Smell

The idea that the social nature of money is related to a constitutive absence does not require metaphysical subtleties. It can be demonstrated simply in recalling the timeless maxim *money has no smell*. This maxim speaks directly of what money does not have; however, the point is that it does not refer this lack to money's social neutrality but rather to its specific social nature. By referring to the fact that nothing sticks to money, this maxim actually invokes the very opposite of neutrality. It suggests there is something dirty in money's cleanliness, that money appears clean precisely because it can hide a dirty secret. This becomes clearer if we notice the performative aspect of the maxim. It is invoked as a means of overcoming social and moral inhibitions when it comes to money. One uses the maxim to make money the means of overcoming such inhibitions.

In theoretical terms, this amounts to viewing money as a medium. Economists sometimes refer to money as a medium of exchange. But the irony is that they are oblivious to what media studies have taught us about the concept of medium. They are unaware of, or choose to ignore, one of the founding concepts of media studies, namely, Marshall McLuhan's idea that *the medium is the message*. Rather than referring to the neutrality of the medium, this idea suggests that the social impact of a medium lies precisely in its transparency. As McLuhan notes, we are accustomed to looking at the content of a medium and thus miss its real effect, which has already taken place behind our backs: "It is only too typical that the 'content' of any medium blinds us to the character of the medium."[24] If the content of money is the commodities it can buy, then the notion of real economy blinds us to the character of money.

Adopting McLuhan's idea we could say that the maxim *money has no smell* refers to money as a medium of time—not just in the sense that money bridges over gaps in time and separates selling and buying, as economists are accustomed to say, but in the deeper sense of the term, meaning that time disappears in the transparency of money. The maxim means nothing but that money carries no traces of its immediate past. This meaning was already evident in the alleged origin of the maxim in Vespasian's reply to his son Titus's complaint about his decision to collect a tax on public urinals. In this maxim we see, therefore, a kernel of the connection between money's temporality and its abject social nature. Its social nature consists precisely of its ability to efface its past. Bounderby exemplifies this connection in his fabricated life story. However, as we shall see, this connection is also valid for the broader issue of money's historicity, for its mode of existence in history.

New Money I

Bounderby actually demonstrates the challenge that the image of new money, or the nouveau riche, poses to economic thought. His character manifests some of the typical lines of the age-old figure of the new-money person. His vulgarity, his mysterious past, his contempt for, or ignorance of, received cultural values, alongside his practical attempts to join higher social circles all unmistakably identify him with the tradition of literary portraits of new money. However, the paradox is precisely that new money invokes such a specific social type.

This is a paradox because there is a sense in which the money-object itself is new: it carries no traces of its immediate past; we do not know from whence it comes, in what exchanges it took part. Only its coincidental material embodiments are given to the wear and tear of the physical world. The money that they represent remains untouched by time. The point is that in orthodox economic terms, this newness of money is related precisely to its social neutrality. Because it lacks use, it is conceived as a means to purchase useful things. Because it is untouched by time, it can serve as a store of value—as a medium to bridge over a time gap. Because it carries no traces of previous social interactions, it is the perfect means for anonymous economic transactions. In short, in orthodox economic terms, money's newness implies that money has no social character.

The Marxist perspective, by contrast, allows us to relate the newness of the money-object with the cultural figure of new money because it conceives

of the various absences that characterize money as its substantial social properties. It allows us to read the cultural trope of new money as related to the
temporality of money. This, of course, should not imply any nostalgia for old
money, which is nothing but a conceptual double of new money. A critical
view of this parallel will be developed in Chapter 5.

In the Marxist framework the absences associated with money mark its
specific social nature—its hostile, devastating nature. Its lack of use marks it
as the carrier of economic forces foreign to the level of immediate experience,
epitomized in the lethal drive of capital to accumulate. Furthermore, from a
Marxian perspective, the anonymous nature of money transactions does not
render money socially neutral but rather renders it a carrier of specific social
relations marked by social alienation.

One should recall Marx's speculation in *Capital* regarding the spread of
the use of money. Marx claims that since money and commodity relations are
impossible in a traditional community with its kinship and close social ties,
they first appear in the interaction between different communities and then
spread inward, into the internal life of the community.[25] The social and historical ontology is of interest here: commodity relations emerge in the interactions between foreigners and then bring this foreignness into the community
itself. The crux of the matter is that foreignness is not seen here simply as a
lack of specific social relations but as itself a social relation. In other words, we
find here a mirror image of Anthony Giddens's concept of *disembedding* as the
key process of modernity.

Disembedding refers to the "'lifting out' of social relations from local contexts of interaction," and money is a prime example of it:

> Money [. . .] is the means of bracketing time and so of lifting transac-
> tions out of particular milieux of exchange. . . . [Money] provides for the
> enactment of transactions between agents widely separated in time and
> space.[26]

Giddens's idea rests on the commonsensical notion of foreignness as a neutral
layer upon which specific relations may or may not be added. It ignores the
senses of threat, fear, and hostility that the image of the stranger carries with
it. In a Marxist framework, by contrast, we can see money as a medium that
can bring these senses into the closest social ties: through money we can relate
as strangers even to the persons closest to us.

From the various types of absence associated with money, its absent past can be seen to hold a primary status. The past, as the prototypical form of real absence, is what confers ontological status on all other forms of absence. This could be formulated the other way around: the ensemble of all absences viewed as positive properties of money comprises the meaning of money's being a historical object, of its past as present in absence (of its being new money in the abject, social sense of the term). Here again we can see the theoretical force of grounding money on desire. Desire is the ultimate mark of absence as a positive quality: money is desired in spite of its uselessness, social neutrality, and so forth. To better understand this relation between history and lack, we can start again from Bounderby's fantasy.

Lack and History

Bounderby's fantasies interrelate in various forms the reality of money with a sense of its absence. Apart from being a key to his figure, these fantasies contain a grid of a purely theoretical question. To see this we must recall that the myth of barter also revolves around a certain lack. This lack is not always explicitly mentioned as it belongs to the motivation for the story more than to its content. The story is summoned to explain a certain absence: How is it that money functions although it has no X? This missing X may change over time. At first money has no use (e.g., in gold), and later it does not even have distinct materiality (within our current monetary system). But in any case although there is something it lacks, still, money functions.

The interesting thing is that one can describe the controversy between Marx and the economists as a reference to the different ways to come to terms with this lack or absence. The economists seem to follow Bounderby's fantasy by treating lack in a simple, factual manner and in relegating it to the past. Marx by contrast exposes the real side of fantasy by attributing an ontological status to lack and referring it to the present form of money.

How do economists use the story of barter to come to terms with lack? In a very simple sense, they use the story to explain away lack. Faced by the mystery of a money-object with no intrinsic value, they invoke a time past when only useful objects were exchanged for each other. Money evolved from this lost time of barter and has gradually shed its uses. In this use of it, the story explains how useless money came into being, but by this very movement it turns lack itself into a mere feature of the story. That is to say, in the framework of the story, money is not useless in itself, as a positive property of it, but only in comparison with something completely different than money, with a form of exchange that belongs to a lost past.

This use of the story has a certain remedial effect: it is invoked to explain a certain lack that is apparent in money but in telling the story, lack is no longer a feature of money itself, but only in a comparison with barter. For that reason, the dismissal of lack as a quality of money amounts to a dismissal of the very relevance of the story itself. Precisely because it explains a certain feature of money through a comparison with a past moment distinctly different from money, it makes this past irrelevant to the present state of money. It may purport to explain how the present situation came into being, but in itself it has no presence in this situation. That is why the narrative of barter is correctly referred to as a myth. In terms of historical ontology, this use of the story refers to change but overlooks the more basic question of what persists through change.

However, the standard use of the narrative of barter also suggests how to turn the story from a mythical to a historical form. The difference between the two is naturally not a question of historical facts but pertains to the manner facts are understood as historical. It can thus be posed in somewhat of an abstract manner before the question of the factual validity of the narrative of barter is posed. The mythical mode presents lack as a feature of the story and not as a positive quality of money in its synchronous state, and, similarly, it views the story itself as absent, severed from the synchronous existence of money. The opposite way, therefore, is to conceive of lack as a real quality, which is precisely the present trace of the past as that which is radically absent. That is actually the way Marx uses a version of the story of barter.

Economy as an "Other Scene"

That Marx refers to the story of barter may appear strange if we keep in mind the ideological weight this narrative has for orthodox economics as demonstrating the efficiency of the market and the benevolent influences of money. However, the general outline of the first chapter of *Capital* follows roughly the stages of the story. It begins with an absurdly lengthy discussion of the significance of a direct exchange of two commodities, of the form "20 yards of linen = 1 coat"; then it raises the notion of the universal equivalent, which is a specific commodity, such as linen, that serves as the measure of value for all others; and it reaches the money-form, which is actually no different from the universal equivalent, except for the fact that now gold assumes the place held by the former plain commodity.

At stake in Marx's intensive investigation of a simple barter exchange is nothing less than an alternative concept of economy. In the views of Marx and the economists, we can pin down competing concepts of economy to the basic act of exchange. Adam Smith's imagined baker, butcher, and brewer already imply the dominance of methodological individualism in orthodox economic thought. Indeed, Smith famously invokes the natural "propensity [of humans] to truck, barter, and exchange one thing for another," and bases exchange on the wills and desires of agents.

When Marx examines the same act of exchange, he comes up with the dia-metrically opposite concept of economy. What he sees is the lack of a common denominator between the things exchanged, which he then elaborates into a concept of economy as a context of action that is radically foreign to the agent's perspective. What motivates his discussion from its beginning is the idea that there is nothing in the use value of commodities that can explain the quantita-tive value relation between them. Use value cannot explain why one coat is exchanged for twenty meters of linen (and not, e.g., ten).

As is well known, this starting point leads him to posit labor as the source of value. However, it also implies a notion of the economy as a context of action marked by foreignness from the point of view of the agents. There is nothing in what an object is to its owner (i.e., its use value) that can explain its economic dimension (value). To borrow a Freudian term, Marx elaborates a concept of the economy as an *other scene*, in which an agent's actions are interpreted in a language unknown to him.

This Marxian notion of economy is also related to an attempt to bring the consideration of barter out of the realm of myth and into history. In a close inspection, one finds a sound reason for Marx's unique view of the act of exchange. His inspection of the systematic form of the exchange, rather than whimsical exchanges of surplus (the butcher who exchanges whatever he has no immediate occasion for), amounts to an insistence to consider the barter *economy* as an original form of economy and not just a plain, unqualified notion of barter. To reconstruct his argument against the standard economic allusion to barter, we can claim that if the notion of barter is to have any rel-evance whatsoever to money, it is in the form of a barter economy.

What places the standard view of barter in the realm of myth is that it turns to an imagined origin before economy—a reality governed by direct uses and satisfactions, by direct relations of people to things, and lacking any sense of a social object. For that reason when Smith turns to his imagined baker and brewer, he does not really turn to an *economy before money* but actually to an imagining of *exchanges before economy*. He purports to describe the emergence of money, yet what sneaks into the narrative together with money is the emergence of economy, or even the social, itself. This use of the story is mythical in nature because it refers to a lost past, radically different from the present, and at the same time finds there a replica of the present—the baker, brewer, and butcher being self-sufficient artisans and merchants.

By considering barter *economy*, rather than sporadic exchanges, Marx can place barter and money within the same conceptual confines. His exploration thus is not aimed at explaining how money came into being, but at finding what we can learn from juxtaposing money and barter economies. That is why he concludes the description of the passage from barter to money with the remark: "the simple commodity form is therefore the germ of the money form."[27]

Marx's alternative approach to history becomes concrete at a point where he explicitly refers to the economic myths of money:

Hence the mysteriousness of the equivalent form, which only impinges on the crude bourgeois vision of the political economist when it confronts him in its fully developed shape, that of money. He then seeks to explain away the mystical character of gold and silver by substituting for them less dazzling commodities, and, with ever-renewed satisfaction, reeling off a catalogue of all the inferior commodities which have played the role of the equivalent at one time or another. He does not suspect that even the simplest expression of value, such as 20 yards of linen = 1 coat, already presents the riddle of the equivalent form for us to solve.[28]

What should be noted is that the dispute of Marx with the imagined political economist is not about historical narrative but about historical ontology. It is not about the alleged facts of the story but about what a story is: what, within the story, comprises the enigma and what counts as its solution. For the imagined economist the riddle is the current monetary system, and the solution for him appears to lie in past forms of money. For Marx, by contrast, "it is a riddle all the way down": what the economist presents as a solution—the direct exchange of useful goods—is not the solution but the primitive form of the riddle itself. What he points out is that there is nothing less mysterious in the basic act of exchange when it is considered as an economy (why one coat is exchanged for specifically twenty yards of linen).

Whereas the economist thinks of the mystery of money as something that must be solved through historical speculation, Marx conceives of the mystery as the historical substance itself. History is a process through which the mystery becomes explicitly articulated. And it is the mystery that accounts for the narrative's continuity, what is handed down in it through time. In a sense Marx simply takes seriously the notion of the mystery of money: he does not take mystery to be merely an epistemological fault, a mere misunderstanding that must be clarified, but a part of the historical reality of money. In his view, "the mystical character of gold and silver" is not something to be explained away by history by invoking less mysterious means of exchange.

Gold, in this view, *is* a mysterious object in the strict sense of the term. That is how it assumes its economic function. Mystery is simply a description of the condition in which gold is the universal means of exchange in spite of its having no real quality that can account for its status. On the other hand, mystery marks gold as a historical object, as a medium of history that carries some unknown vestige of the past. We should not be deterred by the idea that something is really mysterious. Mystery is a basic way to account for the reality of history: to see the present containing an element of a blind inheritance from the past. To see an object as historical means nothing but to see it as transcending the perspective of present agents. A conceptual relation between history and economy is enfolded here: the mystery of gold is, on the one hand, nothing but the economic function of gold, the way it serves as the universal means of exchange, and on the other hand, the manner in which it stands for history, as a vestige that cannot be fully explained in synchronous terms.

The source of the difference between these views of history can be traced back to the difference between the views of the basic act of exchange. For the economist, the enigma is this: How is it that a relatively useless thing (gold, modern money) is exchanged for useful things? For that reason speculation about useful objects that once served as a means of exchange seems to be a solution to the riddle.

To begin with, for Marx, the enigma is the opposite question: How can a *useful* thing (such as a commodity in barter) also carry exchange value, keeping in mind that value is indifferent to use value. This riddle is already present "in the simplest expression of value," and its presence in money is simply its "fully developed shape." The enigma is not solved by history but gives shape to history. Money presents the full development of the original enigma in the sense that it explicitly assumes the indifference of value to use value by embodying value with no use value. In a way, in the simplest form of exchange, the riddle of value is hidden behind the usefulness of the objects exchanged, and it is fully expressed in useless money.

The difference between these views can be described in terms of the different ways to associate history and absence. The economist is confronted with a mysterious absence in his current money and, quite naturally, explains it by a past in which this absence was filled (money was still a useful object). In this use of the story, history is invoked to sustain a notion of a-historical money, detached from its past. By contrast, when Marx pushes the riddle backward in time, he effectively claims that *absence was already present in the earliest forms of exchange*. At the starting point of the narrative, value is defined through its absence from the substantial qualities of things, through the lack of a common denominator in use values. In a monetary economy this absence is embodied in money. Thus, what separates the two *uses* of the narrative—Marx's and the economists'—is precisely the ontological status of lack.

The economic use of the story solves the problem of absence by invoking an absent past and, thus, dismissing the presence of the past and the relevance of the story. In Marx, by contrast, absence is the thread that runs through the story as a whole and, thus, emerges as the positive trace of the past, as an index of historicity. At this point we can formulate a conceptual relation between economy and history engrained in Marx's thought: economy is a context of action defined by its absence from the actor's perspective; and history, as an absent horizon, provides the background against which this absence acquires an ontological status. In other words, viewing history as real provides Marx a way to maintain the reality of lack.

The whole conceptual movement from commodities to money to capital is enfolded in this view of the connection between history and economy. This movement can be seen as an elaboration of the foreignness of the economy in different forms. Barter economy is guided by a principle of value absent from any commodity. Money is a special commodity that embodies this absence because it carries value precisely in it uselessness. It embodies the principle of economy as absent from the sphere of immediate experience. Finally, the proof of the validity of this view of money is capital.

The endless movement of capital is a result of the absence of use being viewed as a positive quality of money. Capital thus reflects a further form of the foreignness of economy because it represents a drive that is alien to subjectivity. What should be noted is that these moments of barter, money, and capital should not be seen as consecutive distinct historical phases. In the Marxian framework their historicity amounts to the way they interpenetrate one another. The notion of barter economy already implies money, and money already implies capital.

In his early writings, Marx already formulated this relation between history and lack. We can notice it in a critical remark that he aims at the economists in *The Poverty of Philosophy*: for the economists, he writes, "there has been history, but there is no longer any."[29] The context of this remark is different from that of the present discussion. The remark refers to Marx's claim that his contemporary economists treat feudal economic institutions as artificial while they conceive of bourgeois economy as natural. In their view feudal economy is steeped in a specific historical political organization whereas their own economy is pure economy, not embedded in a political order.

However, this critique of Marx holds a more general lesson regarding the critical force of a historical perspective. What it suggests is that a historical view that contends that the past was radically different does not by itself hold critical weight regarding the present. The crucial aim of a historical approach is to historicize the *present*, and this should be done not externally, by invoking a past that was different, but internally, by accounting for the mode of the presence of this lost past. To restate Marx's formulation, historicizing the present amounts to conceiving history not just as *has been* but as *what still is*. Historicizing the present amounts to pointing to the absence of the past as a positive attribute of the present.

History and Mystery

The clearest dividing line between Marx and orthodox economics lies in the question of history. It is not a question of this or that historical narrative but of a much deeper one, of what is a narrative, of what is its form of truth.

We can ground large portions of Marx's critique on his having a historical ontology—an understanding of economic entities, such as money and commodities, as historical objects, that is to say, as media or carriers of history. When Marx takes seriously the mystery of money, when he conceives of the mystery as real and not just as a result of our short sight, he conceives of money as a historical object. The mystery marks the manner in which the object punctures the present, brings into it an impenetrable presence that cannot be accounted for in the terms of the present. We know that Marx also refers to commodities as mysterious. And why not conceive of capital in such terms—capital as an object that mysteriously forces subjects to submit their activity to its endless growth.

To realize the full force of this notion of the mysterious object as a medium of history, it should be read vis-à-vis the contemporary discourse of historiography. This notion can actually be seen as a requisite solution to certain deadlocks in the philosophy of history. A good starting point is the work of Hayden White, who elaborates the theoretical challenges of historiography to the extreme of denying the possibility of historical truth in narratives.

White argues that historical narratives cannot be truthful in the simple sense of truth as correspondence. Historical narratives cannot resemble the historical past in the same way that a model airplane resembles a real airplane. Thus, from a sympathetic point of view, White argues that to save itself, historiography must embrace its half-forsaken affinity to literature and abandon its aspirations for scientific truth. His basic argument is quite simple: the historical narrative is composed of historical facts chosen from an infinite reservoir, which are then organized by the historian according to literary techniques. Because there are potentially infinite ways to select and arrange the facts, there can be no one exclusive way to account for the historical truth of a narrative. By selecting certain facts and omitting others and by arranging the selection in a certain order, the historian can decide whether to represent history in the form of a tragedy or a comedy.[30]

In this form, the argument is perfectly valid. Yet it does not necessarily entail the exclusion of narratives from the realm of truth. Its real implication is that there is a theoretical choice between facts and narratives. White's argument forces one to choose: if reality consists only of facts, then there can indeed be no truth in narratives; and, conversely, if one wishes to maintain a sense of truth unique to narratives, one must reserve a place in reality to what is strictly speaking not a fact. Mystery, of course, does not belong to what we usually count as fact. But that is why attributing a sense of reality to mystery opens up a space for a reality of history.

At the heart of White's argument actually lies a positivist conception of a fact. His argument relies on a view of reality as consisting of closed and distinct facts that can be manipulated and arranged in various forms like building blocks. This positivist core is evident, for example, in White's claim that the historian cannot find "stories" in reality but, at most, can find "story elements." This distinction takes for granted that story elements are logically prior to stories. Yet it is doubtful whether it is valid even in reference to literature. Are stories made of their elements, or is it more correct to say that stories confer the ultimate meaning on their elements? This may be true for historical narratives as well. To assign ontological status to historical narratives is to see them not as composed of discrete facts, but as a horizon that confers a final meaning to the facts that comprise it.

In the theoretical choice between facts and narrative, lack is the extreme form of non-fact that can confer reality on narratives. It can be claimed that if the historical narrative is to have any reality, it should leave its mark as something that transcends any single moment or, in its extreme form, as an absence that is nonetheless constitutive of reality itself. This idea actually finds an echo in White's argument that the construction of a narrative depends on omitting facts. He writes:

> The relationship between the past to be analyzed and historical works produced by analysis of documents is paradoxical; the more we know about the past, the more difficult it is to generalize about it.

and, borrowing from Levi-Strauss, concludes that

> [o]ur explanation of historical structures and processes are thus determined more by what we leave out of our representations than by what we put in.[31]

Again, this argument can be read not only as a repudiation of the possibility of the truth value of narratives but also as outlining a condition for a realist conception of history. The idea that the construction of a narrative demands omissions may be taken to mean that all narratives are partial or even false. Yet, if something is omitted in reality, if a historical reality is organized around a constitutive absence, then reality itself can give way to a narrative form. Chapter 4 will elaborate this conception of history in reference to Weber's work.[32]

How would we recount Marx's narrative according to this link between history and lack? In a barter economy, to the extent that the term is applicable, there is no organ that represents value. Value organizes the system of exchange but remains external to all things. In a monetary economy, one organ represents value; however, it assumes this position insofar as its lack of use becomes its property, as it is reflected in the movement of capital, which is indifferent to use value. In this framework, the object money stands for history in its impenetrable presence. Its mysterious lack of use stands for its absent past. Its objectivity is constituted by this impenetrability. That is why Marx can tell the narrative of money as a story of objects, in which the money commodity is set apart from the circle of all commodities. "The social action of all other commodities [. . .] sets apart the particular commodity in which they all represent their values."[33]

Shell remarks that "Marx regards money as the hero of a great historical drama."[34] This observation should not be taken merely as a literary comment. The grand narrative of money is a story in which objects are really, and not metaphorically, the protagonists, because it can take place only as it is saturated in money and commodities and thus confronts the subject as an impenetrable object.

New Money II

Marx's view of various absences as the positive properties of money is supported by the historical nature of his thought. The money-object concretizes the notion of the presence in absence of the past. That is why we find in Marx a parallel to the paradox of new money drawn over the grand historical view of money. The social character of new money is entailed with a disavowal of the past. Similarly, for Marx money assumes its position by effacing its past.

In Marxist terms, a monetary economy entails a necessary illusion: when one commodity functions as money, it appears as if "all other commodities universally express their values in [it] because it is money," whereas the truth is the reverse relation, "that a particular commodity becomes money because all other commodities express their values in it." That is to say, money, being a special commodity, cannot but be a structural effect that involves the whole

circle of commodities. Its unique place in the circle of commodities cannot be described other than in terms that refer to this circle as a whole. Yet
it appears as if its function as money is a substantial quality of it. To this
reversal Marx then adds: "The movement through which this process has
been mediated vanishes in its own result, leaving no trace behind."[35] The
movement that results in money "vanishes in its own result." What does the
preposition *in* mean here? How does a movement vanish *in* the object that
it brings about?

There is actually a highly accurate sense to this formulation. It suggests
that a thing being money is equivalent to its effacing of its past. In a system of
commodity money, such as gold-based money, there is a level of basic similarity of the money-thing to all other commodities in the economy (e.g., they
are all produced by labor; they are all scarce resources, etc.). The uniqueness
of money is not grounded on any substantial property of it. The strange situation is that its uniqueness is equivalent to its obfuscation of the fact that there
is nothing really unique about it. It is unique precisely because it obscures the
fact that it is not unique.

This paradoxical situation can be sustained by viewing money as historical.
In a system of commodity-money, an ordinary commodity emerges as unique
insofar as it effaces its ordinary origin, the fact that at one time or another it
was but an ordinary commodity. That is why it is perfectly logical to think of
history as vanishing *in* the object: it is a social object insofar as it effaces its
past. This consideration is most clearly valid for the time of gold-based money
that Marx had in mind. As he put it: "This physical object, gold or silver in
its crude state, becomes, immediately on its emergence from the bowels of
the earth, the incarnation of all human labour."[36] Yet, the next chapter will
argue that in some respect our own money can still be considered a type of
commodity money. The fact that it appears radically different from gold-based
money is itself an effacement of its origin in it.

The absent past characterizes money in both the local and the grand-
historical contexts. Money is new in that it carries no traces of its immediate past. Dickens's Bounderby demonstrates the robust social meaning of this
newness. He assumes his character by actively renouncing his past, by rewrit-
ing it in the shape of money—the story of the self-made man. But in this he
monetizes the whole of his social relations, to the point of denouncing maternal love (the obscene underside of the self-made man). But this local history

is reflected, according to Marx, in the grand history of money as an object constituted by effacing its lost origin.

How can we account for this parallel? It may have to do with the notion of the historical substance in historical materialism, that is to say, with the manner history is steeped in matter-like substance, in social objects, and the manner in which it is carried forward through them in time. History is embedded in objects in the form of repression. In other contexts we are accustomed to say the opposite. We think of monuments, for example, as carrying memory and shared meaning. But material history is no less involved with oblivion. This is true also for the case of the monument. A monument is itself a historical object, an object that takes part in history, because it also rewrites the past. That is how it partakes in the basic fact that the remembered past is always different from the past.

That the recollection of the past is not its reconstitution is nothing but a basic condition of history. Objects are a medium of history to the extent that they also involve a moment of a negation of the past. Objects carry history not only as carriers of memory but also in the sense that memory entails oblivion. Money, in this context, is the pure form of this moment of oblivion implied by history. That is one way to approach the opposition of history and economics, in which they are often conceived as two extremities in the spectrum of the sciences of humankind. The wrong way to approach this opposition is to conceive of the economy as inherently a-historical. That is precisely what orthodox economic thought holds. The right way is to conceive of economy as the pure embodiment of that moment of history that involves a break with the past *as a form of persistence*.

Keith Hart views money as a form of social memory, equivalent to language. Because the money *stuff* (metals, paper) is all gone, what remains in its place "is little more than traces of memory and the banks which keep it are mechanized minds." It is in this link that Hart grounds his optimistic reference to money: if money could fulfill its potential as a memory bank—could salvage the memory of the past it contains—it could be used to "inform the construction of a better global society."[37] The doubt raised by such optimism is whether money is inherently related to oblivion; whether it would no longer be money if it could serve as memory bank. In a mirror image of Hart's idea, we could speculate that precisely because money erases memory, it impedes the construction of a better global society.

Historicity as Effacement of History

The need to distinguish between history and historicity—between history, as a narrative or a process that takes place in time, and historicity, as a synchronous state of belonging to history, of being historical—lies behind the notion of the money-object as involved with an effacement of its history. The paradox is that for history to have meaning, it must be grounded on a notion of historicity but also be distinguished from it. If history only purports to explain how the present came into being, then in principle it has no consequences for our understanding of the present. For history to have meaning, it must allow for an approach to a historical moment other than merely a point in a process or in a narrative. It must entail a notion of historicity that conceptually is distinguished from history.

One minimal form of this distinction is to conceive of historicity as entailed with an effacement of history. That is what lies at the heart of the controversy between Marx and the economists. Both sides of the controversy can accept money's apparent detachment from its past. However, whereas for the economists this detachment supports a view of the economy as a-historical, Marx understands it as the specific *historicity* of money. The money-object that emerges through effacing its own past embodies the idea of historicity as distinguished from history. Recalling again Žižek's interpretation of commodity fetishism as a form of repression, we can pose money as its focal point.[38] Money is the extreme form of an object that emerges precisely by effacing its history, the extreme form of the element of repression inherent in the social object.

The narrative of money is quite a thin form of historical narrative. Yet the lessons of the Marxist approach to it can pertain to more standard uses of history. We can find them in what Paul Ricoeur termed "a negative ontology of the past" in his attempt to come to terms with the reality of the historical past. Ricoeur arrives at the necessity to *"make the past remote from the present"* as a condition for the writing of history. He sets it against the naive conception that the past can be reconstructed *from within* by its remainders, which leads to a theoretical impasse. The problem is that if such a reconstruction of the past succeeds, it annuls the reality of history itself: it abolishes the very *past-ness* of the past, its specific temporality, its distance from the present. Thus, to maintain a notion of the reality of historical past, we need to conceive of the past precisely through its distance.[39]

This discussion about the writing of history can be framed in terms of historical ontology. The writing of history is possible if we conceive of the residues of the past in terms of traces or, better yet, if we assign a unique ontological status to the trace as a form of presence of the past in its absence. The point is that this conception can be brought to bear not only on the past but also on the present. If the reality of the historical past is sustained by its remoteness from the present, then the historicity of the present should be sustained by the presence of traces of the remote past that make the present other to itself.

Money Is Feces: A Speculative Supplement

The notion of the ontological newness of money calls for some speculative musings with the outrageous Freudian identification of money and feces. This identification has known a strange fate. Among other uses, the term *anal character* is widely used to refer to a trait of people who are not simply thrifty, but have an intense emotional relation to money. Yet, the idea on which this term is grounded, that the place that money fills in adult emotional life is the place that excrement had filled in the life of the infant, is one of Freud's most contested ideas. To some extent, its rejection seems understandable. The reasoning that Freud gives in his first introduction of the idea in his article "Character and Anal Erotism" is sadly meager, keeping in mind the gap that it crosses.

Apart from invoking his clinical experience, Freud brings three types of evidence in support of his claim. The first is evidence from folklore, where money is frequently associated with filth or even with feces. The second is a speculative, and an all too general, explanation:

> It is possible that the contrast between the most precious substance known
> to men and the most worthless, which they reject as waste matter ('refuse'),
> has led to this specific identification of gold with faeces.

The third evidence is coincidental: infants start to show interest in money roughly at the same time as their interest in feces declines.

The partial nature of this justification is highlighted by the boldness of the claim. It is bold not only because it connects something disgusting like feces with something desirable such as money. This in itself is but a trivial transformation for psychoanalytic thought: what we consider disgusting actually is something that originally attracted us but because it went through social prohibition, it became disgusting and was replaced by another, desirable object. There is an additional set of oppositions traversed by this identification between the intimate, concrete, immediate, and singular object and the public, abstract, mediated, and repetitive one. Our disgust toward feces appears as an immediate reaction, whereas money, by contrast, has sense only as a socially mediated object. But maybe this gap underscores the fact that if Freud's speculation is to have any meaning at all, it must have some kind of an *economic* meaning in the form of a social concept of money.

This point is clearly demonstrated by reading Sandor Ferenczi's defense of the Freudian identification in his paper entitled "Ontogenesis of the Interest in Money." Ferenczi unfolds the basic identity into a series of transformations that lead from feces to money. The infant is interested in his feces, which are connected to the anal enjoyment he derives from defecating. When these become repulsive, the interest shifts to mud, which is precisely like feces, but without the disgusting smell. Then, when the moisture of the mud becomes disagreeable, dry sand takes its place. Then, pebbles take the place of sand and later, artificial objects like buttons. Lastly, these objects are replaced by money, which has the advantage of also attracting the interest of adults. The series of transformations is summed up with a charming example of psychoanalytic boldness:

> Pleasure in the intestinal contents becomes enjoyment of money, which, after what has been said, is to be seen as nothing other than odorless, dehydrated filth that has been made to shine.[40]

Elementary! Of course, the series of transformations does not solve the difficulties of the original speculation. No matter how gradual we make this process of cleansing, money—as a social object—remains external to the series. All other objects in the series—feces, mud, sand, pebbles, and shiny buttons—obtain their meaning from within the child's play. Money, by contrast, goes beyond this intimate circle. It is an object that escapes the child's understanding or imagining. In contrast to all other objects, the child simply does not know what money is.

What Ferenczi shows is how the interest in feces gradually shifts until it reaches the little, round, shiny pieces of metal. What this series cannot, in principle, show is why the little, round, shiny objects are also money. But of course, the beginning of an answer lies precisely in the problem itself: in contrast to all the other objects in the series of transformation, the child does not know what money really is. Maybe in playing with, for example, buttons the child also ignores the function of buttons, but it is only with money that we can suggest that this ignorance has something to do with the object itself.

In other words, the Marxian idea of the process that *vanishes in its own result, leaving no trace behind* (not to mention Marx's Freudian description of gold that emerges "from the bowels of the earth" to assume immediately its position as money) provides an appropriate economic supplement. It can be argued that while psychoanalysis explains how the interest in feces is repressed due to social prohibition, Marxist theory can explain why this interest is eventually replaced by interest in money as an object that stands for repression as such. In a way, Marx shows us how the process of repression is completed by the transference to money. The interest in feces is socially repressed and replaced with an interest in the object constituted by social repression.

Freud's second approach to his idea is useful in this respect. In his article "On the Transformation of Instinct as Exemplified in Anal Erotism," Freud adds a new element to the scene, as he presents feces as "the first gift" that an infant gives to its parents and thus as intersubjective to begin with. Here feces are seen not simply as an object of individual interest and pleasure, but they receive their place due to others and their real and imaginary demands: the infant responds to his parents' pleas to use the toilet. It is a difficult act because the infant relates to his or her feces as "a part of his body which he will give up only on persuasion by someone he loves, to whom indeed, he will make a spontaneous gift of it as a token of affection." Complying with the parents' pleas amounts to nothing less than giving up on a narcissistic pleasure for a step of entrance into society.

In this view feces are the first object that stands for intersubjective relations. The Marxist idea that the social object stands for the social in its radical externality to the individual gives shape to the replacement of feces with money. When the interest in this first object becomes socially forbidden, it is replaced by an object that embodies the social in its radical externality to the individual. Viewed in this way, the gap that separates money and feces appears less wide. The gap between the immediate, concrete, and intimate relation to feces and the mediated, abstract, and social nature of money appears as nothing but the basic form of repression. That feces appear as immediately disgusting is in truth only a feature of the repression of our relation them. It is an immediately social relation, in the sense that its social mediation cannot be experienced. The desire for money, as Dickens's Bounderby enunciates it, is a mirror image of this relation. It is inexpressible in itself, but only through the mediation of hostile others.

There is actually one truly compelling argument that Ferenczi posits in his article. Every civilized person, he writes, is abhorred from a public mention of feces, yet anyone can show interest or curiosity when it comes to their own waste matter. Excrement is immediately disgusting, yet *mine* is somehow fascinating. This argument extracts the disgust from its immediacy by articulating it in primitive terms of ownership. A first reaction to this statement would see in it an example of the way the institution of private property is already inscribed in our most basic level of instinctual life. But it could also mean that the institution of private property is inscribed on the most basic level of the *repression* of instinct.

Like so many of Freud's ideas, this one carries a temptation for a clever formulation of the human predicament: as infants we give excrement to our closest loved ones to show our love to them; as adults we give money to people to make them strangers. Maybe this is more than just a joke. It shows a basic proximity of psychoanalysis to historical ontology in the sense that it conceives of human existence in a constant disaccord with time.

Barter Today

Critical perspectives on economics and the economy most often invoke the need to historicize the economy and sometimes set the narrative of barter as their first target. Polanyi suggests that for a true historical account, we first must get rid of this narrative; more recently Graeber has said the same in his book *Debt*. Their refutations may be too hasty in the sense that they are based on the conviction that one knows approximately what this refuted legendary barter stage is. To be more precise, what these refutations have in mind is mainly the classical imaginings of economics of the happy baker, brewer, and butcher at the dawn of economy, who are nonetheless already perfect merchants.

Marx's allusion to a barter economy rather than whimsical barter exchange should remind us that there are other possible ways to conceive of barter. Graeber, for example, points to archaic credit systems, such as the Sumerian system, as a refutation of the historical primacy of barter. It indeed upsets the familiar version of progression from material money, to paper notes, and finally, to credit. However, the point is that an ancient credit system may fall precisely under what Marx conceptualizes as a barter economy. When credit is not yet financial credit but simply a system of registration and settling of debts, it is simply a highly sophisticated system of barter.

If credit is not systematically created from nothing—if it does not bear interest, if central organizations do not issue credit, and so forth—then this situation is reducible to a system of direct exchanges of objects that bridges over time gaps and differences in demand (i.e., which has overcome from the outset the problem of "the double coincidence of wants" that guided the classical economists' imagination). It is only when one object emerges as both a product of labor and the means of exchange, when it is excluded from use—to paraphrase Marx—that a real historical change occurs, and commodity-money emerges.

So the question is how can a notion of barter be a viable theoretical tool? The Marxist approach provides a substantive answer. A barter exchange, as we read in *Capital*, is simply an exchange of two products of labor: 20 yards of linen = 1 coat. This basic definition is most efficient precisely because it does not imply a categorical difference between barter and commodity money. It does not render them as two distinct historical phenomena and, therefore, allows a historical account of both, of the way they interpenetrate and shed light on each other. In this definition, a monetary transaction in a commodity-money system is, in itself, a barter exchange. When, for example, one gold coin is exchanged for one coat, it is, in itself, a barter exchange: two products of labor exchanged for each other. What differentiates a monetary economy from a barter economy is not present in this transaction itself but in all other excluded transactions. It is defined by the impossibility of the direct exchange of twenty yards of linen for a coat.

In a proposition that plays a central role in the next chapter, we should note how Marx eventually defines the position of the universal means of exchange: one commodity "has the form of direct exchangeability with all other commodities [. . .] because, and in so far as, no other commodity is in this situation."[41] The fact that a certain object is money actually means that all other objects are not directly exchangeable. Note that this is a historical view of money because it does not categorically distinguish money from barter. Money is defined by the *impossibility* of certain barter exchanges, that is, by their presence in absence. This absence is not a metaphysical term. It has its real traces in the present—historical traces, to be sure. Its obverse is the mystery of money. It is manifested in a paradoxical structure that desire weaves into money: that money is worth more than anything it can buy.

Consider again the basic proposition that a monetary economy is not a barter economy. The orthodox view, rightly rejected by critical scholars, accepts this proposition as a categorical distinction between two historical forms. From a Marxist perspective, the difference between a barter economy and a monetary economy is what defines each of them as historical phenomena. A monetory economy is an economy in which barter is excluded. Turning this insight to the present, a surprising result is that the claim "money is not barter" emerges as a basic definition of a consumer economy. Our monetary economy positively is not barter because of the strange fact that most of what we buy loses economic value for the very reason that we buy it. The consumer economy is the focus of the next chapter, but in the following section I briefly note one clear example of its perversity in relation to orthodox economic discourse.

The Price of Newness

The 2001 Nobel Prize in economics, awarded to the economist George Akerlof, generally is attributed to his famous paper about "lemon cars," which introduced into mainstream economic thought the notion of markets with asymmetrical information. The paper starts with a question that for the layman would probably appear trivial: Why does the value of a car go down once it is bought? Here is how Akerlof presents it:

> From time to time one hears either mention of, or surprise at, the large price difference between new cars and those which have just left the showroom. The usual lunch table justification for this phenomenon is the pure joy of owning a 'new' car.[42]

Akerlof's answer relies on the gap of information between buyers and sellers. The seller of a used car knows more about the car than the buyer does. Thus, a buyer reduces the price he or she is willing to pay, given the chance that a seller withholds information about the true value of his or her car. The novelty in this paper was that it opened the way to conceptualize imperfect markets. It added a new factor to the simple neo-classical world view. In addition to the preferences and resources that define each economic agent, the concept included the information each agent holds.

The first interesting thing to note regarding Akerlof's argument is that the notion of asymmetrical information should be seen as a euphemism for deception. That is typically the situation in the example that Akerlof chose to illustrate his theory. The seller of a used car does not simply hold more information. The excess of information that he or she holds, most typically means that the seller hides some defect and that he or she does so against the inquisitive efforts of suspicious buyers. In other words, the argument encodes the view that the seller of a used car is, statistically, a liar. It may be true that this situation indeed characterizes the real situation in used car markets.

In my experience, even nice, honest people might indeed lie when it comes to selling a car. A person may appear as a respectable, honest member of the community in every other respect but as a seller of a used car, he or she is nonetheless held to be a potential liar.[43] One view of this contrast would say that the relative anonymity of the interaction liberates the utilitarian, egotistic economic subject hidden beneath layers of civility. However, a Marxist framework provides a somewhat different explanation, which sees the hostile social relation as immanent to the ontology of money, and attributes it not to the anonymity of the encounter but to the context of alienation that money induces. Money allows one to act in a manner that is foreign to one's self image. Regarding monetary affairs, one may cheat and still view oneself as an honest, respectable member of the community.

However, the more important aspect of Akerlof's argument is not his solution to the riddle, but rather the possibility that this solution circumvents. Akerlof pinpoints it quite clearly: what is unthinkable in economic terms is that people pay for "the pure joy of owning a 'new' car." The example that Akerlof chose is perfect in this respect as it isolates newness as a purely formal category. The car that has just left the showroom is identical to the cars in the showroom in every significant, positive quality, yet it is no longer new. That is precisely what motivates the economist to explain the price difference. A price set for sheer *newness* is ostensibly a money-for-nothing exchange.

Akerlof's argument does indeed solve the problem that this possibility sets for orthodox economics. However, taking into account the multifaceted craze for *the new* that characterizes contemporary consumer culture, we must raise the doubt whether the possibility that the economists avoid is precisely the case. That is to say, maybe in a consumer economy, a price is set for newness, and the case of the new car reveals it in its extreme paradoxical nature.

Marx's economic ontology enables us to give a theoretical account for the price of newness. The price of newness marks the extent to which an object loses its exchangeability once it is bought. In other words, it marks precisely, in a quantitative manner even, the exclusion of the possibility of barter. Following Marx, it shows how a monetary economy is still defined as the exclusion of barter—that is to say, how the concept of barter is still relevant to our economy. The economic value of the new marks precisely the extent to which a thing is not money, or more precisely, its mode of being non-money.

Nevertheless, it is in Akerlof's favor that he put quotation marks at the heart of the phrase *pure joy of owning a new car* for this joy cannot exist. That is precisely what his argument shows, namely, that we never own new things. We may have a momentary illusion of having a new thing, but economically speaking they are not new once we own them. Therefore it is more accurate to speak of the *desire* to own a new car rather than the joy of owning a new car. Akerlof formulates quite neatly the basic economic perversity of consumer culture: things are new only in the showroom; the things we own are at best *like new*, to use the common phrase in ads for second-hand items. They may seem new to us, but economically speaking they are at best like new, a close replica of the things in the shop.

For contemporary critical discourse, the consumer economy's craze for the new is far from being a shocking revelation. David Harvey links it to the problem of over accumulation. After capital exhausted the possibilities of extracting surplus value from mass production in economies of scale (the Fordist economy), it moved to new paths of profit making by diversifying the supply of goods and decreasing their life cycles (the post-Fordist economy).

Fredric Jameson pointed out a similar effect in the post-modern experience of time. The nostalgic tone that became dominant in cultural production, he argues, marks a break with the past, and its ultimate explanation is the economic one. Nostalgic uses of external features of past styles, such as retro fashion, disclose the fact that the past can no longer be reconstituted. What should be further noted is the strange, utter deafness of orthodox economics to such arguments, as demonstrated by Akerlof. This deafness suggests that the craze for the new also touches an ontological dimension—that it is related somehow to the social reality of money.

This possibility can be traced to the two uses of the story of barter. In its economic use, it is a story of the separation of money from the circle of commodities in order for money to become a transparent means. The economic mind sees money as the emergence of an ever more efficient way to access things (Adam Smith's baker can more easily get the meat he wants). Dickens and Marx suggest an opposite reading of the story. The exclusion of the money-object from the circle of commodities is accompanied by a social formation of desire for money that gradually colors the circle of things as a whole. The exclusion of money from direct use is associated with its becoming a mark of an impossible pleasure that taints the circle of commodities as a whole. It may afford easier access to things, but it also marks the pleasure of things as partial to the impossible pleasure of money. This is the hidden lesson of Akerlof's argument: our consumerist desire is guided by the idea of the pure joy of owning a *new* thing, but we can never satisfy it. Economically speaking, we can only get a replica.

It is a happy coincidence that an illustration of this idea appears in the movie *A Beautiful Mind*, which is based on the life story of the economist John Nash, who despite his schizophrenia led a fertile intellectual life and was awarded the Nobel Prize in 1994 for his innovations in game theory. A famous scene dramatizes his intellectual breakthrough. It takes place in a bar, where a group of economics students are watching some young girls who have just entered the bar. They are all pretty, but one glamorous blond attracts everyone's immediate attention. In a demonstration of the contaminating nature of the economic frame of mind, we hear them brag of getting the girls in metaphors taken from Adam Smith: "in competition, individual ambition [i.e., to get the blond] serves the common good."

But only Nash, who sits there with his stack of papers, ostensibly indifferent to the sexual overtone of the conversation, is really thinking of Adam Smith. It is then that the idea hits him: "Adam Smith needs revision," he says to the astonishment of his colleagues and, then, explains: if they all go for the blond, nobody will get her, but her friends will be insulted and turn them down, *because nobody likes to be second choice.* The solution to the deadlock goes against the economic tenet of free competition: everybody in the group must ignore the blond, and go, from the start, for his second choice. "It's the only way to win. It's the only way we all get laid," he says and gets up excited. The blond mistakes his intention and smiles at him, but he bypasses her and rushes to the door to develop his idea in his room.

The scene summarizes the two sides of the narrative of the separation of money from commodities. Taking one object out of the picture allows access to all other objects. But it also makes all objects second choices in comparison with the unreachable pleasure of the lost one. The sexual mise-en-scène is appropriate to this idea because of its perfect parallel to the psychoanalytic conception of the lost object that informs man's desire. Once the child accepts the prohibition of incest, he enters society; but this prohibition colors his relation to all other sexual objects.

Chapter 3

MYSTERY

The Materiality of Symbols

Milton Friedman opens his book *Money Mischief* with the marvelous story of the stone money on the island of Yap in the Caroline Islands. Until the twentieth century the media of exchange in Yap were large stone wheels, which were totally useless on the island and had been brought to it on boats from another island about four hundred miles away. Since these wheels were huge, ranging in diameter from one to twelve feet, the islanders did not actually move them during monetary exchanges. Instead, they changed the marks of ownership on the stones themselves. The story tells of a particularly enormous stone that kept on circulating without anyone ever seeing it. This stone was secured by an ancestor of a respected family, but on its voyage to Yap, it sank to the bottom of the sea during a violent storm. For the two or three generations the stone was there, its purchasing power remained intact "as valid as if it were leaning visibly against the side of the owner's house."

The point that Friedman finds in this story is that in spite of its apparent absurdity, the exchange system of Yap strictly resembles the modern monetary system in the age of the international gold standard. Thus, in 1932–33, when the Bank of France feared that the gold standard might collapse, it ordered the Federal Reserve Bank of New York to convert a major part of its dollar assets into gold. Of course, no gold was actually shipped to France. Instead, officials of the Federal Reserve Bank simply marked some of the drawers of gold in the vault as the property of the French. Needless to say that this trivial action, similar in form to an exchange of the sunken Yap stone, had enormous real effects. According to Friedman, it was one of the factors that ultimately led to the banking panic of 1933.[1]

There are a few interesting lessons to learn from Friedman's story. First, money is a genuine historical object. It is historical not simply in the sense that it changes over time, but more deeply in the sense that stories and narratives provide us unique knowledge about it. Friedman's story, which juxtaposes modern and primitive forms of money, forces us to use words such as *still*, *already*, and *not yet* to refer to both Yap money and to ours. We find it necessary to conclude that the Yap money is in some sense already like ours, but not quite, or still something else. These are far from being simple adverbs. They necessitate a philosophy of history that would enable us to see things not simply as what they are, but as already or still or not yet something else. In short, they necessitate an idea of the presence of history in the object. The historical narrative, in this context, is not a concatenation of different and distinct moments, X and then, Y. Rather it is only the narrative that associates them that reveals what X and Y really are.

The second point is that this conception of the historical object of money is possible due to the constitutive place of non-knowledge. The Yap money is already like ours, with the exception that the inhabitants of Yap do not know this. They still think that the stones are important. However, a more elusive type of non-knowledge relates to our own money. The more intriguing point is that Friedman brings the story to teach us moderns a lesson. The islanders' ignorance should somehow teach us something about our own money. This story must raise some doubt regarding the idea that ours is a transparent monetary system, that because our system detached itself from old superstitions, we finally have come to know what our money actually is. In a sense, what Friedman suggests is that our certainty about our understanding of money consists of a double negation: we do not know that we do not know it; we summon an earlier form of non-knowledge in order to recall that we do not know.

The third lesson may clarify the previous point. The story forces us to reconsider the notion of materiality in relation to money. Yap money still has a material form, yet its pinnacle is the sunken stone. Then the question is whether this awkward, ghostly form of materiality is valid also for our own money. Maybe it is not exactly non-material but only seems so because we do not have the concepts yet to deal with its unique form of materiality. If we expand the sunken stone metaphor to include the abyss of time alongside the ocean abyss, then maybe our own money is still material in the same form as the Yap's stone: the gold that we have lost in the abyss of time still confers a form of materiality on our monetary system like the sunken stone that confers materiality on the symbols exchanged in its place.

These points are the central themes of this chapter, which explores the shift from gold-based money to modern symbolic money. The chapter draws from Marx various notions of the shape of this historical shift. It argues that to understand modern money, we must develop a concept of the distinct materiality of symbols that underlines a dimension of continuity beyond the apparent sea change of the dissolution of gold-based monetary systems.

The Shape of History

In Marx's *Grundrisse* we find a seemingly teleological formulation about the way money fulfills its purposes by negating them. The following is the quote in full:

> We see, then, how it is an inherent property of money to fulfill its purposes by simultaneously negating them; to achieve independence from commodities; to be a means which becomes an end; to realize the exchange value of commodities by separating them from it; to facilitate exchange by splitting it; to overcome the difficulties of [the] direct exchange of commodities by generalizing them; to make exchange independent of the producers in the same measure as the producers become dependent on exchange.[2]

The very mention of "purposes" of money and their fulfillment may raise the eyebrows of historians, accustomed to suspect any shade of teleological interpretation of history. However, the idea of fulfillment by negation points to the way that a certain teleological form is a necessary requisite for history. It points to a notion of history as cunning. It points to the manner in which history progresses behind the backs of human agents. It points, in other words, to the level in which a retroactive gaze is necessary for historical knowledge or to the level where the advantage of retroactivity has an ontological status. Fulfillment by negation implies that only at some later stage can a prior point be fully understood. This idea may alarm historians, yet it is actually a minimal requirement for maintaining the advantage of a historical perspective or, better yet, for maintaining that history provides a unique form of truth.

To be sure, the entanglement of desire and money is one way of describing this narrative form of fulfillment by negation. The grounding of money on gold provided an excuse for the way it is desired (gold is beautiful, mysterious, noble, etc.). So what happens when money detaches from gold? There are two principal ways to understand this shift. On the one hand, from the dominant economic perspective, it can be read as a moment when money overcomes the residue of pathological desire associated with gold to become a perfect means in an ever more rational economy. On the other hand, if gold was but an excuse, a misguided aim of desire, then perhaps what remains when gold is left behind is the pathological desire for money, which is now revealed in its most irrational form as fundamentally lacking an object, a horizon of satisfaction.

What should be noticed is that the decision in this dilemma is actually not between history and teleology but between two forms of teleology, a positive one and a negative one. As Ingham argues, the idea that money develops into a rational means, as in Carl Menger's account of the origin of money, actually involves a teleological thought that should be rightfully dismissed. It may be more rational for the economy as a whole if people accept paper notes instead of gold, but since it is not rational for any *specific* subject, this view of the shift to paper money relies on a notion of a rational master plan of history.[3] It is in comparison with this narrative form that Marx's version of negative teleology appears most plausible. Its relation to desire is best seen in his invocation of money as "a means which becomes an end." By becoming a means, money does not detach from desire but is desired *as a means*, that is, it becomes an object of an endless desire. This type of *failed* teleological form is more plausible because it is grounded on a sort of persistence. It is not governed by the image of a rational end point to which history is oriented, but by a movement of explication, where the conditions that were implicitly there to begin with are becoming explicit.

By the end of this chapter, we arrive at the way that desire draws the grand history of money. But to reach that conclusion, we start with more technical questions to which Marx's metaphor of history appears relevant: the question of labor money and the question of symbolic money.

Why Can't There Be Labor Money?

The idea of labor money, which fascinated socialists in Marx's time (and keeps recurring from time to time in utopian thought), occupies an interesting place in the transition from *Grundrisse* to *Capital*. In the earlier work Marx devotes several pages, in three different attempts, to an explanation of the impossibility of time-chits—money that is a direct representation of labor time. In

Capital, by contrast, these deliberations are replaced with a simple statement in a footnote declaring that if money is equated with labor time, the economy would simply not be a commodity economy.[4]

This change in the manner of explanation between *Grundrisee* and *Capital* represents a shift from thought about the economic mechanism to thought about the economic object. In the beginning Marx tries to find the mechanism that prevents an identification of money and labor, but in the end he understands this impossibility as constitutive to money. That is to say, in the later phase, its differentiation from labor is what makes the money object what it is. Thus, in a way, it is *Capital* that elaborates more fully the question of the object. The change in the manner of explanation represents a shift in the focus of attention from the attempt to find the laws that govern economic objects to an attempt to understand what is an object, what is the economic object. However, for that very reason it may be useful to examine the earlier attempts to explain the impossibility of labor money. They may disclose the theoretical complexity that later became enfolded within the money object.

The idea of labor money poses a theoretical challenge to Marx because it might seem as the most sensible way to revolutionize society. In terms that belong to *Capital*, labor money precludes the possibility of extracting surplus value. If every hour of work is paid for by a note whose value is "one labor hour," it is clear that no one can live off the work of another. Marx is well aware of the difficulty that this utopian thought poses for him. "Thus," he writes, "it may seem a very simple matter that labor time should be able to serve directly as money" but then adds that "[t]he truth is that the exchange-value relation [. . .] comprises contradictions which find their objective expression in *money which is distinct from* labor time."[5]

In *Grundrisse* Marx returns to this question of labor money, or time-chits, a number of times within a relatively short range of text. I want to examine here the first answer he gives to the question though it may at first seem somewhat bizarre. In this answer Marx does not focus on the possibility of an economic system of labor-money, that is, he does not focus on the internal structure of such a system. Instead he speculates as to how such a system could appear, how it could emerge out of a capitalist reality. His general line of argument goes like this: suppose that a bank issues these time-chits, which directly represent labor and serve as money. This bank, says Marx, would hand out notes in exchange for real commodities. A producer who prefers to hold these notes, would sell his products to the bank. Thus, if the system succeeds, the bank would end up holding all the commodities.

> [P]recisely seen, then, the bank would be not only the general buyer and seller, but also the general producer. In fact either it would be a despotic ruler of production and trustee of distribution, or it would indeed be nothing more than a board which keeps the books and accounts for a society producing in common. The common ownership of the means of production is presupposed, etc. etc.[6]

In other words, if the system succeeds, there are only two possibilities, which are nonetheless complete opposites. On the one hand, it may be that the bank has become a "despotic ruler." On the other hand, it may be that this bank is only a bureaucratic organ of accounting in a communal society. However, this latter possibility is dependent upon the abolishment of private property beforehand. It cannot result simply from the institution of time-chits.

What lies at the heart of this thought experiment is the question of the historical object, that is to say, of the object as a medium or bearer of history. When the system is considered in synchronic terms, it is possible to imagine the workings of the system of time-chits. But this speculative thought in itself is not sufficient to resolve the true nature of the system, which remains thus suspended between two extreme opposites: either a totalitarian regime, where the bank holds all property and everybody is enslaved to it, or a utopian society that has abolished private property altogether.

The choice between the two interpretations remains undetermined by the formal description of this society. It is decided only by considering how it could have come into being, by considering what the money object carries into it from its past. In more concrete terms, what decides the dilemma is the question of value. What would render the speculated time-chits as the bearers of capitalist relations of exploitation is that they would assume the function of money as both representing value and having value. For the time-chit to function as money, Marx explains, "this symbol has to have the property of not merely representing, but *being*, exchange value in actual exchange."

If they only *represent* value, time chits could indeed be a tool in the economic administration of a just society, in which a laborer gets the full one hour worth for every hour of labor. However, if they emerge from a capitalist economy, they must emerge in place of capitalist money, which has the property of being an exchange value precisely by representing value. Strangely enough, in such a case, time-chits turn from being a tool for the eradication of exploitation into the diametric opposite: the embodiment of pure surplus value. If time-chits succeed capitalist money, they concentrate in one point all surplus value. Every exchange in society would be allegedly fair: one hour of labor for a one-hour time-chit.

But the bank that would issue time-chits would absorb all surplus value. Its transactions would be pure surplus: a product of labor exchanged for a note produced with no investment of labor whatsoever. One may still wonder: What is really the meaning of this distinction between representing value and being value? It is not that simple to pinpoint precisely because it touches the heart of capitalist reality. It is what lies at the heart of the phenomena of finance and financialization, in which anything that represents value is prone to enter transactions as a thing on its own.

On a more abstract level, this consideration of the status of time-chits shows us the outline of money as a historical object, that is to say, as an object that stands for the opaque and persistent presence of history. In the play between representing value and being value, the money object demonstrates a principle of historical persistence through change similar to Marx's notion of negative teleology. By representing labor time, the time-chits seem to expose a secret of capitalist economy, namely, the fact that value is created by labor.

But aside from exposing the secret of the system (representing value), they also have to function within it (having value)—that is the meaning of their emerging from within reality. And that is why their establishment cannot change it into a transparent, fair system. In their appearance they expose a secret of the system but because they also function within the system, it is no longer the same system whose secret they have exposed—the system itself is somewhat changed by their very emergence and, therefore, the secret they expose is to some extent partial and misleading.

Throughout these changes something is always omitted from the picture, and the historical object stands for this omission. The historical object stands for this shifting stain that prevents society from achieving full transparency. It stands, in other words, for certain non-knowledge that is constitutive to society. A hidden principle of a social system may be revealed in time, as embodied in a specific organ of the system. That is, for the revelation to be not merely theoretical, it must be embodied within the system. But upon this revelation, the system itself changes precisely because the hidden principle is now embodied in an organ of the system.

Is this wild speculation of Marx relevant to modern economy? One element in it seems to be fulfilled. Humanity has not yet developed a system of labor money like the time-chits; modern fiat money appears to be produced with no investment of labor but nonetheless can be exchanged for products of labor, thus embodying surplus value. Indeed, there are real impediments to the production of money by governments and banks. But to the extent that it is indeed produced with no investment of labor, it resembles Marx's speculation. This concept is the focus of the rest of this chapter. It addresses the emergence of valuable symbols in the spheres of money (in coins and notes) and commodities (in brand names) and dwells on the correct way to conceptualize the historical narrative of this emergence and its relation to surplus.

Symbolic Money

The following is how Adam Smith explains the institution of coins:

> The inconveniency and difficulty of weighing those metals with exactness gave occasion to the institution of coins, of which the stamp, covering entirely both sides of the piece and sometimes the edges too, was supposed to ascertain not only the fineness, but the weight of the metal. Such coins, therefore, were received by tale as at present, without the trouble of weighing.[7]

The symbol ascertains the amount of material substance in the coin. It is a symbol that serves as material evidence. Its completeness testifies to the wholeness of the coin. This is a very familiar explanation, but it should be read retroactively. The full significance of this story becomes apparent only when its missing ending is taken into account, that is, when the story is read from the standpoint of modern symbolic money. Considering this end point we find one more instance of Marx's formula that money fulfills its purposes by negating them.

In the context of modern money, the relation between matter and symbol is diametrically opposed to what the story elaborates. In place of the symbol signifying material substance, in modern coins the material substance is but one component of the symbol. In the beginning of the story, a fault in the symbol suggested that the quality or quantity of material is incorrect. In this respect the situation today is the complete opposite: a suspicion in the material identity of a coin is meaningful only as a possible signal that the symbol is a fake. Whereas in the beginning, the symbol attested to materiality, nowadays the material substance attests to the authenticity of the symbol.

Thus, the real, thought-provoking result is brought about by taking the story seriously and incorporating in it its unexpected ending. The symbol is instituted to attest to its material substance but by this very attestation, it makes the material substance redundant; it renders materiality secondary in importance in comparison to the symbol. The symbol replaces in its function that which it symbolized. This inversion seems even more paradoxical when formulated in relation to ownership: in the first moment the symbol supports the ownership of the material substance of money; in the second moment it prohibits this ownership.

In a *full-bodied* coin, the symbol attests to an ownership of a certain amount of material substance. By contrast, the functioning of a fiat coin is conditioned on the prohibition of ownership of the material substance of the coin by the possessor of the money. In this coin the symbol signifies that the material substance does not belong to the possessor of the money. It should be noted that the fiat coin achieves a similar materiality to that of the sunken Yap stone: a material substance beyond our reach secures value. In this transition from material coin to fiat money we find an exact replica of the logic of Marx's history as deceit: the coin fulfills its purpose (signifying material substance) by negating it (relegating material substance to a secondary status).

Indeed, the fascinating feature of the story is that if taken at all seriously, it raises the most profound questions of the history of money. These stem from the fact that it seems fundamentally impossible to locate the transition between the two forms of money that the story, in its full version, portrays. It is theoretically impossible to determine when money shifts from being matter supported by symbol to being symbol supported by matter. The only possible temporality of this change is that which *has already happened.*

Indeed there can be points in time when people acknowledge the fact that a change has already taken place. That is what actually happened in the 1971 Nixon shock when the United States withdrew from its obligation to convert dollars to gold and, thus, officially put an end to the age-old connection of the international monetary system to gold. But it is not that the dollar replaced gold at that point in time. The only way such a replacement could have effectively taken place is if the dollar had *already* practically replaced gold. The official announcement, in this case, was nothing but the explicit recognition of what had already happened. It should be noted that questions in the philosophy of history arise here in their simplest forms. Accounting for the dissolution of the gold standard in 1971 compels us to instill the adverbs *already*, *not yet*, and *still* in any narrative of change. Just before the Nixon shock, money was already symbolic money but not yet recognized as such.

To push the riddle further, this form of posterior recognition in the shift does not really solve the problem of change. A posterior recognition in change implies that a real change has already happened beforehand. Simply put, if we accept that there is a real difference between the two forms of coin in the story, between a gold coin and fiat coin—a distinction which does not seem at all far fetched—then the real transition between them must have occurred sometime. Yet it is theoretically impossible to locate this point in time.

The solution to this enigma is actually very simple and exemplifies again the logic that guides Marx's speculation of time-chits, where the object stands for both non-knowledge and the opaque presence of history. This logic can be applied to the enigma of the shift from material to symbolic coin. The answer to the enigma is twofold. First, it can be claimed that money has been so all along: from the moment of inscription of the symbol on the coin, the symbol had already replaced matter. So, again, when did the real change take place—granted that there is indeed a real difference between a gold coin and fiat money? The second half of the answer is that the real change is nothing but the posterior recognition that the change had already occurred.

This seemingly paradoxical formulation is made intelligible only if we keep in mind the fact that the act of recognition itself also must be historical. That is, if the act of recognition itself is viewed not only as a recognition *of* a historical fact (that money is not X but Y) but is viewed as a historical event. The posterior recognition is itself a real change if it changes money. But this requires that we consider non-knowledge and misrecognition as parts of a historical reality or even as elements of reality that account for historical persistence. Before money is recognized as already symbolic (i.e., before 1971), something is clearly missing from people's knowledge of money (they think it is gold while it is already the dollar).

The more enigmatic factor is what happens after the moment of recognition. If this moment is viewed as a historical event that actually changes money, then something must slip away from our view in the very moment that we recognize money. But what exactly is omitted? What disappears from our sight at the very moment when money explicitly assumes the position it already implicitly held?

If before the shift money was already symbolic but misrecognized as such, then perhaps after the shift we must consider how it is still material but mis-recognized as such. In other words, what we must consider is a notion of the distinct materiality of the money symbol. This possibility is the central theme of the rest of this chapter.

As a somewhat abstract starting point for its consideration, we can turn again to Friedman. There is actually something quite surprising in his ac-count of the workings of fiat money. Friedman addresses the question: How can purely symbolic money form a stable monetary base? How is it protected from the temptation of rulers to issue money at will? It is in his favor that Friedman does not provide an unequivocal answer:

> [I]t remains an open question whether the temptation to use fiat money as a source of revenue will lead to a situation that will ultimately force a return to a commodity standard—perhaps gold standard of one kind or another. The promising alternative is that over the coming decades the advanced countries will succeed in developing monetary and fiscal institutions and arrangements that will provide an effective check on the propensity to inflate and that will again give a large part of the world a relatively stable price level over a long period of time.[8]

Following the logic of this argument to its extreme, what Friedman actually claims is that in principle our monetary system can still be considered as a sort of gold-based money; that money has never really detached itself from a mate-rial base. Governments and central banks see to it that fiat money behaves like the gold it succeeded. They artificially limit its reproducibility to force it to function *as if* it is of a material substance.

But the argument does not stop here. These actions of rulers are not sim-ply autonomous acts of governance. There is an economy to which these rul-ers themselves succumb. Gold itself—or some other commodity—hovers over the system as a potential that forces governments and central banks to restrain their money. If they do not limit the production of money, then automatic economic mechanisms, far stronger than their own powers of influence, will lead to the abandonment of fiat money in favor of some form of commodity money. In this respect there is a strict continuity between gold-based money and symbolic money.

In all its forms, money behaves *as if* it is of a material substance. Even before the dissolution of the gold standard, money notes functioned *as if* they represented gold. Gold guaranteed their value and restrained their endless reproduction only as a potential, in the same way it guarantees the value of contemporary fiat money according to Friedman. Moreover, even if we go back to earlier times when gold may have directly exchanged hands, there is still some sense in saying that it behaved *as if* it was of a material substance. Even gold can be claimed to behave *as if* it is gold, in the sense that its function as money had nothing to do with its material properties. Rather, it depended on a secondary, contingent property—on its rareness, which strictly speaking is a not a property of gold, but a geological fact about the surface of the planet.

From Symbolic Matter to Material Symbol

How then should we tell the story of the transition from gold-based money to modern symbolic money? It is not really a story of transition between two different and distinct forms. Rather, the story shows them to be two complementary, interpenetrating forms. Put simply, it is no longer a story of transition from material money to symbolic money. Rather, the real transition is from symbolic *matter* to material *symbol*: from *matter* that obscures its own symbolic function to *a symbol* that obscures its own materiality.

What is usually conceived of as *materially* based money is constituted by the oversight of its symbolic aspect. To be sure, we can locate this aspect even before the institution of the coin: even *pure* material money, if there ever was such a thing, has an aspect that belongs to the order of a sign because it always possesses a social function. From its very beginning it should be conceived as symbolic matter. (In other words, it is not that material money *has* value but that it always *signifies* value to some extent.) At the other edge of the spectrum, we find fiat, ostensibly purely symbolic money, but its symbolic nature is actually constituted by the oversight of its ongoing materiality.

What persists through the shift from material substance to symbol is the fact of oversight. The change is simply in what is omitted from the picture: the material aspect or the symbolic one. This shifting oversight is what holds the narrative together. It also renders money as a genuine historical object in the further sense that only the narrative as a whole reveals its true face. Any synchronous view of money is essentially misleading.

This is the true meaning of Simmel's claim that credit is the original form of money. In this claim Simmel does not try to provide an alternative narrative for the evolution of money by reordering the stages and setting the last stage first (credit money before material money). He does something more radical because he situates the structure of credit as already within the material forms of money. That is why, he writes,

> the development from material money to credit money is less radical than appears at first, because credit money has to be interpreted as the evolution, growing independence and isolation of those elements of credit which already exist in fact in material money.[9]

What should be added, to fully realize the potential that this view holds for a historical account of money, is the parallel movement where the first stage, the allegedly *material* form, persists in an implicit form within the last. Keith Hart argued that money is always both heads and tails just like the coin in our pocket: the heads side marks authority and social organization while the tails side marks monetary value, like the price of a commodity.[10] This simile is especially telling if we recall that one can never see both heads and tails at the same time.

The Structure of Value: Neither . . . Nor . . .

A concept of historical ontology creates a fundamental break with a-historical, abstract economic thought. One meaning of this break is evident with regard to the social structure of the value of money. The classical economic mind is puzzled by the value attributed to a mere symbol. The answer it gives is the commonsensical one: the symbol is valuable because it symbolizes something. The symbol enhances material value as it guarantees the quantity of a precious substance. In other words, it is a conception of conjunction: the coin is matter with a symbol.

Historical ontology, which in a way is nothing but the attempt to take the story seriously, eventually leads to an opposite conception, whereby value is seen as based on disjunction. The value of a coin is constituted by its being neither material nor symbolic. This approach eventually demonstrates that at every stage, value is constituted on the cohabitation of symbol and matter in spite of their fundamental opposition.

There is a commonsense opposition between symbol and matter: where the former is abstract, referential, and replicable, the latter is concrete, unique, and self-contained. This opposition lies behind the common narrative, which orders these forms as distinct stages in the evolution of money: as if at first money is a pure material thing (gold), then it becomes material and symbol (the gold coin), and in the end it remains purely symbolic (fiat coin). The alternative view sees the opposition not as distinct stages of the story but as constitutive to value at each of its moments. It suggests that the unresolved opposition between matter and symbol is itself the secret of value.

Why does this contradictory structure account for value? A possible answer can be found in the Marxist logic of alienation; according to this theory, dispossession or in-ownership is logically prior to private property. Consider a condensed formulation of it from Marx's comments on Mill—a formulation that runs through the different themes of this chapter:

> We ourselves are excluded from true property because our property excludes other men.[11]

This should be read not just as a moralistic critique of capitalism but as a conceptual analysis of private property as a social phenomenon. Its logic is that the social dimension of private property is essentially foreign to its *private* features, to what a thing of property is to its owner. If private property is predicated on others not having our property, then this social dimension transcends the experience of ownership of things. What Marx says is that we cannot *own* the essential social aspect of our property. Money, in this logic, is the culmination of private property: it is an object that represents property and for that reason has nothing private in it—it simply has no sense in a strictly private context.

Following this logic of alienation, it could be argued that for an object to be money depends upon the inscription of its social aspect in a form that upsets possession. The material substance can be simply possessed, but this only means that it is not yet money, which represents ownership. It becomes money only when the social dimension is inserted in it in the form of that which cannot be possessed, namely, the symbol (the fact that the symbol is the privilege of the ruler only underlines that a symbol in principle cannot be possessed). At the other end of the spectrum, that of fiat money, we find the peculiar entity of a symbol that can be had, that can become an object of ownership. However, it is symptomatic that this symbol emerges together with the exclusion of the possibility of the possession of the material substance in the modern coin, whose function entails that people cannot materially own it. In this respect, modern fiat money can be said to represent a culmination of the logic of ownership, but what it develops to the extreme is the moment of dispossession constitutive to money.

Symbolic Commodities

Friedman suggests that symbolic money can function as long as fiscal institutions maintain it as a simulation of irreproducible material substance. He suggests, moreover, the threat of a potential return to gold is one of the factors that forces these institutions to maintain symbolic money as a simulation of matter. An implicit idea in this argument is that with reference to money, we should not conceive of symbols simply as the opposite of material substance but instead consider the distinct materiality of symbols. However, what I argue in this chapter is that this materiality is maintained not through the relation of symbolic money to gold but through its relation to the sphere of modern symbolic commodities as a whole.[12]

For that reason it is necessary to turn our attention now to brand names. The intriguing point is that we can find an exact replica of Adam Smith's story of the coin in the explanation that orthodox economics provides for brand names. The standard economic explanation of brand names reproduces Smith's story in three ways: in what seems to be the basic motivation for the explanation, in the structure of the explanation, and, most importantly, in the type of error or blindness that is embedded in the explanation.

The first similarity between the coin story and the explanation of brand names is in the motivation for the explanation. As in the case of the coin, the feature of the brand name that annoys the economic mind is a certain symbolic excess. What disturbs the economic point of view is again the fact that a mere symbol seems to carry economic value. The question challenging economists is: What do people pay for when they buy Levi's, Coca Cola, or Nike?

The second similarity is found in the answer to this question. The standard economic answer grounds brands in a situation of imperfect information. Benjamin Klein argues that brands "lessen the costs of acquiring product information."[13] Thomas Sowell formulates the same logic in everyday language (notice the suspecting, cynical economic view):

> When you drive into a town you have never seen before and want to get some gasoline for your car or eat a hamburger, you have no direct way of knowing what is the gasoline that some stranger at the filling station is putting into your tank or what is in the hamburger that another stranger is cooking for you to eat at the roadside stand that you have never seen before. But, if the filling station's sign says Chevron and the restaurant's says McDonald's, then you don't worry about it.[14]

The seemingly irrational symbolic excess is domesticated and incorporated in the calculating, utilitarian view of economics, much the same as was the stamp with regard to Adam Smith's coin. Here, again, the symbol testifies to the quality of something else, namely, of the familiar product.

These first two similarities—in the motivation for the question and in the structure of the answer—remarkably underline the third and most symptomatic similarity: the similarity in a structure of blindness. The economic explanation conceals the most typical feature of the object that it explains, namely, the fact that in the world of brand names, symbols themselves have somehow become economic entities. It may be that brand symbols do assure quality, but this does not mean that quality answers the question of what type of an object the brand name is. The insistence of high quality might be aimed to prevent poor quality from harming the reputation of the brand as symbol. It does not mean that the object is indeed simply signified by the brand symbol.

In a sense, what economists oversee here is what every child knows: when children demand from their parents, say, new Nike shoes, they do not demand the shoe whose symbol attests to quality but simply the shoe with the Nike symbol (and the quality of the shoe may help the parents comply with the demand). In a typical brand name, the symbol is an indistinguishable and inherent part of the thing. As Naomi Klein puts it in her best-selling *No Logo*, the "brand name revolution" involved a change of paradigm: "The old paradigm had it that all marketing was selling a product. In the new model, however, the product always takes a back seat to the real product, the brand."[15]

This is a replica of the reversal that structures the coin story: the product, allegedly signified by the symbol, becomes the material support of the symbol. Nike shoes, for example, must indeed be of high-quality material, as the economic explanation holds, but in contrast with this explanation, this material quality is a support to the symbol: it is a part of what maintains the reputation of the brand name. Poor quality would simply harm the symbol. Precisely as in the case of the coin, the thing symbolized (material substance, quality of product) itself comes to be a component of the symbol. That is why in especially successful brand names, the physical object assumes a contingent status in relation to the symbol: the Nike symbol can be applied to a vast, almost unlimited, array of objects—sneakers and sportswear and watches; so why not also cars and furniture? The immaterial symbol assumes the true persistence in comparison with the contingent thing.

The brand name that most clearly demonstrates this paradoxical reversal is probably the most ubiquitous brand name of all, namely, Coca Cola. Coca Cola has inadvertently proven this in an empirical way, in the remarkable New Coke incident of 1985. This new version of the drink was developed with great effort to counter the increasing competition from Pepsi. Blind tests had shown it to be overwhelmingly tastier than both Pepsi and traditional Coca Cola. But then the public announcement of the drink caused an unexpected reaction: consumers protested the insult to tradition until the increasing protest eventually forced Coca Cola to return to its old secret formula.

This incident poses a paradoxical logic of the brand name against the background of history. In the economic conception of brand names, Coca Cola signifies the material substance—it assures consumers that it is the same substance they know and like, that it has exactly the same positive qualities as the substance they know and like, and so on. However, the protests against the insult to tradition exposed an elusive yet crucial difference from this conception: it is not that the symbol attested to the persistence of the same material qualities, but that persistence *as such* has become one of the most identified properties of the brand name Coca Cola. The symbol does not vouch for the persistence of the material substance. Rather, the material substance provides an anchor of persistence for the symbolic object.

The inert persistence of the material substance enabled Coca Cola to become something quite different from mere material substance, namely, a bearer of tradition. It is the same drink produced according to the same secret formula from 1888 to our day. Through this elusive reversal, persistence shifts from being an ordinary property of physical objects to being a remarkable, mysterious property of a symbolic object. In this sense, Coca Cola is a historical object par excellence. We have claimed that a notion of historical ontology points our attention to that which persists through change, to a thing whose very identity is disclosed through its transformations. Coca Cola, then, is the exact mirror image of this realm: it changed by remaining precisely the same. By remaining the same for such a long time, Coca Cola evolved into something different; it changed into the *thing that remains the same.*[16]

The Real Symbol

Because brand names are comprised of symbols and images, there is a natural tendency to understand them in terms of meaning and identity. Brand names afford consumers a meaningful use that partakes in the construction of their personal identity. Setting aside the limited reservoir of connotations of brands (they are young, fresh, cool, exotic, etc.) and focusing on the level of meaning obfuscates the real economic question: How can something of the order of *meaning* be sold and bought? Under what conditions can meaning, which quite obviously is not a thing and belongs to the sphere of what is shared, be sold and bought?[17] Furthermore, the focus on meaning may sterilize the discussion, because it eventually presents us with another form of utilitarianism. Because utility is an infinitely flexible term in economics, indeed, because economics refuses to have any positive knowledge of utility, it can easily include meaningful use. The focus on meaning may therefore duplicate the oversight of economics concerning brand names.

So how can meaning become an economic object? The beginning of an answer can be found in a quote from Nike CEO Phil Knight that Naomi Klein includes:

> For years we thought of ourselves as a production-oriented company, meaning we put all our emphasis on designing and manufacturing the product. But now we understand that the most important thing we do is market the product. We've come around to saying that Nike is a marketing-oriented company, and the product is our most important marketing tool.[18]

This statement proves again that the brand name poses a real ontological question (and aims, again, at its being a historical object—if you notice the retroactive nature of understanding involved with the brand). Taking his statement literally, what Knight says is that to sell the brand object, there must be a product that carries it. This idea is not as trivial as it may seem. It suggests that *meaning* can be an economic object insofar as it is attached to a meaning-less object. The immediate theoretical context against which this statement should be read is the shallow version of the postmodern concept of simulacra, identified with Baudrillard, according to which the order of the sign has come to replace the real, and mere symbols fill the place of real, material products.

The urgent task for an alternative economic understanding of brand names is to account for how this real level is sustained for the symbol to become an economic object. In other words, what Knight alludes to is the distinct form of materiality of the brand symbol. The product, in a way, confers materiality on the symbol. This may seem similar to the economic explanation of brand names, which also relied on a relation between the symbol and the thing. However, a closer examination reveals a diametric opposite to the economic explanation.

Economists attribute the value of the symbol to the way it attests to the quality of the thing. By contrast, we can speak of the thing as conferring materiality on the symbol insofar as there is a fundamental gap between the symbol and the thing or insofar as the symbol fails to attest to the thing. This paradoxical relation is brought to the extreme in the image of Coca Cola's secret formula. The apparent paradox in this case is that one of the most recognizable and reproducible symbols attests to the material identity of an unknown substance. In formal terms the symbol cannot attest to the identity of the substance. However, it is precisely through this formal failure of sig-nification that the relation is reversed, and the unknown material substance confers materiality on the symbol. That is to say, the substance may well be different than Coca Cola. There is no guarantee in the symbol itself for its identity. But if the material substance is the *wrong* one, then the symbolic object is a fake. It is the possibility of the symbol failing to attest to the thing that sustains the peculiar notion of *true* symbol or *real* symbol that is essential to the field of brand names.

Within a formal conception of the sign, there is no sense to the ques-tion of whether a sign or a symbol is true or fake itself (whether this is a real, authentic "A"). But in reference to the brand-name symbol, it is a basic question: Is something a *real* Nike or a *real* Gucci? It can be conceived as real insofar as the object that carries it is the real one (the real Coke substance). But this can be sustained only when the object can, in principle, be a fake. *The failure of the symbol to fully attest to the thing is the way that the thing con-fers reality on the symbol.* Thus, brand symbols may indeed have meaning, but they are economic objects insofar as they consist also of a meaningless object. It is this excess of the thing, the way it escapes symbolization, that eventually confers authenticity on the symbol.

Coca Cola's secret formula actually poses an ontological question for economics. The question is simply: What is Coca Cola? What is it in relation to the secret formula? A commonsensical economic answer would be that Coca Cola is the material substance that the secret formula describes. Its secrecy defends the firm's property rights over it. This answer ignores the place of symbols and images as constituting part of the reality of the brand name. More specifically, it ignores the fact that the secret formula, as a cultural trope, holds a central place in the Coca Cola image.

The firm has actually put the formula, secured in a sealed box, in its museum. It is set within a film-like, huge vault, above which we see the title "The Vault," thus allowing people to get close to the real essence of Coca Cola. However, concluding that this real essence is not the material substance but the image itself forces us to accept the peculiar answer that Coca Cola *is* the fact that we do not know what Coca Cola is. This statement should be read as a prototypical form of economic symbolic objects, whose very objectivity is symbolically constituted. In the case of material objects, our non-knowledge is a basic predicate. The object is opaque, impenetrable, and unapproachable for the subject. We cannot fully know it because it is an object. Coca Cola shows that with symbolic commodities this relation is reversed. It is constituted as an economic object by our non-knowledge of it. It is an object because we do not fully know it.

Here we can find further evidence for the potency of the comparison between symbolic money and symbolic commodities. The example of the coin should have warned us from the beginning to suspect the question of the meaning of the symbol. Monetary symbols have meaning, too. Yet as Adam Smith already noted, their economic function is utterly indifferent to this meaning (in Smith's terms, for an economic function, it suffices that the symbol is intact, regardless of its content). Furthermore, as in the case of the coin, the economic reality of brand names relies on the tension between the symbol and the thing. It is based on their cohabitation in spite of their unbridgeable gap.

Here one cannot miss a basic similarity to Lacan's dialectic of desire. It is found in the way desire traverses speech precisely through the failure in signifying. According to Lacan, desire is intertwined with speech because we cannot fully articulate what we want, or more precisely, because the very articulation of what we want implies that we really want something else. Verbal demand can never capture pre-verbal need because of the gap of language, and desire results from the difference between the two.

In parallel we can claim that brand names are entangled with desire insofar as they are characterized by a similar gap in which the thing exceeds in some way its symbol. In this sense, brands are made of desire. Their very identity, their unique form of materiality, is related to the way they are desired.

As in Lacan's dialectic of desire, the gap between the symbol and the thing reappears on the symbolic level. That is why the imagery associated with brand names typically refers to the unreachable. Consider, for example, the breathtaking, almost surreal natural landscapes identified with Marlboro cigarettes. It is wrong to understand these landscapes as an attempt to persuade an idiot-consumer that smoking a Marlboro cigarette provides a pleasure that is somehow similar to the experience of a lone rider in the Grand Canyon. Rather, these ads simply tell the truth. What they say is that the real experience of Marlboro is unreachable, utterly different than the experience of smoking a cigarette on the sidewalk outside the office. Their message is quite direct: it's not *smoke Marlboro and you'll feel like a real man* but simply you never *really* enjoy Marlboro.

The comparison with the coin is again fruitful: possession is entangled with what cannot be had. Symbolic money and symbolic commodities are perfect mirror images in this respect. With money one can own the symbol but not the material substance whereas with brand names, one can own the material object (e.g., a Marlboro cigarette) but not the symbol.

The discussion thus far has explored the phenomenological aspect of brand names: the way they are constituted by the relation between the symbol and the thing; the way they confront the economic subject. A fuller exploration of the mode of materiality of symbols must take the homology between symbolic money and symbolic commodities one step further. It requires an inquiry of how materiality is maintained by the *real* relation between money and commodities.

Modern Money as Commodity Money

There is a basic similarity in the manner the symbol inserts itself in the history of money and in the history of commodities. In both cases this insertion sneaks behind the back of the economic view. While this view insists, at least initially, on the a-historical reduction of the value of the symbol to a real quality of the thing, a retroactive view reveals an opposite process, through which the thing becomes subsumed under the symbol.

The similarity in the form of these two replacements suggests a radical alternative to the historical narrative of money. Considered on its own, the dissolution of the gold standard in 1971 is quite naturally conceived of as the final breakdown of the long-lasting tradition of commodity money. By detaching its last, formal connection to gold, money appears to separate itself from the circle of commodities to become a pure symbol and a means in the administration of commodities. However, taking into consideration that in a parallel process, commodities have also become more and more symbolic, we should consider the possibility that this transformation is actually a part of a broader narrative of persistence. Both money and commodities went through a radical transformation during the twentieth century, but the similarity in the forms of this transformation suggests that the relation between money and commodities persists. And this relation is nothing but the Marxist concept of commodity money.

This alternative narrative becomes most visible when brand names are considered according to their entanglement with desire and to the place of money in this desire. The anthropologist Robert J. Foster opens his discussion of brand names with a simple formulation of this entanglement of desire, money, and commodities:

> [Brand-name] vendors market them as singular and incomparable ('Accept no substitutes!') in order to enhance their desirability and hence exchangeability—that is, their substitutability for money and, by this token, all other commodities.[19]

The enigmatic nature of this allegedly basic insight must not escape our attention. We usually relate economic value to exchange, but brand names represent an opposite logic, in which a thing is desirable/valuable only insofar as it is incomparable, and thus in a sense un-exchangeable. Note that we can trace here the mirror image of the logic of surplus that Marx associates with money in his early writings. Money, he writes, is "the *object* most worth possessing" precisely because it can appropriate all other commodities.[20]

From the viewpoint of desire, money is worth more than anything it can buy because it can be exchanged for other things as well. This formation is mirrored in relation to brand names, which are desirable insofar as they are un-exchangeable. In both cases desire is related to a fundamental upset of equivalence, to the way equivalence itself leads to its disruption, in a way that reminds us of Lacan's definition of object *a*, the object-cause of desire, as what is "in the subject more than the subject." Is there a real connection behind this mirroring of desire in relation to money and commodities? To pursue this possibility, we should turn to the later work of Marx.

The surprising point is that Foster's enigma is already foretold in *Capital*. When Marx refers to the situation where one commodity assumes the function of a general means of exchange, he describes it thus:

> A single commodity, the linen, therefore has the form of direct exchange-ability with all other commodities, in other words it has a directly social form because, and in so far as, no other commodity is in this situation.[21]

And in a footnote he clarifies:

> It is by no means self-evident that the form of direct and universal ex-changeability is an antagonistic form, as inseparable from its opposite, the form of non-direct exchangeability, as the positivity of one pole of a magnet is from the negativity of the other pole.

These should be read as minimal formulations of the structure of commodity money. What Marx argues here is that a commodity being money is equivalent to all other commodities not-being money or to the way they are non-money. The fact that an object occupies the place of money is equivalent to the fact that all other objects are not in this situation.

At first sight this formulation may appear circular: an object is money inso-far as other objects are not money. Yet it is the basic requirement of any system of commodity money. In such a system, money is a commodity like all the rest, yet somehow different, but this difference cannot be accounted for in terms that refer to the money object itself. An attempt to ground this difference in qualities of the money object itself is but a fetishistic error. The uniqueness of the money object can be described only in terms that refer to the structure of commodities as a whole. And the minimal requirement from it is that all other objects are not money. Strictly speaking, an answer to the question of what is money cannot comprise solely in terms that refer to the money object. The an-swer must include the whole web of commodities in which money is situated.

In other words, an answer to the question of why gold is money is that, for example, iron and wood are not directly exchangeable.

This formulation is quite obviously valid for a system of gold-based money, where the difference between the money commodity and other commodities clearly does not reside in any property of the specific object that serves as a means of exchange. What about modern fiat money? Regarding fiat money, economists follow the basic impression that money really belongs to a different category of things. But impressions can deceive. The fact that the property of being non-money is now positively inscribed on commodities suggests that the basic structure of commodity money may persist in contrast to appearances.

The enigma that Foster exposes is actually a direct formulation of the place that commodities occupy in a system of commodity money. This is precisely the paradox of brand names: they are desirable as un-exchangeable, that is to say, as being directly, in themselves, non-money. In relation to brand names, desire articulates the way that the commodity positively assumes its position in the structure of commodity money. Marx's formulation seems prophetic in this respect. The universal exchangeability of money is simply the other side of the "non-direct exchangeability" of commodities. This "non-direct exchange-ability" or, I suggest, *direct non-exchangeability*, is a characterization of the desire entangled with brand names—and if we accept that desire is indeed of the substance of brand names, then this is a characterization of the economic position of the brand object.

This view of brand names provides an elegant, broad formulation of the historical narrative of the shift to fiat money. The common view presents this change as a demystification of money, but the brand name suggests that this demystification was made possible by a mystification of commodities. The mystery of money was expelled but was replaced by the mystery of commodities. A system of gold-based money is haunted by the notion of *the mystery of money*, which has fascinated economists throughout the ages: How is it that gold occupies such a peculiar position in the economy although there is nothing really unique about it in relation to other commodities? The point, of course, is that this enigma has no solution. The mystery is nothing but the description of the way gold fills the role of money.

As argued in the previous chapter, this mystery can be conceived as a real property in a historical framework. It denotes a historical property of gold that exceeds any formal, a-historical view of the economy. That is why desire is the correct term to explain the role of gold: desire marks the mysterious quality that gold possesses beyond its positive qualities, the untraceable quality that makes gold unique.

What should we say then of modern fiat money? The standard view says that money became demystified, liberated from the mystery of gold and the pathological desire associated with it. Our exploration of the brand name suggests a radical alternative view: money has become demystified because the commodity is now directly mysterious. In a system of gold-based money, the fact that all other commodities are *non-directly exchangeable* is sustained by the mystery of money. Modern fiat money appears as demystified, on the account that now commodities directly assume their position as un-exchangeable. It is true that even at the time of gold-based money, commodities were un-exchangeable. But at that time their un-exchangeability was related to the mystery of gold or even a description of the mystery of gold. Today, when money appears demystified, the same mystery is sustained by commodities.

Economics can hold a notion of a process of rationalization that characterizes money precisely because it cannot see the irrationality of the modern commodity. Better yet: it purports to know what money is on account of insisting not to know what commodities are. For example, economics holds that commodities differ from money in that they hold utilities. But the brand name provides a further proof of the futility of the concept of utility. That is the root of the distinction between products and brand names. A branded object has something that transcends the utilitarian qualities of the respective product. By incorporating commodities into the narrative of money, the pathological desire is not overcome through history but appears as the substance of the historical narrative, the secret of its coherence.

The Mystery of Commodities

In what ways are brand names mysterious? They appear directly mysterious if we consider the imageries that typically accompany them in advertising, where they display all sorts of miraculous powers. This imaginary mystery has a real economic counterpart that can be detected in an aspect of them that escapes economic understanding. What focuses the economic *perversity* of a brand object, its aspect that is most foreign to the economic utilitarian view, is that with a brand name, price can be a property of the commodity. This possibility is inconceivable in economic terms: price is conceived of as what is paid in return for the beneficent properties of the thing. Listing it among the properties themselves amounts to a money-for-nothing exchange (consider, e.g., putting up for sale a very expensive rock, whose high price is justified by its unique expensiveness).

It appears that this is the normal case in a consumer economy. The previous chapter examined one manifestation of this economically perverse logic in the price set for newness. Newness is a quality that disappears through the very act of purchase and, thus, can be seen as reflecting the extent that the price has become a property of the object. However, brand names represent a pure form of this perverse logic. In relation to the brand name, price is a part of what constitutes the notion of *real* symbol. The fact that an object is too cheap suffices to render it fake, un-real.

In a famous episode of *Sex and the City*, Samantha, the most provocative and daring character in the female quartet, buys a cheap, fake Fendi bag and is dramatically punished for it in a humiliating scene at a party at Hugh Hefner's mansion. She publicly accuses a *Playboy* model of stealing her bag and demands that the model open the bag she carries and reveal as proof of her accusation the "Made in China" tag inside. To her great embarrassment, the bag that the *un-real* model carries turns out to be a real Fendi, and Samantha is disgracefully thrown out of the party.

In this case the narrative establishes the difference between the authentic and the fake brand in a real, even if minor, property and thus obscures the real challenge that brand names pose to economics. This challenge is more directly represented by the main character Carrie Bradshaw, who is initially thrilled at the idea of buying a cheap replica. Samantha takes her on a long drive in Los Angeles to the yard of the dealer, but then as she stares at the bags in his trunk, she changes her mind. "I should have liked them," she confides in a voice-over monologue, but in the trunk "they no longer looked like elegant Fendi bags. They just looked cheap. And even if everyone else thought it was real, I'd always know that my bag came from a cardboard box in a trunk deep in the valley."

Carrie spells out explicitly the mystery of brand names. The mysterious aura of the desirable object is sustained among other things by its price (the exact replicas look *cheap*). And this mystery is very real in the sense that it goes beyond the grasp of economics. Carrie's conduct is unthinkable in economic terms. In economic terms, an agent cannot deter from buying an exact replica of an object solely on the grounds that it is cheap. However, this economic agent is presupposed in an economy of brand names. Intellectual property laws indeed prohibit the production of such replicas, but by themselves they cannot explain the brand-name economy. The brand-name market supposes the existence of an economic subject who prefers the expensive thing precisely because its price guarantees that it is real.

This last point should be taken at face value. The reality of brand names, their unique materiality, is sustained by their relation to money. In a sense, brand objects can be understood as being *made* of money. If substance is what guarantees the identity and irreproducibility of an object, then money is part of the substance of brand names. This is true not only in the local context of the consumer but also at a macro-economic level. What limits the reproduction of Fendi bags is indeed nothing but their price. Had the company decided to lower their prices, there would have been many more of them around. Taking these two points into account, it appears that in contrast to the impression of a growing distance between money and commodities, in their symbolic form they actually interpenetrate each other.

Economists have a name for a situation where a firm, like Fendi, limits production in order to maintain high prices. It is called a monopoly, and it is considered an aberration of the market economy. Yet, economist Paul Krugman has recently acknowledged that in the American economy, monopoly rents are no longer an accident but are becoming the rule. The most significant characteristic of the American economy in the twenty-first century is "profits that don't represent returns on investment, but instead reflect the value of market dominance." His prime example is Apple: "To a large extent, the price you pay for an iWhatever is disconnected from the cost of producing the gadget. Apple simply charges what the traffic will bear, and given the strength of its market position, the traffic will bear a lot."[22]

What could have enabled such dominance of monopoly rents in a market economy? The rise of the brand name provides us with a fundamental cause. Brand names are essentially monopolistic when we take into account the role change between the symbol and the thing that characterizes them. If symbols are indeed a part of the economic object, then there is actually no sense to the idea that Coca Cola and Pepsi are competitors—no more than any random pair of goods is in competition.

The best example of the way the price turns into a property of a thing is found in art, in relation to the various forms of its dematerialization. Without going into detail, we can easily point to the way money has become the substance of the work of art. In fields such as photography, digital art, or video art, there is less and less meaning to the distinction between an original work and a copy. The extreme case is conceptual art, where every physical instance of the work is but an execution of it ("a perfunctory affair," to quote the conceptual artist Sol LeWitt). Yet even conceptual art works can be sold and bought. What one buys in this case is the abstract right to execute the work. But this means that as an economic object, the very identity of the work is comprised of its price.

Note the switch of the role of money in relation to traditional forms of art. In traditional forms of art, an original work is a very scarce resource, and this accounts for its price. In dematerialized works of art, it is the other way around: the money price artificially maintains the possibility of an original. Something can be an original art object because it was paid for.

Things as Non-money

Brand names directly assume the role of non-money, of a thing that is valuable as un-exchangeable, the role that commodities play in the structure of commodity money. In this role we can see the connection of the phenomenon of the brand name to the circulation of capital. As discussed in the Chapter 1, Marx's concept of capital relies on his unique concept of money. Economists do not conceive of money as a thing but as an external organ to the circle of economic things. Marx, by contrast, elaborates a topology in which money is both external and internal to commodities. He sees money as a commodity abstracted from *thingness* and, therefore, as indeed external to the circle of things but at the same time as the hidden secret of economic things, commodities. To quote again the beginning of the chapter in which Marx introduces capital:

> If we disregard the material content of the circulation of commodities, i.e. the exchange of the various use-values, and consider only the economic forms brought into being by this process, we find that its ultimate product is money. This ultimate product of commodity circulation is the first form of appearance of capital.[23]

What should be noted is that this transition between things, money, and capital does not draw categorical distinctions between them. Eventually the distinctions between things, money, and capital can be sustained only by including the subject positions in which they are entangled. The capitalist is the subject who actually disregards "the material content of the circulation of commodities, i.e. the exchange of the various use-values." The capitalist is the one for whom commodities are just another form of money; he is the subject who can actually buy money with commodities. The complete description of the distinction between things, money, and capital would be: an object is a thing for the laborer and money for the capitalist. But on another level, what is money for the laborer is capital for the capitalist. Subject and object are reciprocally determined (insofar as use value for one person is money for another, then this latter is a capitalist).

An important point that should be emphasized is the elusive, yet central, part played here by use value. In a first approach to *Capital*, use value can be understood as a critical anchor for a moral and political critique of capitalism. In this reading the problem with capitalism is that it submits use values— people's needs, their immediate relations to their material environment—to exchange value. In this reading, in capitalism the fate of our needs and desires are actually determined by alien forces—the indifferent considerations of exchange value that motivate the economy. This is only a partial reading. What this reading misses is the theoretical part allocated by Marx to use value. Use value is that which differentiates a commodity from money, that which sustains its difference from money. As such, use value is an essential part of the circulation of capital. Its economic function is that of a necessary middle term in the movement of capital from M to M'.

In this further reading, use value does not necessarily mark authenticity as answering the immediate needs of people and as refering to the truth of the thing (i.e., to its substantial properties, to its immediate value for a person). Rather, use values also can be understood as fashioned by the drive of limitless accumulation that characterizes capital. Use value does not simply mark the way the economy operates in a dimension that is foreign to people's everyday experience but the way this alien dimension can eventually shape everyday experience.

This view of use value has immense theoretical implications. What it says is that Marxism holds a possibility of an economic knowledge of use values, that is, of the commodities themselves. The novelty in this possibility is best viewed against the obstinate refusal of orthodox economics to have any substantial knowledge of commodities. Any substantial knowledge of economic things is done away with through the concepts of utility or preferences, which, in principle, cannot be inquired by economics.[24] As Becker puts it, "economists generally have had little to contribute, especially in recent times, to the understanding of how preferences are formed."[25]

The apparent flaw with this line of thought is that it can't approach the weirdness of commodities in the consumer economy. Take bizarre merchandise such as a ringtone—a sequence of sounds sold for a mobile phone to differentiate incoming calls. Although people do use and like them, it would be absurd to claim that they emerged to satisfy people's preferences. The simple truth is that they emerged as means to further capitalize on music property rights.

It is precisely this philosophical difference that explains why Marxism is ever more relevant to the understanding of the contemporary economy. In contrast to orthodox economics, Marx's thought possesses the possibility of incorporating consumption within economic theory because of the theoretical function he assigns to use value. It is this theoretical stance that enables Marxist thought to easily leap from economies of scarcity to those of abundance—from the gray industrial economy of nineteenth-century England to the modern, bright consumption economies of the contemporary, affluent West.

In terms of the theoretical (as opposed to the merely critical) place afforded to use value in the system, there is a perfect symmetry between the basic questions that these two economies raise: Why do people have too little? Why do people have this sickening abundance of things? In both cases the answer is that use value—whether it is scarce or nauseatingly abundant—is an effect of the circulation of money and is determined by its unique considerations and, therefore, alien to the subject's point of view. According to this reasoning, we should learn from Marx that the most radical critique of the economy lies in inquiring after the use value of things, that is to say, after what economics hides from itself beneath the concept of utility.

Desire as Substance

Applying the question of use value to brand names reveals their place in the circulation of capital. Things are brand names insofar as they comprise an element that goes beyond their direct utility. They are desired insofar as they comprise *something more* than mere objects of use. But this is also the manner in which they can be said to be made of money. Desire marks both the unique identity of the brand item and the manner its price has become its property. In this sense, it is desire that articulates the place of the thing in the circulation of capital.

This line of reasoning is mirrored with reference to luxury goods. These goods also owe their identity to their minimal difference from money. A marvelous example of this grammar of luxury is found in Robert H. Frank's *Luxury Fever*. Frank tells of Patek Philippe watches, whose prices range up to a few million dollars. What causes the more expensive models to be so expensive are not the traditional jewels or gold embellishments but rather what the firm calls mechanical *complications* that have been added to the watch. The most elaborate of these complications is the *tourbillion*, a mechanism based on a gyroscope that turns very slowly, at the pace of about one round per minute, to compensate for gravity's distorting effect on the mechanical apparatus of the watch. As Frank notes, the absurdity is that a simple five-dollar quartz watch is actually free of this distorting effect (and, therefore, the term complication is actually very apt; the firm finds complicated ways to fulfill simple tasks).

In both standard economic terms and Marxist terms, there is a certain justification for the extremely high price of a tourbillion watch given the vast amount of sophisticated development and production work invested in the mechanism. However, this justification does not account for the use value of the watch. Inquiring about the use value, we would say that the use value of the watch actually lies in its extravagant uselessness. What is extreme here is not just the effort invested in the mechanism and its sophistication, but also the obvious redundancy of it—a mechanism that hardly moves (an inertial movement of one round per minute), installed to fix an almost unperceived error, which can be solved in the simplest manner—a masterpiece of redundancy. Of course, it is this redundancy that enables the watch to signify expensiveness.

Luxury is produced through a certain inversion, whereby the thing-properties of the watch are expressively annulled, so that in their redundancy they come to signify the price. Like the brand name, the Patek Philippe watch can be said to be made of money (the difference, as we shall see, is that with luxury, the owner appropriates the labor of others, while with a brand name, the labor of the consumer is appropriated by capital). They both occupy the same position in the circulation of capital, namely, that of associating value with un-exchangeability. This structural position is explicitly stated in the second half of the Patek Philippe slogan: *You never actually own a Patek Philippe.*

You merely look after it for the next generation. What it says is that the watch permanently arrests (for all generations) the circulation of value. In Marxist terms this means that the watch is a means of preventing value from entering back into circulation, avoiding what Marxist thinkers refer to as the problem of over-accumulation.

What the examples of brand names and luxury goods both demonstrate is the explosive force of the concept of desire for economic discourse. Viewing things in light of their direct uses and thing-properties supports the economic distinction between things and money. By contrast, turning to the perspective of desire as a certain surplus over direct use and over mere *thingness* blurs the distinction and unearths the way things come to assume their position in the circulation of capital. In a sense, desire emerges as the substance common to money and commodities.

This amounts to adopting one of Žižek's basic arguments regarding the way that fantasy and desire are not simply opposed to reality but are intimately intertwined with it:

> [Fantasy's] function is similar to that of Kantian "transcendental schematism": a fantasy constitutes our desire, provides its co-ordinates; that is, it literally "teaches us how to desire."[26]

What Žižek suggests here is a sphere where an identity of a thing comprises the way it is desired. The economy is probably one the most typical such spheres—the economic function of a thing can be seen to depend on the way it is desired.

Indeed this is not very far from our experience of brand names: Can we think of Coca Cola, Nike, or Marlboro *objectively*, apart from the way they are desired? Desire is inscribed in their very form. But this claim is just one more way to describe the inversions between symbol and thing that characterize the brand name if we consider advertising in this light. If brand names are comprised of symbols, then advertising should not be seen simply as communication about merchandise, an attempt to attribute false qualities to objects, but as a part of the object itself. Strictly speaking, Coca Cola is the advertising for Coca Cola. Advertising, in this respect, does not lie. It shows us the commodity as it is. But this means that desirability must be a feature of the thing. Indeed, this is highlighted by a common form in advertising, where things are portrayed not as good but as desirable. This form, for example, lies at the heart of the aesthetic of food in commercials, where the typical case is that no one is seen actually enjoying the food. Such advertisements simply show us what the economic object really is: not something tasty or delicious, but a desired object.

In a sense desire enables us to form a unified theory of the economy, which encompasses both production and consumption. In the first chapter of this book I showed how Marx's concept of capital entails a notion of desire at the limit of subjectivity. The M-C-M' circulation (money exchanged for commodities and then back to money of a higher sum) can be read as designating desire that can take effect as long it is transferred to the object. Thus, in relation to capital, money embodies the principle of its foreignness. It embodies that dimension of economic action that is foreign to one's substantial wants and wishes marked by use values, which indeed annuls such wants and wishes.

The marvelous point is that a precise echo of this pattern informs modern consumption when we view brand names as non-money. Being non-money marks, at the same time, the way a brand name transcends mundane wants and wishes and the way it is made of money—the way its higher price has become its property. A fuller exploration of this link is provided in Chapter 5, but for now we can note that the slogan "there are some things money can't buy" is used by MasterCard in credit card commercials, that is, in advertising expensive money. In both cases money embodies a principle that annuls the thingness of things. In the context of production, things are effects of the drive of capital to accumulate. In the context of consumption, things appear as effects of the parallel de-centered drive to spend. The desire of the consumer is inseparable from the desire of capital.

To bring this discussion closer to standard economic discourse, we turn from desire to the more down-to-earth notion of labor. It is the question of labor that actually provides a final proof that Marx is essential for the understanding of brand names.

Surplus and History

Marx's speculation about time-chits portrays surplus value as a stubborn historical kernel. An imaginary attempt to eradicate surplus value by a fair monetary system leads to the equation of money itself with surplus value: money notes produced with no investment of labor being exchanged for labor products, leading to a concentration of all property in an issuing bank.

This is indeed only an imaginary scenario, yet its outline can be traced around the emergence of symbolic money. The economic explanation for the value of the symbol, represented by Adam Smith's account of the emergence of coins aims precisely at avoiding the possibility of surplus value. By anchoring the symbol's value in the value of metal, the narrative circumscribes the possibility that a mere symbol, produced with no investment of labor, carries value. Of course, by this very effort, Smith's explanation only underlines the fact that in a historical view, a certain notion of surplus value must have asserted itself. His account can explain how in any synchronous state of affairs, the value of the symbol is reducible to the value of the metal (e.g., it saves the additional costs of measuring and uncertainty). But by that very movement, it prevents the possibility of accounting for the way symbols eventually take the place of metal.

The same applies, of course, to symbolic commodities. The orthodox economic explanation aims at avoiding the sense of a surplus exchange: money paid for mere symbols. But that is precisely the direction to be pursued for a true economic account of brand names. Foster spells out this relation between brand names and surplus value. The surplus value associated with brand names can be traced by asking exactly how and where they are produced. Granted that brand names are indeed symbolic objects, the answer cannot be the work done in factories (many of which are in the developing world, in China, etc.) because these factories produce only the product, the *material support* for the brand name.

It also would be wrong to attribute production solely to the designers and the advertising agencies that create the symbolic aspect of brand names (the design, the logo, the images, the commercials, etc.). Indeed, they design the brand name and manage its public life, yet they cannot account for the massive public aspect of the symbol. For that reason Foster allocates the production of brands to the consumers themselves. Brands are produced by what he terms *consumption work*.

In the actual daily use of branded merchandise, consumers invest them with meaning and thus turn them into a part of their own identity. In this way brand names can be seen to dispossess the consumer: "In effect, consumers transfer control over aspects of their persons to corporate owners of the brand, who defend their brands legally as protected intellectual property."[27]

In this sense, brand names represent a sort of pure surplus value, folded into the thing itself. In industrial capitalism, surplus value is spread through the system of production. It is theoretically detected in the difference between what a laborer produces and what he is paid. Adopting Foster's view, we would say that in the case of brand names, surplus value is what constitutes the economic object itself. The object becomes what it is through the unpaid consumption work invested in it. A practical demonstration of this paradox is found in brands that allow the consumer to personalize the object: when a consumer invests labor in designing his own personal Nike sneakers, he ends up paying more for the object—that is to say, he pays for his own labor.

Foster's view of brand names in terms of labor and surplus value points in the right direction. But formulating it in terms of meaningful use and its role in the construction of identity seems to put it on the wrong track. It suggests that the consumer does get something for his labor: meaning and identity.

A more fruitful path is to consider consumption work along the lines Marx attributes to capitalist production, namely, that the laborer produces what is not his own. Consider the following basic example. Fast-food chains often display images of the hamburgers they serve right above the counters. It is a genuine philosophical riddle as to how these images can look better than real hamburgers. (Saying, e.g., that these photos are digitally retouched or that the photographed object is not real does not answer the question but simply paraphrases the riddle. This answer simply shows that the language of the visual image runs counter to experience.) The point is that a photo of a good hamburger is something different from a good photo of a hamburger.

Yet a strict consideration of the economy of brand names forces us to accept that the perfect image is a part of the economic object called McDonald's, alongside the real burger we get. This image, strictly speaking, presents us with the hamburger that we cannot have. What should be noted is that in this interpretation, McDonald's replicates the position of the object in Marx's concept of alienated labor. His formulations in the *Economic and Philosophic Manuscripts* seem prophetic when they are read with an eye to the idea of the unreachable image as completing the economic object:

> the object which labor produces [. . .] confronts it as an alien being, as
> a power independent of the producer [. . .] The worker becomes poorer
> the richer is his production, the more it increases in power and scope.[28]

These are precise descriptions of McDonald's images if we think of the confrontation with the image in terms of production.

The image that produces the McDonald's brand renders the real hamburger a lesser thing. The consumer as viewer produces wealth (the image of the hamburger as an image of abundance, of full satisfaction) only to render the hamburger he really gets as lacking.

This is one key to reading Guy Debord's attempt to conceive of "the spectacle" (mass media, advertising, entertainment) in Marxist economic terms. In a typically abstract formulation, Debord writes that "the spectacle that falsifies reality is nevertheless a real product of that reality."[29] If this formulation seems vague, we need only replace here the hamburger image for the spectacle and the burger for reality. Thus, what we get is a description of the uncanny effect of the McDonald's image: it works by declaring itself the real thing (which is true in the economic sense: the image is an essential part of McDonald's as a brand name) and, therefore, by falsifying the reality of the burger.

This basic example provides a way to consider consumption work more concretely, by focusing it on the confrontation with images. Accordingly, rather than the meaningful use of brand names, we can consider Sut Jhally's idea to consider the watching of advertising in terms of labor.[30] Advertising, in this view, should not be thought of in terms of persuasion (commercials manipulate us to believe that if we buy certain merchandise, we will be perfectly happy) but as a form of production. It is where images related to brands become public and where the brand is actually produced.

Furthermore, conceptualizing television as a production site of brand names has the additional advantage in that it offers an economic answer to an enigma of our time: How is it that broadcast television survives? Television survives because it is a social space compatible with brand names and consumer culture, as can be observed through the topology shared by celebrities, commercials, and brand names. To put it briefly, all three supplement the mundane household reality with an unreachable horizon.

What Is Television?

In terms of a technology of transmission and consumption of video content, broadcast television has become an idiotic, superfluous tool. Compared to the wide array of alternative video technologies: cable TV, video-on-demand (VOD), web-TV, DVD, and others, it has only drawbacks. This situation has led some theorists to speculate about the end of television and an era of post-television. Yet it is more fruitful to use this peculiar historical moment to reconsider what television really is. That television survives despite its drawbacks requires us to conceptualize it not simply as a technology but in terms of a distinct social space.

Daniel Dayan characterized television as distinct by its *sharedness*—the sense of implied others who watch the same content at the same time as we do.[31] This observation is certainly true, yet it does not take us very far from the basic description of the television form. The point, naturally, is to show its relevance to the understanding of television content. The wrong way to search for this sharedness is the obvious one, namely, the experience of sharedness in the broadcasting of national events—what Dayan and Elihu Katz termed "media events."

The crucial point is to explore the shared dimension in the ordinary realities of television. In this respect we can point, for example, to the rise of reality-TV as a genre that thematizes the shared dimension of experience. Television shows like *American Idol*, in which amateur performers compete for the love of the anonymous audience, invoke the presence of this faceless crowd—indeed, they are meaningless without the implication of a watching crowd. Thus, these shows can be understood as a struggle of television to assert itself against the threats from neighboring media by underlining the unique characteristics of the medium. In this light, reality-TV can be seen along the lines of the artistic avant-garde, as a moment when a medium reveals itself by exploring its underlying material conditions.

Another basic example of the shared dimension of television is the institution of celebrity. The celebrity is a social phenomenon. When we watch him or her on television, we are interested in the celebrity as a person that captures everyone's attention. Others are implied in our relation to the celebrity. Of course, the celebrity appears to us as a unique personality. We need not experience our relation to him or her as *shared*. But that is precisely the importance of a celebrity. The celebrity enables us to locate the social dimension of television in a way that bypasses experience. To paraphrase Marx, the celebrity is immediately social. The celebrity enables us to situate the social in the ontological dimension of television.

Two observations are in place here. First, network-based media cannot produce celebrities. People can become celebrities as an outcome of their activity on the web. But they typically become celebrities when television turns its attention to them after they have acquired some fame on the web. This is actually a theoretical distinction. We should recall Daniel Boorstin's sharp definition of celebrities, as "people who are known for their well-knownness."[32]

That is precisely the difference between television and the web. On the web people can be well known, for example, when thousands of people follow them on Twitter or Facebook. Only on television can they be known for their *well-knownness*, precisely because there is an anonymous crowd watching them. They represent everybody's attention because their following is not reducible to concrete others.

The second point refers to the wide variation that spawned celebrity types, together with the emergence of reality-TV. In addition to the traditional glamorous celebrity, we now see celebrities being humiliated and suffering. We see them ridiculed, we see former celebrities trying to enliven their bygone fame, or we see anonymous people motivated by the desire for celebrity. Perhaps the most enigmatic of these new forms is on the *Big Brother* show, where people become famous for being themselves—famous for their ordinariness.

All these new forms do not signify the dissolution of the institution of celebrity but, rather, mark its intensification. The celebrity who is famous as an ordinary person folds back into what the celebrity was from the beginning, namely, a marker of the difference between what's *on* television and what's outside it or a code name for our relation to the television screen. It is the pure form of celebrity precisely because it dismantled the illusion of a substantial difference (a special talent, etc.) between ordinary people and celebrities. By becoming ordinary, the celebrity underlines the difference between the world of television and the world outside it: the celebrity is a perfectly ordinary person, just like us, but nonetheless he or she is famous.

The theoretical frameworks that best capture this spatial feature of television are those that refer to it in terms of religion or ritual. Nick Couldry applies to media some anthropological concepts of religious rituals, mainly in a Durkheimian approach. In examining these concepts in terms of ritual, Couldry looks for the ways the media strengthen and naturalize the basic categories of media space. First and foremost, the media recreate "the basic category difference between anything 'in' or 'on' or associated with 'the media,' and anything which is not." This distinction echoes Durkheim's opposition of the sacred and the profane in the sense that it is content-less: the scared is defined by nothing but its opposition to the profane, just as the media-person is defined by nothing but his or her opposition to *common* people.[33]

What should be noted is that this ritualistic view of the media is uniquely valid for television. The distinction between an inside and an outside is precisely what characterizes the unique topology of television in contrast to the web. There is no sense in which one can be *in* the web because at any moment we are both inside it and outside of it. Of course, one cannot really be *on* television. But what the present moment teaches us is that there is no life to television without the idiotic illusion that being on television is somehow better than ordinary experience.

That is the structural reason why *Big Brother* participants stress the unique experience of being in the house.[34] When a participant is evicted from the house, the show's host eagerly interrogates him or her about life in the house, to which we have already been intimate witnesses. What confers meaning on this scene is the one question that cannot be asked but hovers over the dialogue as a whole: What's it like to *really* be on television? However, what connects this topology to the consumer economy is that the difference between the inside and the outside of television can be articulated in terms of enjoyment. Celebrities enjoy pleasures inaccessible to us (such as going to parties with other celebrities).

This feature also became more visible with the rise of reality-TV. When a judge in a *Pop Idol* show describes the extraordinary thrill of a nice performance that we have just witnessed together with her, what she really is saying is that *inside* television there is access to a more intense enjoyment, denied to the passive viewer. This is also the secret of the rising popularity of cooking shows on television. They are so numerous precisely because flavors cannot be broadcast and therefore demarcate the difference between the inside and the outside of television in terms of enjoyment.

At this point we can see the topology shared by brand names and celebrities. The celebrity is an ordinary person who has access to intense enjoyment that is inaccessible to us. The brand name is an ordinary object, often accompanied by images of intense, impossible pleasure. This parallel allows a preliminary outline of television in terms of production. When we watch television we reaffirm the precedence of what's on television over our everyday, immediate reality. When we watch celebrity-related content, we reaffirm the superiority of the celebrity over ordinary people. We actually produce celebrities by watching television. One should notice the fetishistic reversal that characterizes this situation: we may think that we watch someone on television because she is a celebrity, but in fact she is a celebrity because we watch her on television. But in watching celebrity-related content on television, we also reproduce television itself as the space where the unreachable pleasure of commodities can be presented, a presentation through which brand names are produced.

The well-known series of commercials for Nespresso coffee makers demonstrates precisely this topology. In the first commercial the actor George Clooney buys a Nespresso machine but as he leaves the store, he is crushed under a piano, which mysteriously falls from the sky. In the next frame we see him at the gates of heaven, meeting John Malkovich, who is dressed in a blazing white suit. As he slowly understands his situation, Clooney pleads for his life until Malkovich hints that "maybe we could make an arrangement": Clooney would get his life back in exchange for the coffee machine that he would leave in heaven.

The religious imagery ("heaven can wait, but not for its coffee") may seem exceptional. Yet, it demonstrates to an extreme the paradox that characterizes television advertising at large: consumer goods, and especially those like food and drink, which provide an immediate experience, can hardly be advertized with images of merely *possible* pleasures. However, this allusion to heaven would strain attempts to read this commercial in the standard terms of persuasion. One would have to be an idiot to be convinced that Nespresso coffee machines provide a heavenly pleasure. Actually, the commercial itself suggests that it is not aimed at persuasion. It is built in the form of a double, and not a single, shift in reference to reality, which spares it the need to persuade.

The experience of coffee is hyperbolically transformed to heavenly pleasure, yet this transformation is accompanied by transferring the pleasure to celebrities, whose position is defined to begin with by access to unreachable pleasures. In this sense the commercial actually tells us that we do not have to believe. We know that Nespresso will not give us heavenly pleasure, but that's okay because we know that we are not Clooney or Malkovich either. In this sense the commercial simply tells the truth: you can never enjoy your coffee like that. But in telling the truth, it joins itself to the realm of production. The commercial produces the unreachable pleasure that defines the brand name and distinguishes it from the mere product—coffee.

That the religious nature of the commercial should be taken literally is evidenced not only by contemporary theory that conceptualizes television in terms of sacred space and ritual. It also echoes Veblen's analysis of religious sanctuaries. A sacred structure, Veblen writes, is usually "more ornate, more conspicuously wasteful in its architecture and decoration, than the dwelling houses of the congregation." Yet the luxurious build of the shrine must not serve the comfort of the worshiper. Taken together, these two principles base the economy of religious expenditure, what Veblen terms *devout consumption*, on the notion of *vicarious consumption*. Just like the members and workers of the aristocratic household consume not for their own comfort but to display the wealth and power of the head of the household, worshipers consume for the grandeur of their divinity. That is precisely our situation vis-à-vis television consumer discourse. It presents more luxurious pleasures than our own. Our consumption, in this context, is devout vicarious consumption. We consume for the ideal of consumerism, embodied, among others, in celebrities who actually enjoy it.[35]

To return to the perspective of production, television commercials manifest the characteristics of Marx's analysis of capitalist alienated labor. The first thing to note is that when advertising is conceived in terms of production, it recapitulates the root form of alienation as a relation to an object. This root form is: in capitalism the laborer produces that which is not his. According to Marx, this is the basic form of capitalist production. In advertising, this relation to the object seems to fold into the object itself. What we produce when we consume commercials is precisely what we will not get when we buy the object. We produce the difference between the coffee that we will actually have and the brand name, which is the real economic object at stake.[36]

We can also find in television echoes of additional senses of social alienation that Marx lists, which in Chapter 1 I presented as secondary conditions that make possible the primary sense of alienation as a relation to an object. To recall, Marx characterizes capitalist production in terms of alienation from the work process, alienation from others, and alienation from the human essence. The celebrity brings to an extreme the social alienation of production, because its social dimension is completely masked under the guise of an infatuation with a unique person. It is the epitome of social alienation because in our relation to the celebrity, we are social even in the solitude of our living room. This relation to the celebrity confers concrete meaning even to Marx's most vague idea of alienation from the human essence. Vis-à-vis the celebrity, and particularly, the ordinary celebrity of reality-TV, we experience ourselves as somehow lacking.

Debord formulated a general proposition regarding the viewer:

[T]he alienation of the spectator, which reinforces the contemplated objects that results from his own unconscious activity, works like this: the more he contemplates, the less he lives; the more he identifies with the dominant images of need, the less he understands his own desires.[37]

Renata Salecl poignantly diagnosed a similar situation in reference to advertising. Salecl refers to the seemingly revolutionary advertising strategy of Nike characterized by slogans such as *be yourself* and *just do it*. Her argument is that such slogans do not represent the liberation of consumers, who are now begged to relax and just be themselves. Rather, the possibility of not being true to oneself is actually the most forceful source of anxiety. Along these lines, the shift from glamorous to ordinary celebrities marks an intensification of the intrusive effect of television. We can more easily concede to the idea that we will not be like Brad Pitt or Angelina Jolie than to the idea that we are not being ourselves—not fulfilling all of what we can potentially be.

So why does television persist? There seems to be a simple economic answer. Broadcast television will survive as long as it can sell advertising air time. In fact this answer is not that simple. It seems simple—and by the same token empty—only if we consider television advertising as a neutral medium for marketing preexisting merchandise. It is not that simple if we keep in mind that advertising is not external to the merchandise advertised. As a social form, television fashions specific forms of advertising, and these forms are compatible with specific economic objects. In this way television is intimately entangled with the consumer economy. Much more than our ways of consuming video content would have to change if television were really to disappear.

Possible evidence that watching television can be considered a form of labor is the strange fact that on the iPad screen, the most individual of all screens, so many games are fashioned directly in the form of labor: preparing hamburgers, digging for gold, cultivating fields, and so forth. In "Ninja Fishing," for example, the player catches fish and then cuts them as they are thrown in the air. With the money the player earns by cutting the fish, he or she can buy better fishing equipment, which will enable the player to fish in deeper waters, catch more expensive fish, and so forth—a marvelous demonstration of the shared futility of both endless profit making and monotonous labor.

This explicit form of labor may result from the solitary confrontation with the iPad. With television, we need not be aware that by watching the celebrity we are actually producing a real social phenomenon. This is true because of the social formation involved. The celebrity will be a celebrity regardless of the relation to any specific viewer because by implication there are always others who watch. By contrast, with the iPad there is no way to make the simplistic, two-dimensional fish sketches feel real except by explicitly investing effort in catching fish. The sketches are real only because the player worked so hard. Otherwise the fish would be simply two-dimensional sketches that no one would glance at a second time. Strangely enough, the game itself provides the proof that it should be conceived seriously as labor. One can buy the virtual fishing equipment with real money, which means that one can pay to play for less time.

In the same vein, note the irony of the famous 1984 Apple commercial that preceded the release of the first Macintosh computer. The commercial alluded to IBM's PC, (i.e., Apple's competitor), with images of a totalitarian regime. The commercial presented a dictator speaking from a screen to crowds of faceless gray zombies, saying "we are one people, one will, one resolve, one cause. . . . Our enemies will talk themselves to death . . . we shall prevail" until a young woman dressed in red shorts and a tight, white shirt enters the frame. She throws a big hammer that smashes the screen signifying a promise of liberation.

The historical irony is not just that Apple eventually prevailed economically but that it did so in a way that resembled the totalitarian image more than its competitors ever resembled it. The PC is indeed colorless in comparison to an Apple product as are the zombies in the commercial. But for this very reason it is and never was an emotionally charged object. Apple won because from the very beginning its products succeeded in becoming very personal matters for its users, objects that reflect their users' identities. In this way it extracted a form of devotion from its users.

The *i* in Apple's most recent series of products not only signals extreme individuality but at the same time, it signifies its opposite—a symbol of submission, namely, of investing one's identity in an external, inanimate object. The final twist in the irony is that the iPad, as one of the defining objects of our time, is a tool that enables one to work practically anywhere, which gives the 1984 commercial its ultimate meaning: you cannot enslave people in a free society unless you make slavery seem sexy.

Brand Names and the Problem of Labor

Adhering to Marxist thought can sometimes lead to a view of our economy as radically different from that of early capitalism. Steve Fleetwood concludes his illuminating presentation of the Marxist theory of commodity money with the seemingly wild suggestion that we no longer use money: "whilst the system still uses something called money, something that appears to be money, this something might not really be money at all. Appearances might be deceptive."[38] In a complementary article Peter Kennedy takes up this line of thought. He explores symbolic money and presents it in terms of a break with commodity money.

Kennedy's main argument is that modern money is no longer a form of commodity money insofar as it no longer fills the place of both *the form of value* and *the content of value*. According to this argument capitalist money regulates economic life because it both governs the social relations of labor (people are paid money wages) and is produced by the investment of labor (gold is produced by labor). This double function allows for the organization of an economy in the absence of any direct social relations—a society where the relations of production are totally mediated by impersonal *things* (commodity money). As for modern capitalism, Kennedy argues that because money is no longer produced by labor and can no longer automatically regulate economic life, this function has been taken up by "professional/administrative bureaucracies, which operate at corporate, quasi-state and state levels."[39]

Kennedy's narrative is a story of the declining power of money, which creates a vacuum filled by the state and other organizations. He claims that "a large part of the macro history of the twentieth century can be understood as the attempt to establish relations of direct social dependency in the context of the declining power of money to regulate social relations indirectly."[40] Thus, Kennedy associates two distinct and complementary historical changes: on the one hand the twentieth century was characterized by a gradual transition to managed money; and on the other hand, this period saw the rise of social welfare, which entails a measure of direct management of labor by the state. Thus, with the weakening of money as an automated mechanism of labor control, there appear mechanisms to directly control labor: "instead of labor flowing to the requirements of capital accumulation, capital flows would be determined in the interests of regulating labor through the policing of social needs."[41]

The crucial point is Kennedy's explanation of the cause of this decline in the power of money. It is what is sometimes referred to as the problem of the third volume of *Capital*, namely Marx's analysis of the tendency of the rate of profit to decline. To put it briefly, the rate of profit tends to fall because of the constant process of technical innovation. Each capitalist is motivated to increase the efficiency of production by technical innovations, which afford a local increase in profits, until the innovations are adopted by competitors. But the overall effect of these accumulated local innovations adds up to tendency for a decrease in the share of labor in the composition of capital. Because in principle surplus value is the source of profits, as production processes become more mechanized, the rate of profit for all capitalists falls. This change can be understood, Kennedy claims, as a movement whereby capital consumes its own power to regulate the economy and, thus, is the background for the move from commodity money to symbolic money.

When the automatic market mechanisms fail, political mechanisms of direct management take their place in the regulation of both labor and money. The change, according to Kennedy, was swift: "the turn towards national agreement on the partial decommodification of labor was equally as sudden as the conversion to managed money."[42]

As noted throughout this chapter, the choice between break and persistence as the keys to a narrative is a theoretical historical question and not an empirical one. Focusing at the level of continuity beyond the change from gold-based money to managed money, we would say that on the one hand, managed money is managed within constraints that appear objective and force it to behave like a material substance; on the other hand, that gold-based money appeared as an automatic mechanism because the social relations that accounted for it were disavowed. To recall Simmel, material money already contained an element of credit in the simple sense that it entailed the belief of buyers and sellers.

It is more important to formulate this dilemma between persistence and change in terms of labor. The point is that if we think we know in advance what labor is—in other words, if we hold onto the images of industrial labor—then we would certainly accept the narrative of break. By contrast, if we want to understand what persisted beyond the change, we have to forgo substantial notions of labor and use the narrative itself to inquire what labor is. We have to ask what labor is today under the assumption that the conceptual relations between labor, capital, and surplus value have not gone through a fundamental change.

The answer provided in this chapter is quite simple: the brand name is the economic reaction to the problem of the diminishing share of labor in production. The emergence of consumption work invested in the production of brand names enables capital to keep investing labor in objects that are technically easy to produce. The brand name is an indefinitely flexible instrument that allows any measure of investment of labor in any commodity, simple as it may be. Considering the consumption of advertising as one of the main sites of consumption work, capital can keep investing labor in production simply by purchasing more air time for commercials.[43]

Even chewing gum can be made a brand. A series of commercials for 5 Gum shows people entering into various ominous machines, where they are attacked in a simulation of the taste experience (e.g., a man lies strapped to something like a surgical table in a net cage while cannons shoot fruit at the net so that the mash sprays his body). Strangely enough, these commercials put forth images of the hostile object that lies at the heart of Marx's concept of alienated labor. Perhaps because of the pettiness of the object advertised, the commercials revert to the naked function of advertising.[44]

Can this new form of labor be applied to money? This chapter focused on the way brand names manifest a persistence of the relations between money and commodities and of the way commodities persist in their function in the structure of commodity money. Fleetwood and Kennedy point to an additional theoretical requirement for a thing to qualify as commodity money: commodity money is an object produced with the same type of labor as other commodities. We can offer a somewhat speculative reply to this challenge. If brand names are indeed made of money in the sense that they are inherently expensive, then in some sense the labor invested in the production of commodities is by the same token also labor invested in the production of money. This may be especially true if we follow the idea that desire is the substance of money, that is, that a certain form of desire sustains the role of money. Commercials give visual representation for the desire for things as made of money.

Revisiting the Labor Theory of Value

Marx's labor theory of value has been widely disapproved of—even within Marxist circles—among other reasons because of the problem of the diminishing share of labor in production and the parallel diminishing rate of profit. However, because it is precisely this problem that provides an economic explanation for the truly bizarre phenomenon of brand names, this theory seems to deserve a second look.

The concept of consumption work suggests a way to theoretically reaffirm the concept of value. The labor theory of value may indeed be rejected if it is read with substantialist conceptions of labor and of value, that is to say, if we have in advance a good notion of what labor is and accordingly treat value as an empirical reality that lies behind prices and market mechanisms. But the labor theory of value can still prove fertile if we reject a substantial notion of value and conceive of it as an analytic category designed to unearth power relations in the economy. For that purpose, it is enough that the economy can, in principle, be described in terms of the aggregate labor invested in all the objects that exchange hands in it and of the way these labor products are distributed. As an analytic category, there is no sense in asking whether value is valid or not. This category of value can serve theoretically to detect who lives off the work of whom. But what this means is that the concept of value is meaningful only insofar as there is also surplus value—only if the equivalence of values in exchange is disrupted at some point.

A comparison with the concept of utility may be useful in demonstrating the purely theoretical advantage of the concept of value. With the rise of neoclassical economics, utility pushed away the concept of value that Marx shared with classical political economy. Both concepts occupy the same theoretical place. Both utility and value are theoretical concepts that stand behind the empirical fact of price as magnitudes that allow the comparison of two qualitatively different objects. In neoclassical economics, an exchange is explained by the utilities that the two parties gain from it. In Marxist economics, value measures the distribution of labor involved in an exchange.

Furthermore, both utility and value can never be directly discerned. Utility, in orthodox economic thought, can never be directly approached. It is only implied by the fact of price itself. But value is also never directly revealed. Value is theoretically distinguished from price, and prices are not held in a direct relation to value (there are many additional factors that affect prices, such as coincidental shortages in supply, technological innovations, and others). But this similarity underscores the theoretical advantage of value, in terms of its contact to reality. By conceiving of utility as an empirical magnitude, economics actually turns it into a purely metaphysical concept. Utility is implied only by the facts that it explains.

Furthermore, by fending itself from reality, utility turns into an ideological notion. It prevents economics from the possibility of conceptualizing coercion (e.g., if someone points a gun at me and demands my wallet, an economist would have to argue that I freely gave my wallet to the pointer, namely, I weighed the utilities of the courses of action open to me). Compared with the concept of value, utility circumscribes in principle any formalization of the idea that someone works for someone else or that someone lives off the work of other people. In utilitarian concepts, they simply exchange utilities. The capitalist forgoes the utility of spending his fortune for consumption to obtain greater utility in the future, while the workers prefer to suffer the disutility of working for the greater utility of their wages.[45]

What rescues the concept of value from the circular absurdities of utility is precisely its systematic suspension by surplus value. In a world with no surplus value, the concept of value would be fended from reality and would be useless, precisely like utility. Through the concept of surplus, it escapes the circle of self-reassuring equivalencies. Like utility, value is never directly approached. Yet it is a meaningful concept nonetheless because even if all values exchanged are equivalent, it forces us to account for surplus.

Why Do People Buy Brand Names?

Our discussion of brand names and consumption work has probably brought forth a reservation: Why is it, then, that people buy brand names? Why do people pay for what in principle they cannot get? The first point to make in this regard is that it is futile to expect a simple answer to the question of why people do certain things. Economics has conditioned us to expect an unequivocal, model-like explanation of human behavior. But no other science of humankind shares this idea that human behavior can be reduced to a mechanism following a clearly defined set of principles (ideally a minimal one if we listen to economists!).

A more realistic account, aided by practical observations of the consumer economy can suggest a spectrum of possible answers. For one thing, there may be those naive consumers who actually believe. There may be people that in some way or another are taken by the images of supreme pleasure and confuse them with reality. (Although not empirically confirmed, in conversations with young students, I get the impression that many people do believe that the right type of car can provide some sort of a thrill, qualitatively different than the usual experience of driving.)

At the other edge of the spectrum, we find people who buy brand names simply because they want the product—a soft drink, sneakers—and have no choice but to buy a branded product. Here we should recall that the main economic reason for the spread of brand names has little to do with consumer demands. Everyone in the business—producers, vendors—finds it more profitable to sell brand names. As recently as ten or fifteen years ago, freezers in grocery stores in Israel were about half-packed with primitively branded ice-pops, costing about 50 cents each. Today, they are almost fully stocked with brands with names such as Magnum or Knock-Out, costing about five times as much. These brands are indeed of better quality. Yet it seems naive to attribute their expansion solely to consumer demand for better quality, ignoring the obvious fact that it is five times more profitable for the stores to use limited space for branded merchandise.

Between these two poles of the spectrum we can formulate other possibilities. An Israeli Sprite commercial spells out such a possibility. It spans a para-natural narrative that takes place in Africa and America simultaneously. A young man in a cabin in the Arizona desert is drinking Sprite; as he puts the bottle on a map of the world, a small drop slides down on it directly toward Africa. Meanwhile a group of children in Africa play football in the blazing sun. At the moment when the drop hits the map on one side of the world, on the other side the ball miraculously turns into a huge drop of water that explodes and refreshes the players. The clever slogan that closes the commercial can be read as a precise phenomenological account of enjoyment in consumer culture: *Whenever you drink Sprite, someone gets refreshed.*

The narrative puts the unique pleasure of the brand beyond reach, yet by transposing pleasure to the third person, the slogan replaces its immediate experience with detached knowledge: *someone gets refreshed.* Maybe the true meaning of the slogan is: when you drink Sprite you know that you enjoy. This conforms to the way people sometimes use a can of soda as a reward or a prize or to mark a break from work. It is not that they necessarily enjoy the drink. It could be that the can provides them with material evidence that they enjoy.

Baudrillard has formulated a similar observation in his ironic characterization of consumer culture as a modern cargo-cult:

> [T]he beneficiary of the consumer miracle also sets in place a whole array
> of sham objects, of characteristic signs of happiness, and then waits (waits
> desperately, a moralist would say) for happiness to alight.[46]

To seriously consider the parallel between consumer work and Marx's concept of alienated labor implies that the question of why people buy brand names is the wrong one. The parallel question with reference to industrial capitalist production is why workers toil over machines and then give away the product of their labor, which is clearly an incorrect formulation for an important question. Marx does not seek a psychological answer to the question. Rather, he starts with the fact that the object that the laborer produces confronts the laborer as an alien being and asks what the social conditions are that make this possible. By pointing to the object, from the outset Marx bypasses the realm of psychological explanations. The object that confronts the subject as external and independent of it marks the incompleteness of any psychological answer to the question of why.

The object, in a sense, comes in place of the answer. What Marx explores, instead, is the question of how: What are the social conditions of labor that maintain capitalist private property as an objective reality, ostensibly independent of the workers' relation to it? Transferring this idea to the question of consumer work, we could say that the object is the ultimate answer as to why people buy brand names. In the first instance, this simply means that brand names are the primary economic object today. We satisfy a growing number of our needs with brand names.

But the lesson to be drawn from Marx's analysis of alienation is that what needs to be asked is how this economic object is maintained by a web of social conditions, one of which is television and celebrity culture. In both cases, of industrial and post-industrial capitalism, the object marks the closure of the subject. It is the answer to the question of how this precarious entity, the subject, can have some kind of ontological persistence. In the case of industrial capitalism, the object answers the question: How does the subject persist as proletarian? He persists insofar as he relates to the machine as not his own. A revolution is the actual recognition by the workers that the product of their labor does not *objectively* belong to someone else. In the case of post-industrial capitalism, a revolution is entailed with the actual recognition that celebrities are not really different from us. Television cannot prevent this recognition (just as the machine cannot prevent the worker from incorporating his labor product). As a matter of fact, in the reality genre, television has gone some distance toward showing that the celebrity is just like us. But the fact that television persists attests, among other things, that we still behave as if the celebrity is different from us.

Here we should recall Marx's second thesis on Feuerbach:

[T]he question whether objective truth can be attributed to human think-ing is not a question of theory but is a practical question. Man must prove the truth—i.e., the reality and power, the this-sidedness of his thinking in practice.[47]

The objective truth of thought is not measured by its correspondence to real-ity but by its ability to intervene with reality; not by correspondence to the object but by overcoming the object.

In this context this idea can be reduced to a very concrete meaning: the laborer can know very well that the machine is not really not his and still give away the product of his labor, just as the viewer can know very well that the celebrity is not really different from him or her and still watch. But the ulti-mate nature of knowledge, as knowledge, is decided by one's conduct. These are two different types of knowing: to know that the celebrity is just like us and therefore not watch and to know this and keep watching nonetheless.

Economy and Ecology

There is a tendency today to conflate economic critiques with ecological argu-ments on the grounds that capitalism's blind forces of economic expansion lead to the destruction of nature. Although it may be true that nature is de-stroyed because of capitalist economy, from a critical-economic perspective, this is an effect and, therefore, cannot be the basis of a critique. To remain true to its concept, an economic critique must first and foremost address social cat-egories such as exploitation, labor, freedom, or power relations, which are eco-logically neutral. Furthermore, the speed with which the ecological message has spread within affluent societies, where alternative economic regimes are far from sight, raises the suspicion that the ecological discourse is to some ex-tent a replacement for an absent, fundamental social and economic debate. In this respect, the avidness with which we separate our garbage for recycling or refrain from taking an extra plastic bag from a store may appear as a sterilized redirection of a political motive. It is as if we practically believe that we can act politically in our conduct of things rather than in our relations to humans.

The question of brand names delineates in a precise form the theoretical gap between ecology and economy. In a sense, brand names are the partial solution that the capitalist economy has developed by itself for the problem of ecology. With branding we drastically reduce our use of natural resources. This is a simple arithmetic truth. If a branded shirt costs, for example, ten times more than an unbranded shirt, nine fewer shirts are produced; presumably, this is positive from an ecological viewpoint. Because in a capitalist economy, money cannot sit idle in the absence of symbolic commodities, it would have to buy many more material ones.

This is not to say that brand names will solve environmental problems or that we should not devote efforts to ecological issues, but simply to underline the conceptual difference between the two discourses. What in one context is a solution (channeling production to non-material ends) is a problem in another (paying and working more for even basic goods). From a critical economic perspective, the ecological threat is a side effect—maybe an important one, but still, a side effect. Its popularity seems to lead social and economic critics to jump on the bandwagon. But by presenting the ecological threat as the reason why a fundamental change in the economy is required, these critics actually turn ecology into a mask that hides the real and necessary critical discourse about the economy.

Globalization and Solidarity

In *No Logo*, Naomi Klein situated brand names at the center of a geo-political map of exploitation and impoverishment. On the global scale, the labor of producing the material aspect of commodities is typically relegated to poor countries. After centuries of perceiving material production as the epitome of national wealth, during a relatively short span of time, production has become a symptom of poverty. Nowadays the global South produces the material aspect of commodities, but its control over material production does not save it from poverty because the real value of commodities lies elsewhere, in brand names owned by the affluent North.

Although the above can be seen as an accurate description, an examination through the lens of the ontology of brand names gives us a better understanding of the relation between the consumer in the North and the laborer in the South. A commonsensical view ties the exploitation of the South with the affluence of the North. The laborers in the South are impoverished because the consumers in the North thrive at their expense. Such a view does not hold. It is based on the assumption that what the laborers produce and what the consumers purchase is essentially the same thing. But the truth is that a brand name can indeed be a part of global exploitation only because it stands between producers and consumers, that is to say, because the consumers in the North buy something essentially different from the object produced in the South. Thus, a more correct formulation would say that the brand name impoverishes the laborers in the South by impoverishing, in a different way, the consumer in the North.

The difference between these two conceptions can be mapped in two different ways to understand the relation of brands to non-knowledge. Foster claims the function of *constructed ignorance* is central to the creation of brand value. The brand name is sustained, among other things, by withholding from the consumers information about the real conditions of production, such as the working conditions in developing countries: "Such conditions of ignorance and segmentation facilitate the investment of brands with meaning by consumers and the appropriation of such meaning by brand owners."[48]

One interesting aspect of this formulation is that there is a twisted parallel to it in economic thought. This ignorance is echoed in the notion of *asymmetrical* information that is central to the economic explanation of brand names. Brand names, according to this explanation, replace missing information that characterizes the typical consumer situation. Consumers cannot check all the different makes of all the products they buy, and brand names supply them with a replacement for the missing information. There is a stark difference between these two notions of non-knowledge related to brands. Whereas for economic thought, asymmetrical information is an anomaly solved by brand name, the notion of constructed ignorance indicates the reverse connection: it is essential to sustain incomplete information in order to support a brand name. That is, the brand name is one of the mechanisms that sustain the anomaly.

This shift in the function of ignorance, from an anomaly of the market to a basic principle of the economic system, suggests yet a third and the most important meaning of non-knowledge as inherent in the economic thing itself. Non-knowledge refers not only to the conditions of production but also to the mode of existence of the economic thing itself, as epitomized in Coca Cola's secret formula.

The well-known Happiness Factory commercial for Coca Cola perfectly illustrates this. It begins with three young people standing by a Coke vending machine. One of them inserts a coin; immediately the scene changes, in parallel with the movement of the coin, from the street to the inside of the machine. There we find a fantasyland populated with a variety of little, marvelous, and colorful creatures toiling on a magical coke production line. Some fluffy creatures shine the bottle, some icy ones cool it, and all together they merrily accompany the bottle in what seems like a long journey to the dispensing hole of the machine. From there, one young man picks it up and drinks joyfully, laughing with his friends at a joke. An important point in this commercial is that the three young people are totally ignorant of the miraculous activity that takes place inside the machine. In a way, it is this last twist that renders the commercial perfectly reasonable. The commercial does not try to persuade that there is a marvelous secret in Coca Cola. It suggests, rather, that we need not believe there is a mystery about it to enjoy its good, albeit not exceptional, taste, just like the young man in the commercial.

How does this commercial stand with respect to the other two notions of non-knowledge? With respect to the economic notion of asymmetrical information, the stark opposition can be presented as a real theoretical challenge. If, as economic thought perceives it, the brand name solves a certain lack of information, then how is it that a commercial openly invokes such a lack? The role of brand names cannot exclusively consist of compensating for the absence of information because their function frequently includes an invocation of their mysterious natures.

With respect to Foster's argument of constructed ignorance, the commercial can be seen to suggest a supplement. Foster's argument situates ignorance in a geo-political scene: the brand name can function *here* (in the affluent North) because the consumer does not know how the product is actually produced *there* (in the South). This view rests on the commonsensical identification between non-knowledge and an exclusion of information. According to this identification, ignorance surrounds brand names in the form of the nasty information about their production that is withheld from consumers so that they can consume the brands with a clear conscience. This seems a partial argument. In a world of ever more elaborate flows of information, we can imagine that it becomes harder to maintain constructed ignorance about the production conditions of merchandise.

The horrific collapse of the eight-story building in Savar, Bangladesh, in April 2013, which caused the deaths of 1,129 people, again brought public attention to the working conditions in factories in developing countries. The building housed garment factories that manufactured apparel for several brands, including Benetton, Mango, Bonmarché, Walmart, and Primark. Would the protest that followed bring a major change? It is hoped that these firms would more carefully monitor the working conditions of their subcontractors. But even in such an optimistic scenario, the cruel, excessive form of exploitation would be replaced with regular exploitation based on the gap in the standard of living between the North and the South.

In other words, we can imagine a world of more socially sensitive media, but what we cannot yet imagine is a world without brand names. The Happiness Factory commercial suggests that ignorance refers not only to production conditions somewhere else but to the object itself. It is not simply that people don't know enough about Coca Cola and therefore are willing to consume it. To the contrary, non-knowledge is what makes Coca Cola what it is; it is non-knowledge that constitutes it as an object. It is most telling therefore that this commercial invokes the image of the assembly line. By relegating labor to such exotic spheres of imagination, it hides its blunt truth: production is actually accomplished here, in front of the television screen. It is by consuming this commercial that the consumer actually produces the object as unknowable (our immediate reaction to the commercial, *we know that it is not really like that*, could actually mean *we do not know what it's really like*—we do not know where the mystery of Coca Cola lies, but it's certainly not inside the vending machine).

Returning to Naomi Klein, a parallel change—from the contemplation of the global scene to its reflection in the economic entity—also is essential with reference to the thesis of the impoverishment of the developing world. It is inaccurate to say that the fruits of production are withheld from the manufacturers because consumers in the North are enjoying goods that are produced in the global South. The brand name stands between these producers and consumers, disowning both. The correct view is that the impoverishment of the manufacturers is made possible, or supplemented by, the manner in which consumers are withheld from really owning a branded object.

Another famous Coca Cola commercial is a perfect example. It starts with a series of scenes of daily life characterized by simple, yet twisted, enjoyments, produced through a constant irony between image and text (when the voiceover says "start a band," we see a young man playing guitar in his room while his girlfriend jumps on the bed behind him; when the voiceover says "dance to the rhythm," we see, among a fashionable crowd in a club, a guy dancing in a clumsy yet very personal manner; when the voiceover says "feel the music," we see a man lying on the floor listening to his neighbor, a young woman, of course, playing the cello in an apartment downstairs). In all these scenes, Coca Cola is hardly visible—at most, the bottle is present as an inert object in the background. Then the climactic scene arrives, which depicts a complete and ecstatic pleasure: a lone traveler standing on the sharp edge of a high cliff, surrounded by a wide landscape of wild nature, drinking Coca Cola; or, in another version, someone drinking Coca Cola on the deck of a yacht sailing in the wind.

The simple explanation of this would be that the commercials attempt to persuade the viewer that drinking Coca Cola is somehow similar to the ecstatic experience of climbing a sharp cliff in the middle of a wild, untouched landscape, or the experience of sailing alone in heavy seas. As any explanation of advertising that is based on persuasion, this one presupposes an idiot consumer who would believe such a claim. But what is worse is that this explanation misses the contrast that structures this commercial, the difference between daily life with its awkward, broken pleasures and the ecstatic, complete pleasure of Coca Cola. Taking this contrast into account, the commercial seems to say something different. Instead of *drinking Coca Cola is like sailing on a yacht*, it says *this is how one really enjoys Coca Cola: by drinking it while sailing alone on a yacht*. Thus, what the commercial shows is that one can never *really* enjoy Coca Cola. It might be nice drinking it in the cafeteria—just as daily life can provide its unexpected moments of minor pleasures—but it is, at most, a shadow of the real experience of Coca Cola. Again, this explanation does not have to presuppose the idiot since the daily experience of the consumer who drinks Coca Cola actually confirms the advertising message: "Yes," the consumer might say, "this is indeed not like drinking Coca Cola on a yacht."

There is a political lesson to be learned from this conception of the brand regarding the form of solidarity between citizens in affluent and impoverished societies. Instead of the familiar position: *we have enough, but as progressive people, we sympathize with those who have less*—a position that cannot be cleansed of a patronizing overtone—we can suggest a form of true solidarity: *they are impoverished because we are impoverished.*

Chapter 4

REVELATION
Weber's Midas

The myth of Midas can be read as the kernel of any manifestation of desire for money. Its traces can be found in the numerous narratives that revolve around the way the desire for money punishes the desiring subject in its very satisfaction—the way the eventual satisfaction of the lifelong desire suffocates the desiring subject amid a cold and lifeless reality that surrounds him or her.

The myth is remarkably simple: Midas loves gold and in the end, he is punished for his excessive desire for it. His wish that everything he touches would turn into gold is fulfilled in a horrendous and literal manner: his food and drink turn into gold. Yet, despite its simplicity, there is a trick to the story. It would not be accurate to say that Midas is punished for his sinful wish because sin and punishment coincide perfectly in the story. It is not correct to say that Midas wants money *too much*. It is actually the other way around: by wanting something—gold in this case—too much, this something becomes money.

Because his desire for gold desubstantializes every other mundane wish, we can appropriately see his gold as a form of money. It is the lethal desire invested in the object that turns it into money. Incidentally, Paul Krugman demonstrates an economic reading of the myth: "Midas' true sin was his failure to understand monetary economics. What the gods were really telling him is that gold is just a metal."[1] As we do not believe in Greek gods, we should reverse this lesson: gold was not "just a metal" precisely because of the crazy way it was desired.

Furthermore, a retrospective view is essential for the true recognition of this desire. It is only when his desire confronts him in the shape of a lethal object that Midas can acknowledge what his desire was to begin with. This is so because desire for money is not simply opposed to money being a means. Rather, money owes its lethal aura to the fact that as a means, it is desired for itself. Thus, the desire for money is best portrayed retroactively, as it appears beyond all specific wishes to which money could serve as means.

Can the myth of Midas be taken as a key to the real history of money as it is entangled with desire? In Max Weber's *The Protestant Ethic and the Spirit of Capitalism*, we find a certain parallel to the myth of Midas. Toward the end of his book, Weber presents his famous notion of the "iron cage" of capitalism, which explains how the spirit of capitalism outlives its origins in the Protestant ethic as it becomes entangled in the fabric of economic activity. One cannot fail to see the similarity in imagery between Midas's suffocating trap of gold and Weber's iron cage of modern capitalism. This is not just a similarity in metaphors because it also gives expression to a conceptual point. In one sense, the ending of Weber's narrative recapitulates on a larger scale the story of Midas; in both narratives the insatiable desire for money becomes objectively embedded in money.

In the initial stages of the development of the spirit of capitalism (in the religious and quasi-religious forms), it was wrapped in intensely emotional language. But the eventual victory of the spirit of capitalism is marked precisely by the disappearance of this language. This disappearance does not necessarily signify the disappearance of desire itself; on the contrary, in a surprising replica of the myth, it might be interpreted as the manner in which desire has materialized, just like Midas's desire that becomes embodied by the objects that confront him. That is to say, the disappearance of the intensely emotional language in the final stages of Weber's thesis can be seen to be nothing but the way in which desire has become embedded in the objective existence of money, in the web of practices and beliefs that surround and sustain money in the capitalist economy. In this way desire has become inseparably entangled with money—precisely like Midas's gold.

Of course, this similarity, if taken at all seriously, brings with it some complications. In the literary narrative, the true nature of the desire for money is made clear only in retrospect because it is revealed in its satisfaction. This is not a problem for literary artifacts. In any good story, the ending reveals something about the beginning. But when this revelation is imported to a historical discussion, this pattern becomes suspect to a dangerous proximity to teleology. Historians today are suspicious of the procedure of explaining something by what has succeeded it. Reading Weber through Midas amounts to claiming a sense in which Protestant dogma already articulated in religious language an inexpressible desire for money. My aim in this chapter is to characterize what precisely this sense is.

This mission is conceptually tied to a need to fundamentally rethink what money is. If we think that we already know what money is, and consider desire simply as one possible relation to it, then there is not much sense in presenting Weber's Protestants as articulating a desire for money. The situation is different if we conceive of the ways that money is desired as inherently related to it. In that case we can consider the possibility that something in the Protestant religious ethic eventually finds its true articulation in money.

For that reason, my mission in this chapter entails reading Weber against the grain. Weber himself insisted on a strictly causal explanation, which distinctly separates cause (religious dogma) and the effect (economic behavior). But as Alasdair MacIntyre has argued, Weber's thesis owes its force not to his causal view but, on the contrary, to a certain inherent relation between the Protestant ethic and the "spirit of capitalism," that is, between the cause and its effect.

This idea has far reaching consequences for the nature of Weber's historical narrative. It implies that we should insert a retroactive reading of Weber, in which the effect is already implied by the cause, and the end point explicates the beginning. In more concrete terms: the causal explanation shows how a religious ethic helped mold the capitalist mind and behavior; but in a retroactive view, we should ask: Why did it take a religious commandment to articulate the traumatic, inhuman desire for money? Thus, fixing on the desire for money as the axis around which Weber's thesis turns forces a certain teleological form upon it.

This form is unavoidable due to the fact that historical knowledge, as a unique form of knowledge, cannot be completely freed of retroactivity. A certain element of retroactivity taints historical knowledge. History is a unique form of knowledge because some things can be seen properly only retroactively. For that reason it can be claimed that there are things that are necessarily embedded in a teleological form.

Money and Death

Weber famously argues that the origin of the spirit of modern capitalism—namely, of the incessant, calculated pursuit of gain for its own sake—is to be found in the Protestant ethic of the Puritan sects, principally in Calvinism. That is, it is to be found in a religious doctrine that preached intensive worldly activity in conjunction with prohibiting the enjoyment of the material fruits of this activity. Such worldly activity is conceived as a calling, a vocation, and an end in itself that later becomes associated with salvation, not as a means to achieve it but as a sign of being among the elect.

Thus, a religious doctrine encourages people to engage in a form of economic conduct that over time develops a life of its own that is independent of its religious origins. It persists as in the objective reality of a capitalist economy. The only remnant of its religious origin is to be found in the stain of irrationality that Weber sees as lying at the heart of a rational economy: in the inability of the economic subjects to account for the reason for their endless pursuit of more, more, and more gain. The following is how Weber described this capitalist spirit:

> [T]he *summum bonum* of this ethic, the earning of more and more money, combined with the strict avoidance of all spontaneous enjoyment of life, is above all completely devoid of any eudaemonistic, not to say hedonistic, admixture. It is thought of so purely as an end in itself, that from the point of view of the happiness of, or utility to, the single individual, it appears entirely transcendental and absolutely irrational. Man is dominated by the making of money, by acquisition as the ultimate purpose of life. Economic acquisition is no longer subordinated to man as the means for the satisfaction of his material needs. This reversal of what we should call the natural relationship, so irrational from a naïve point of view, is evidently as definitely a leading principle of capitalism as it is foreign to all people not under capitalistic influence.[2]

This famous paragraph is a historical description. It is the basic description Weber gives of capitalist economy, and it is especially appropriate to early, entrepreneurial capitalism. Yet it can also be read as a conceptual analysis of the desire for money.

The desire for money makes sense only insofar as it is contrasted in some manner to the desire for things that money can buy. The deadly presence of money depicted in the myth of Midas is echoed here in the way the capitalist relation to money is entangled with a denunciation of life itself—of "all spontaneous enjoyment of life." This conceptual reading poses a challenge to a straightforward historical reading of Weber. Read as a historical description, Weber presents us here with an accident, in which money somehow became involved with pathological desire. The conceptual reading leads to a different story. If the forms in which money is desired are part of the historical reality of money, then Weber's description looks more like a moment when a certain aspect of money becomes explicit.

This dilemma between a historical and a conceptual reading is underscored by the strange way that Weber characterizes capitalism in this quotation. To historicize capitalism, to extract it from its naturalness, Weber contrasts the conduct of the entrepreneur to what he calls the "natural relationship." Capitalism is weird, which is to say, historical, when it appears "irrational from a naïve point of view." One must admit that this is a poor way to historicize. Not only because it implies a *natural* economy prior to capitalism, but more generally, because it suggests there was a time before history, that history begins with a deviation from a natural state.

The dilemma between the historical and the conceptual reading is complicated further if we notice that the question: What is money? is at the center of Weber's paradigmatic expression of the spirit of capitalism, namely, in Benjamin Franklin's famous maxims of daily economic conduct, two of which follow:

> Remember that *time* is money. He that can earn ten shillings a day by his labor, and goes abroad, or sits idle, one half of that day, though he spends but sixpence during his diversion or idleness, ought not to reckon *that* the only expense; he has really spent, or rather thrown away, five shillings besides.

> Remember that *credit* is money. If a man lets his money lie in my hands after it is due, he gives me the interest, or so much as I can make of it during that time. This amounts to a considerable sum where a man has good and large credit, and makes good use of it.[3]

Weber comments that these recommendations are not "simply a means of making one's way in the world" but expressions of "a peculiar ethic," where "the infraction of its rules is treated not as foolishness, but as forgetfulness of duty."[4] Indeed, they seem suspended half way between religion and economy. They speak of basic economic facts such as credit and interest, but they do so in an austere, quasi-religious tone. What should be noted is that this austerity is related to an identification of *is* and *ought*. This chapter asks whether we can take this identification at face value; whether Franklin did reveal what money really is, and by this revelation changed it.

In a way, Franklin does here precisely what David Hume warned us not to do: he derives an *ought* from an *is*, a moral imperative from the revelation of what money *really* is. However, it is precisely because an inert object cannot be a source of a moral imperative that Franklin's ethic is so severe. It appears as emanating directly from the objective reality of money, and that is what gives it its nature as an external, incomprehensible, even traumatic imperative. Just as Midas reveals what money really is when it confronts him as an objectification of an inhuman lethal desire, Franklin reveals what money is when he reveals the inhuman moral imperative embedded in it. In both cases the true nature of money is revealed by an ought: Franklin's moral ought or the ought of desire of Midas.

What makes this similarity even more perplexing is that Franklin is not simply wrong. That is, even as an error, his revelation is part of the modern history of money, a phase in its development. This can be demonstrated by what Michel Callon termed a "performative" aspect of economic knowledge.[5] Franklin actually demonstrates the imperialist nature of economics. In claiming that "*time* is money" he includes within the scope of economic calculation what formerly may have been seen as non-economic, namely, idleness. But once idleness is viewed as something economic—that is, as abstinence from work—it actually becomes economic—that is, it becomes an actual loss of money. Franklin's maxims are of the form of a revelation of the true nature of money. But the disturbing issue is that their performative aspect forces us to consider them as true revelations.

This issue is more pressing with regard to Franklin's moral fervor. His revelation of the true nature of money is entangled with a revelation of the moral imperative embedded in it. Is there a dimension of truth also in this moral fervor that accompanies Franklin's revelations? Notice how he recounts the elementary fact of money interest:

> [R]emember, that money is of the prolific, generating nature. Money can beget money, and its offspring can beget more, and so on. Five shillings turned is six, turned again it is seven and three-pence, and so on, till it becomes a hundred pounds. The more there is of it, the more it produces every turning, so that the profits rise quicker and quicker. He that kills a breeding-sow, destroys all her offspring to the thousandth generation. He that murders a crown, destroys all that it might have produced, even scores of pounds.[6]

Note that at the heart of this zealous fantasy stands nothing more than an elementary economic fact, which today is normally expressed in completely neutral formulations. Furthermore, the fervor stems from an objectification of the fact of interest, of its detachment from social relations. The moral fervor is associated with the idea that money grows by itself (and not, e.g., by lending it to other people or investing it, not to mention exploiting the labor of others).

Yet Franklin's idea is still a fantasy of objectivity—a fantasy of the object that exerts a severe moral imperative. It raises a question regarding our own monetary systems, in which the mechanisms of interest have really become objective. How should we understand his revelation: Was Franklin's misguided moral fervor overcome and replaced by neutral, impersonal monetary institutions, or was it simply objectified in these institutions? In other words, no one today would speak about money interest with such moral fervor. But can't we understand the silencing of this language as the ultimate fulfillment of Franklin's vision of a moral imperative embodied by the object?

The Moral Substance of Money

We can point to a somewhat distant, yet important echo of Franklin's money in economic thought. Consider, for example, Joseph Schumpeter's explanation of the uniqueness of money. In his seminal *History of Economic Analysis*, he explains why bankers can increase the quantity or velocity of money—a feat that cannot be achieved with any other commodity:

> The only answer to the question why this is so is that there is no other case in which a claim to a thing can, within limits to be sure, serve the same purpose as the thing itself: you cannot ride on a claim to a horse, but you can pay with a claim to money.[7]

This differentiation between money and things can be read as capturing the ontological status of money. What should be noted is that this identity between the thing and the claim to the thing is not simply a positive property of the money object. Rather it points to the way money is constituted by its difference from things. If horses were money, one could indeed pay with a claim to a horse, though, still, one could not ride it. That is to say, the coincidence of the thing with the claim to the thing cannot be counted among the thing's positive properties, but it is a property that occurs only through the suppression of the thing's properties.

It is not accurate to say that money has unique properties that distinguish it from things. Rather, the negation of its thing-properties constitutes it as money. This conception of the uniqueness of money provides an ontological basis for Franklin's *moral substance* of money. What we should keep in mind is that claims belong to the moral sphere. Identifying money with the claim to money suggests then that in the most technical terms of economics there lies the identification of the *is* and the *ought*. This becomes more evident if we change the terminology slightly and define the uniqueness of money through the coincidence of the real and the potential. To paraphrase Schumpeter: you cannot ride on a potential horse, but you can pay with potential money.

This coincidence of the real and the potential clearly stands as the basis of Franklin's revelations and of his moral zeal: "*time* is money" means that the potential money not earned because of idleness is real money in every respect. Maybe the attribution of a moral status to money is first made possible by the opening up of the inert object through the insertion of a dimension of potential to its very objectivity. This touches the most perplexing aspect of Franklin's text: the need to consider the possibility that in his moral craze, he did develop logic inherent in money. When he discovers what money is, he actually reveals the fundamental link between money and finance.

The Protestant Ethic as a Phenomenology of Money

The idea that Franklin, with his moral zeal, is in some sense right in his money revelations—that he does literally reveal what money is—directs us to a reading of Weber that in some sense is opposed to his professed view. It confronts us with an uncomfortable notion of revelation, abhorred by those historians who insist on the need for strictly causal explanations. However, this possibility is implied by MacIntyre's critique of Weber. Weber's conception of causality, MacIntyre claims, is basically Humean, namely, a conception of a causal relation between two "distinct and separately identifiable social phenomena."[8] This conception of causality, he claims, is fundamentally inadequate for the social sciences at large.

In the case of Weber, this conception harms his thesis. His ideas are persuasive in spite of his explicit use of Humean causality. Yet they are convincing because of an obvious internal relation between the cause (Protestant ethic) and the effect (capitalist spirit). Following McIntyre's argument we can see why the shadow of revelation accompanies Weber's thesis. Accepting the idea that the effect is already implied by the cause portrays history as a process of becoming explicit. It presents us with history that necessarily wears a teleological form. To be precise, it does not point to teleology but to a real dimension of the historical process that can be grasped only in a teleological form.

This interpretative dilemma can be put in concrete terms in relation to Weber's thesis. At the center of the causal view lies the idea that the religious ethic influenced economic behavior. This ethic demanded irrational devotion to labor alongside the suppression of any drive to enjoy the fruits of labor. Later this practice crystallized in the conduct of the capitalist entrepreneur who irrationally strives for more wealth.

The opposite view directs us to read the Protestant ethic as an economic phenomenon to begin with. There is actually something quite trivial in this suggestion. A religious ethic that is involved with the everyday practices of work, savings, and consumption is ipso facto an economic phenomenon. The fact that it relates these practices to a divine being should not deter us from conceiving of it as economic. It is only the domination of utilitarian economic ideology that blinds us from seeing this basic point. What needs to be asked is: What exactly is the economic function of factors like God, heaven, and salvation? What function in the economy do divine beings have? Why is it necessary or appropriate at some stage to relate certain economic behavior to God?

It is also obvious why this reading raises objections. The causal view would portray capitalism as a diluted form of the religious origin—as practices that persist beyond their cause. The reverse, retroactive view portrays the latter stage, modern capitalism, as revealing the secret of its predecessor, the religious ethic. The capitalist entrepreneur who strives for profit for its own sake only dispels the illusions that previously masked this conduct with divine images. Such a reading is grounded in an alternative view of the relation between economy and history: instead of viewing capitalist economy as a vestige, a web of practices that survived the disappearance of cause, this reading relies on a view of the economy as the realm of the absent cause. Following this suggestion amounts to reading the Protestant ethic as articulating, from the outset, the unspeakable voice of money. This unspeakable element in money is precisely its relation to desire, which goes against the formal, rational, *natural* view of money as means. That is what is at stake now: reading the Protestant ethic as a phenomenology of money as it is entangled with desire.

Omniscient Gaze as a Means of Moral Accounting

Franklin's maxims are a good starting point for an exploration of the aptness of religious language for an articulation of a logic of money. This is so because they stand precisely at the junction of economy and religion. Although they are no longer viewed as religious expressions but only practical economic maxims, their articulation displays a clear religious tone.

> The most trifling actions that affect a man's credit are to be regarded. The sound of the hammer at five in the morning, or eight at night, heard by a creditor, makes him easy six months longer; but if he sees you at a billiard-table, or hears your voice at the tavern, when you should be at work, he sends for his money the next day; demands it, before he can receive it, in a lump.[9]

The moral lesson is rooted again within a conceptual view of money. Because of the identification of the potential and the real, of credit and money, money becomes a specific social relation that rests on suspicion. This social situation embodied by money associates it with a hostile, omniscient gaze. In this way a formation of religious conscience is inherent in money as such.

A full development of the identification of credit and money—allegedly a technical economic procedure—leads to an ever-expanding reach of the social gaze inherent in money, which comes to include "the most trifling actions" of man and their monetary effect. Although this gaze is only the gaze of other people, its structure is similar to the gaze inherent in religious conscience: one might be seen at all times, even when immersed, unaware, in work or pleasure.[10] Thus, although Franklin's maxims are practical economic ones, they are also directly religious. It is an economy that can be described only in religious terms.

Taking a step backward in time to Weber's Calvinists, a mirror image of Franklin's economic wisdom appears, namely, a religion that is directly economic and that can be described only in economic terms. This mirror image is to be found in the view of life as a totality that distinguished the Protestant ethical conduct from Catholicism. Thus Weber writes that "the God of Calvinism demanded of his believers not single good works, but a life of good works combined into a unified system."[11] This religious notion implies a formation that is similar to Franklin's omniscient gaze of money: in a system of moral accounting of life, any trifling action is registered and affects the overall balance. Note that we must take the economic metaphor at face value. What the Calvinists inserted into the religious dogma was a notion of accounting, which is not strictly speaking a religious notion (if there ever is a strictly religious notion) but an economic view. It is not a shift in the view of what the good is but only in the system of accounting for goods.

Predestination, Salvation and the
Endless Deferment of Satisfaction

As is well known, at the heart of Weber's thesis stands his brilliant argument regarding the dogma of predestination, which negated any relation between man's behavior and his destiny in the hereafter. The strength of Weber's thesis lies in his demonstration of the way that the dogma, rather than leading to an indifferent or even a nihilistic attitude to this world, led to the ascetic work ethic that characterized the Puritan sects. This ethic became so austere precisely because of its total separation between good works performed by individuals in this world and their fate in the next world. In a formulation that might be somewhat foreign to Weber, the demand of good works as a calling is severe precisely because it assumes the form of an unconditional demand— that is, precisely because it is excluded from calculations of means and ends, deeds and retributions.

When this unconditional demand for good works in this world became effective in the realm of the economy, the religious ethic led to a sort of forced enrichment: the believer was commanded to an austere work ethic and to his occupation as a calling, while at the same time he was prohibited from enjoying the fruits of this work. In Weber's words, this led to "accumulation of capital through ascetic compulsion to save."[12]

In this demand we see the connection that lies at the heart of Weber's historical explanation. The religious ethic explains irrational, capitalist devotion as exhibited by Franklin. It explains the pattern of action that seeks material profit only for its own sake, combined, as in the case of Franklin, with an aversion to any spontaneous enjoyment from this profit.

But again, there is no reason to see this religious ethic as penetrating the economic realm from without. It is directly economic if we keep in mind the basic fact that it relates to work and occupation. However, reading this ethic as economic to begin with, it simply articulates the logic of desire for money. It manifests precisely the structure of desire for money as it is elaborated in the myth of Midas: in formal terms, people hold money to defer consumption; desire for money emerges beyond this formal view, where the indefinite deferral of satisfaction appears as one's relation to money. The hereafter can thus articulate desire for money in a double sense. First, it can stand in for the place of infinite deferral. Second, salvation marks the supreme form of a benefit that cannot be bought or achieved.

It would be wrong to consider this category, of what money cannot buy, as a non-economic category. It is, on the one hand, the economic articulation of the sublime. And on the other hand, it is the direct articulation of the entanglement of money with desire. Desire for money in itself is conceptually distinguished from the desire for things that money can buy, and it is articulated as the excess beyond the wishes for such things, as the desire for what money cannot buy. Understood as an economic category, it signifies the desire for money as a desire *beyond* the desire for things.

Salvation, when it emerges within a discourse that is economic in nature, is thus the prototypical articulation of desire for money. The insertion of salvation into the economic discourse articulates the capitalist motive of action, if we conceive of the capitalist not as an agent who wants more money, but as the agent who wants more *than* money. It is the excess above the mundane uses of money that can explain the unconditional character of profit-seeking activity. Indeed, the ongoing presence of the category of what money cannot buy in the economy—in the Protestant ethic as well as in modern consumer economy—suggests that desire for money should be conceived of as a central economic category. In Chapter 5, I present the work of Veblen as a systematic exploration of this category.

We find evidence that these considerations are effective in the Protestant ethic in the evolution of the peculiar status of wealth as a proof or sign of election. Wealth, of course, does not bring salvation, yet within the dogma it is seen as not necessarily unconnected to salvation: it belongs to the order of the sign of being among the elect.[13] This status captures the way desire is associated with what is only a means. That is to say, wealth is desired for what it cannot achieve—as a means separated from its end by an unbridgeable gap of the indeterminate sign. The religious language exposes the paradoxical nature of a substitution of ends by means, namely, that when means are desired for themselves, desire wears a much more severe form. In other words, this religious end is nothing but a symptomatic articulation of the means becoming the ends, which is the conceptual definition of the desire for money.

Money as a Foreign Body

The third phenomenological feature of the desire for money can be termed its *inner foreignness*. This alienation is already found in the basic structure of the Puritan religious experience. How could worldly activity bring relief to the horrible distress of a believer in predestination? An assurance of grace was associated, according to Weber, with the very nature of action as a calling, with the basic experience of such an action. Weber describes it thus:

> The community of the elect with their God could only take place in that God worked through them and that they were conscious of it. That is, their action originated from the faith caused by God's grace, and this faith in turn justified itself by the quality of that action. . . . The religious believer can make himself sure of his state of grace either in that he feels himself to be the vessel of the Holy Spirit or the tool of the divine will. In the former case his religious life tends to mysticism and emotionalism, in the latter to ascetic action; Luther stood close to the former type, Calvinism belonged definitely to the latter.[14]

The religious believer feels himself, in his ascetic action, as "the tool of divine will." Outside the sphere of religion, this is precisely the structure of action implied by the notion of the desire for money. That is one lesson of the myth of Midas: a desire for money necessarily entails a submission to the object, a pattern of conduct as if according to an opaque, unintelligible, inhuman injunction. That is also how Marx defines the conduct of the capitalist, as a subject who behaves as if it is money itself that wants to grow. We can wonder whether this topology is manifested in more common examples, in the various ways money makes us act as strangers to ourselves.

The inhuman voice of the Calvinist God seems adequate to articulate the desire for money. In its entanglement with desire, money reveals its most foreign face, in which an intense desire confronts the subject from without, in the shape of an opaque object. This conceptual adequacy raises the question of history in the most urgent manner. Insisting like Weber on a strictly causal history amounts to the notion of a historical accident, in which at some point in time, the economy is invaded by this irrational pattern of action where money becomes an end in itself. The problem with this notion is similar to that which haunts so many economic mythologies, such as Locke's idea of the origin of private property in the work of individuals, or Adam Smith's idea of the origin of money in barter. What Weber's history shares with these myths is the invocation of a time before economy, signaled by Weber in the term "natural relationship" quoted above, in which labor, production, and exchange are all governed by people's direct needs and enjoyments. Of course, this does not mean that we should reject Weber's thesis. It just means that we should consider the idea of history that rescues this text from the mythical illusion.

Money and the Question of History

A starting point for the question of history can be found in the forms that Weber himself attributes to his narrative. His view follows the pattern of history as a process of *emptying* or of a movement away from a lost source. The irrational element at the heart of modern, rational economic conduct was once explained by a certain belief. Nowadays, this belief is gone, but the pattern of action that went with it has persisted. In broad terms, it is a movement from *full* action to *empty* action:

> The people filled with the spirit of capitalism today tend to be indifferent, if not hostile, to the church. [. . .] If you ask them what is the meaning of their restless activity, why they are never satisfied with what they have, thus appearing so senseless to any purely worldly view of life, they would perhaps give the answer, if they have any at all: "to provide for my children and grandchildren." But more often and, since that motive is not peculiar to them, but was just as effective for the traditionalist, more correctly, simply: that business with its continuous work has become a necessary part of their lives. That is the only possible motivation, but it at the same time expresses what is, seen from the viewpoint of personal happiness, so irrational about this sort of life, where a man exists for the sake of his business, instead of the reverse.[15]

A metaphor of history as an emptying movement is invoked here by Weber. The modern capitalist lacks an explanation for his way of life and that is how we see this way of life as historical. A certain absence is the index of the historicity of this modern moment. It points to a dimension of inheritance from the past. Weber's historical account explains this empty present with a full past, namely, with reference to a time when economic agents did hold the missing explanation for their conduct.

This pattern of explanation—a movement from a full moment to an empty one—brings to attention the requirement for a supplementary retroactive view. The point is that in viewing that past as full, as wholly explainable by the agents' self-understanding, we no longer see it as historical. One way to reinstate a historical dimension in it is to consider it from the perspective of the present. The fact that an empty pattern of action was inherited from this past amounts to the fact that to some extent past agents' explanations of their conduct were mystified. They perform a religious duty, but what they really do is something else: they already act like the rational entrepreneur seeking endless profit.

The radically historical narrative in this case is the shift from a mystified self-knowledge to a lack of it. Within this narrative, the rational capitalist who lacks a raison d'être sheds light on his or her religious predecessors no less than they shed on his or her conduct. One's lack of explanation for one's conduct reveals the truth of the illusory explanations of one's predecessors. From this perspective the narrative of emptying is not simply a forgetting of origin, but, at the same time, a process of revelation of the truth of the origin.

What Is Economy?

Adding the retroactive view to the causal narrative of Weber unearths a conceptual connection between history and economy. This point must be emphasized given the background of the widespread conception of a fundamental opposition between the sciences of history and economics. In the spectrum of the human sciences, the former is considered the pole most dedicated to change and contingency, whereas the latter represents the pole of permanent a-historical laws. Weber's thesis, if utilized to the full, points to a conceptual relation between these two poles. It points not simply to the way specific economies are immersed in history, that is, to economic history, but to the way a certain concept of history is the complement of a concept of economy, to an idea of a genuine historical economy.

In brief: if we conceive of the economy as a realm of absent cause, where human action cannot be explained in the terms of the agents, then history is its conceptual complement insofar as it refers to that which persists without a cause. What persists through the shift from the Calvinists to the capitalist entrepreneurs is precisely the absence of a cause of action, an absence that wears different forms (the divine injunction, business as a way of life). And it is the persistence of this absent cause that we can call history. This persistence confers on history a shape beyond the first impression of contingency.

This connection between history and economy is comprehensively rejected by contemporary economics by its insistence on a utilitarian, individualist framework. In the cosmos of individuals maximizing utility, there can be no place for history, precisely because the conduct of the agent is transparent to it or fully contained within it. Indeed, preferences of agents may change historically with fashions, tastes, and trends, yet these fashions are themselves *not* a subject of economic knowledge. What economics purports to know is only how an agent handles properties that are already given—how it allocates resources between competing ends.

The alternative notion of economy, as one that designates that framework in which the cause is seen as most external to the action, has its own history, both in common language and in heterodox thought. We can discern its presence in the use of the term *economy* in highlighting some hidden level of explanation in expressions of the form *economy of gifts, economy of guilt, economy of feelings*, and so forth. Indeed, in all these phrases we find the familiar sense of economy as grounded in exchange, in the give-and-take of the object at stake. In addition, however, in those cases the appendage of *economy* to a term results in a complete reversal in relation to its formal, explicit meaning. An *economy of gifts* not only designates exchanges of gifts but also means that these are not gifts in the full sense of the term; and an *economy of feelings* points to a level that renders those feelings inauthentic.[16]

This alternative meaning of the term *economy* is shared by Marx and Veblen (discussed at length in Chapter 5). For Marx, this meaning is precisely how he finds a radically alternative starting point for *Capital* in the conservative theme of barter exchange: "1 coat = 20 yards of linen." As noted in Chapter 3, it is because Marx sees exchange as part of a barter economy and not just as a whimsical exchange that he traces in this basic form the externality of value in relation to use value and to the realm of experience.

Chapter 5 shows how this conceptual connection between economy and history lies at the heart of Veblen's thought. It suffices if we mention an affinity of Veblen's critique of the theory of marginal utility to Weber's thesis. Veblen accepts that the theory of marginal utility, which dominates the modern economic conception of the person, may have some explanatory power of human behavior. Yet it cannot explain how the hedonistic economic agent came into being. As proof that the hedonistic economic agent is not a natural phenomenon but a historical effect, Veblen invokes what surpasses hedonistic behavior, namely, profit making, and the way it is embedded in business life:

> Business men habitually aspire to accumulate wealth in excess of the limits of practicable consumption, and the wealth so accumulated is not intended to be converted by a final transaction of purchase into consumable goods or sensations of consumption.[17]

In an echo to Weber's thesis, Veblen punctures the a-historical framework of economics with the aid of the most common business practices that are aimed at profit as such. In other words, Veblen's and Weber's arguments point to a basic idea that desire for money can be an anchor for a radical historicizing of economy. If the conceptual relation between economy and history lies in the view of economy as characterized by externality of the cause of action, then money when it is entangled with desire represents the pure form of this externality.

The Shadow of Teleology

An evidence for the need to add a retroactive view to Weber's thesis is provided by the way this possibility is actually avoided by the text. In *The Protestant Ethic*, Weber does not pose explicitly fundamental questions of history, but an idea of history is implied by a distinction he makes between the moment of emergence and change and the process of expansion and persistence.

> [T]he capitalism of today, which has come to dominate economic life, educates and selects the economic subjects which it needs through a process of economic survival of the fittest. But here one can easily see the limits of the concept of selection as a means of historical explanation. In order for that manner of life so well adapted to the peculiarities of capitalism could be selected at all, i.e., should come to dominate others, it had to originate somewhere, and not in isolated individuals alone, but as a way of life common to whole groups of men. This origin is what really needs explanation.[18]

A stark contrast separates the moment of emergence from the process of expansion and persistence in terms of the types of knowledge these necessitate. The eventual victory of the spirit of capitalism is explained in evolutionary terms (*survival of the fittest*) and through the workings of blind economic mechanisms. In other words, it is explained as a process governed by law. The moment of the emergence of the spirit of capitalism lies precisely beyond the realm of law, beyond the "limits of the concept of selection as a means of historical explanation." Thus, although both the emergence of the capitalist spirit and its eventual victory are processes that take place over time, Weber's thought implies that it is actually only the moment of emergence that fully deserves the term *historical*.

The expansion and victory are explained by other types of knowledge of processes—knowledge inspired by economic and evolutionary thought; whereas the emergence, marked by contingency and the absence of law, necessitates a purely historical explanation. Similarly, while the expansion of the capitalist spirit is seen as internal to the realm of economy and, thus, as governed by economic dynamics, the moment of emergence is stamped with a surprising association between different fields: a development within religious thought that eventually influences a totally different field, economy. It is the gap between the fields—religion and economy—that confers on the moment of emergence both the impression of contingency and its status as historical in the full sense of that term. In somewhat crude terms, Weber's overall view is: before capitalism there was history but not economy, in the era of capitalism, there is economy but not history.

It is important to put things in this somewhat simplistic way because it exposes a real weakness in Weber's thesis, which as Braudel commented, haunts historians. Many of them reject the thesis, but somehow it keeps surfacing. The weakness does not lie in the argument itself, or in the association between religion and economy, but in the idea of history enfolded in the argument. It lies in the strange position, similar to that which Marx attributed to economists, namely, the idea that "there has been history, but there is no longer any."[19] For Weber, only the past is historical in the sense that it is contingent, not given to law. The present, by contrast, is thought of in terms of the "iron cage" metaphor, of inevitable progression according to law-like principles of economics and evolution.

It is equally absurd to accept the difference between economy and religion as given, as a difference between two autonomous fields. It is this difference that confers a contingent, historical character on the moment of emergence as Weber presents it. But the truth is that to the extent that a religious doctrine refers to work, consumption, leisure, and so on, it is, in this context, directly an economic phenomenon.

It is probably this historical-philosophical weakness that lies behind a strange gesture that Weber reverts to from time to time, of invoking an impossible gaze from the past to the present. To historicize capitalism, Weber brings in a somewhat sentimental image of a pre-capitalist person, who would not be able to understand the "perverse" capitalist conduct. To the pre-capitalist person, "that anyone should be able to make it the sole purpose of his life work, to sink into the grave weighed down with a great material load of money and goods, seems explicable only as the product of perverse instinct, the *auri sacra fames*."[20]

However, these theoretical weaknesses of the text point quite simply to a more fertile way to read Weber. If the weakness of the thesis lies in the artificial separation between a moment of change and a process of persistence, then the correct way to read it is to reconnect them. The story is not either of change or of persistence but of persistence through change: of something that can only be observed through the changes in its form. This can be clarified by referring to the other crude distinction Weber makes between religion and economy. His thesis is not really about the way Calvinism brought about capitalism but about the different articulations of religion and economy. It is most forceful when it is read as showing both how Calvinism was, among other things, already an economic phenomenon and how modern capitalism is still a religious phenomenon.

Desire as Historical Substance

The weakness of Weber's thesis is found in his insistence on the externality of cause (religion) in relation to its effect (economy). However, this weakness opens the way to another reading that sees this externality as constitutive to economy. This reversal can be formulated in relation to money. Desire for money can play a crucial role in the text, when one does not see it merely as an external relation to money. If we accept that the way money is desired is part of what money *is*, then the externality of the religious cause can be understood as reflecting the traumatic, inconceivable nature of desire for money. My proposal, therefore, is to view desire for money as an axis of Weber's text. In Žižek's terms, desire for money can be seen as the a-historical impossible-real that is a condition of history.[21] In this reading desire for money emerges as a deep kernel, which in no moment of the story is fully present yet informs the narrative as a whole.

How should we recount the story from the perspective of desire for money? Desire draws the story as a picture that is never complete. In its initial form, the religious imperative does not include any reference to money. Yet it dictates a pattern of behavior identical to obsession for money. Later it transforms into secular, rational economic conduct directed explicitly at money, but it becomes so on the condition that it has shed its religious attire. When its kernel appears as desire (that is, in the intense language of the Puritan ethic), it is not aimed directly at money but is expressed in the language of salvation and damnation. When it is aimed directly at money in the later stages of capitalism, it does not appear as desire (but is now expressed in the language of rationality).

One should recall in this context Shell's brilliant reading of Shakespeare's *The Merchant of Venice*.[22] Shell shows that the basic opposition in the play is not between Jewish greed and Christian nobility. Rather, it is between two languages and forms of thinking about usury: while the Jew thinks of usury in terms of people (whom one is allowed to charge interest), the Christian thinks of it in terms of objects (money that begets money). Similarly, while Shylock is explicitly accused of usury, Bassanio and Antonio are no less occupied in *spiritual* usury: they exchange and circulate not simply money but also friendship, love, and emotional obligations. This can be seen as a reflection of a basic chasm characterizing the fact of interest: one cannot grasp both its emotional and rational projections. It is seen either as an objective, impersonal economic fact or as an embodiment of a pathological emotion.

The intriguing question, however, is how we should conceive of the money object in light of this elusive movement of desire. Situating desire for money as an axis of Weber's thesis necessitates a consideration of the way money itself changes together with the change in the way it is desired. An additional idea of Žižek is helpful in this respect, namely, the concept of the *parallax object*. Parallax usually refers to a change in the appearance of an object caused by a change in the point of view from which it is seen. In the parallax object, by contrast, the difference is not merely subjective but is a part of the object itself:

> It is rather that, as Hegel would have put it, subject and object are inherently "mediated," so that an "epistemological" shift in the subject's point of view always reflects an "ontological" shift in the object itself.[23]

The idea of the parallax object is perfectly demonstrated by the perplexing role of objectivity in Franklin's economic maxims. We can take his maxims seriously, as referring to the money object—to what money really is—if we keep in mind the idea that social objects are necessarily entailed with a misperception. Franklin finds a perverse moral imperative in money, whose harsh tone is derived from the illusion that it emanates directly from the object. Later, this moral language is indeed abandoned, but only on the condition that it has already been materialized—that the perverse moral imperative has truly become entangled with objective economic reality. This is the only true meaning of Weber's idea of the "iron cage" of capitalism:

> Since asceticism undertook to remodel the world and to work out its ideals in the world, material goods have gained an increasing and finally an inexorable power over the lives of men as at no previous period in history. Today the spirit of religious asceticism [. . .] has escaped from the cage. But victorious capitalism, since it rests on mechanical foundations, needs its support no longer.[24]

Franklin speaks of money as exerting uncanny influence over people, with a language that still carries a remainder of its religious origin. In modern capitalism this language is forsaken but not really overcome. Rather, Franklin's ideas are materially fulfilled: "material goods have gained an increasing and finally an inexorable power over the lives of men." The complete description of the evolution from Franklin to the iron cage of capitalism can be described not as a correction of an error through the historical process, but as a movement of an error that defines that process. *Franklin falsely attributes a moral imperative to money, but later economics falsely overlooks the moral imperative that is already embedded in money.* The real paradoxical nature of Franklin's maxims is that they are really fulfilled only when they are abandoned. When economics leaves behind Franklin's harsh moral tone, it fully realizes his vision: an imperative emanating directly from the neutral fact of money, without the need of an intervention by an austere subjectivity.

So what is money after all? It is neither Franklin's ominous object nor the neutral object of economics but the movement between the two. It is a genuine historical object in the sense that it can be really perceived only through the change in its form.

This movement strictly mirrors the Freudian conception of the course of human sexual development. In his paper about the sexual theories of children, Freud presents some recurring false theories that children develop when they start to assume a sexual identity. Since no one tells them the truth about these ideas, they come up with their own silly, funny answers, such as that marriage is when "two people show their behinds to each other (without being ashamed)."[25] But what happens later on when the child grows up and knows better? It is not that he has overcome the false theories and now knows the truth about sex. His real knowledge is but a most cunning form of disavowal. He knows better, but only on the account that the previous false theories have already colored the whole of his sexual identity and are now embedded in his whole psychic system: behavior, symptoms, character, and so on.

The mature, full assumption of sexual identity is not characterized by overcoming infantile ignorance but consists of forgetting that one does not know. The ultimate proof of this is that when one's own children inquire about sex, one cannot simply give a true answer: one laughs or tells a story or answers with some embarrassment and lets them complete the apparent lack with their own sexual theories. This parallel to the story of money is no accident. It rests on the fact that Freud, too, is a truly historical thinker, as apparent in his famous remark on femininity:

> In conformity with its peculiar nature, psychoanalysis does not try to describe what a woman is—that would be a task it could scarcely perform—but sets about inquiring how she comes into being, how a woman develops out of a child with bisexual disposition.[26]

This should be read not as an apology but as a theoretical statement. The questions: What is a woman? and How does one become a woman? exclude each other. Presuming to answer one of them excludes the possibility of answering the other. That is, it is either the story that exists or the synchronic moments of it. One cannot have both.

To return to money, the historical transition can be presented as a transition between two meanings of objectivity. The first is objectivity as a specific subjective position (the position involved in asceticism); the second is objectivity as a form of existence outside of the subject (the indifferent impersonal existence of economic reality). The importance of this formulation is that it precludes the possibility of a basic economic objectivity. It points, rather, to a structure of objectivity in which the two opposed meanings are also necessarily complementary to each other: a certain subjective *as if* necessarily accompanies objective economic reality. On a first reading, Weber's notion of the iron cage seems to point to an objective economic reality that somehow became indifferent to subjective positions within it, reality that persists on its own force, regardless of the subjects ("an immense cosmos into which the individual is born, and which presents itself to him . . . as an unalterable order of things . . . "[27]). But Franklin's passion suggests another option: the iron cage is objective not because it is independent of subjective positions but, rather, because the subjective positions it implies are now no longer articulated as such—that is precisely the manner in which we can see them as *objectified*.

In other words, the movement between *as if* objectivity and *external* objectivity exposes the incompleteness of both meanings and the way they complete each other. The appearance of *as if* objectivity, objectivity as an explicit subjective position, as in Franklin's maxims, implies that his understanding of money had not yet become embedded in diversified economic mechanisms, that it was as yet not fully objectified in economic reality. On the other hand, the objectification of this understanding of money, its embodiment in external objectivity, means that there is no longer a need to explicitly articulate the supplementing subjective position.

Appadurai's reading of Weber provides another view of this narrative possibility. Appadurai reads Weber's thesis outside its immediate context. He brings it to bear on a type that is conspicuously missing from Weber's view of capitalism. The "heroes" of the last decades in global finance, Appadurai writes, are far from the spirit of "the ascetical Calvinist businessman, who was deeply opposed to greed, excess, exuberance, and worldly pleasure"—the type that Weber had in mind as representative of modern rationalized capitalism. Rather, these characters—individuals such as Michael Milken, Ivan Boesky, and Bernard Madoff—represent "a gaudy, adventurous, reckless, amoral type, who embodies just the sort of avarice, adventurism, and charismatic self-motivation that Weber saw as the absolute enemy of systematic capitalist profit making."[28]

For that reason Appadurai focuses his attention not on financiers who specialize in rational, or pseudo-rational, risk management but on "bears," who make a profit by wagers against the market, and against the common wisdom of financial institutions (e.g., those who made tremendous profits by short selling toxic financial assets at the time of the housing bubble). The point in his analysis is twofold: first, that this contrarian type is actually a prototypical form of the profit seeker, taking into account that profit making is involved with economic action in conditions of radical uncertainty and not just manageable risk; and second, and more importantly, that precisely this type manifests a dimension of continuity with Weber's religious ascetics. Like Weber's Calvinists, they conduct their business confronting a sense of radical uncertainty. And like their religious predecessors, they also manifest a sense of inner certainty, an ecstatic confidence, and an irrational sense of election—a belief in their power to outguess the market.

Appadurai actually points to a further sense in which the story of capitalism is built around a fundamental split. A lesson from his reading is that Weber's overarching notion of rationalization is fundamentally limited. Rationalization of the economy, in principle, can never be complete. There always remains a stain of *charisma*, a certain subjective, irrational attitude that accompanies it.

Teleology and Retroactivity

This reading of Weber may entail a more general lesson in relation to history. Weber insists on the causal aspect of his thesis by avoiding a teleological form that threatens it. But perhaps a teleological form is a necessary condition of historical knowledge. If there is a unique form of historical knowledge, it is knowledge colored by retroactivity. If there is a unique object of historical knowledge—if history is something at all—it is an object that can be recognized only in retrospect. And knowing in retrospect amounts to conceiving of something according to a later development. In short, it amounts to thinking against the direction of causality, namely, projecting backward in time from an end point to a beginning.

Gordon Graham refines this theoretical dilemma in his attempt to revive an interest in the philosophy of history despite historians' aversion to it. Strangely enough, he begins his argument by partly conceding to those historians who would oppose any knowledge tainted by retroactivity: "[H]istorians may, if they choose, restrict themselves to recording how events were contemporaneously perceived." This is a strange theoretical position because a historian who insists on a contemporaneous view, at least as an ideal, actually avoids the unique advantage of his own perspective as a historian, namely the advantage of hindsight. What are the grounds for such a position? It is the theoretical difficulty entailed with the alternative position. Constructing a narrative that makes use of historical perspective and the benefits of hindsight "will commonly employ ideas of success and failure, advance and decline, and these are concepts which frequently require philosophical analysis and conceptual imagination."[29]

The theoretical choice presented by Graham can be refined in light of the notion of teleology as the main threat for historians. Retroactivity confers a shape on history. And the idea that history has a shape—and not just "one damn thing after another" (Arnold Toynbee's reference to the view of some historians)—comes dangerously close to teleology. It raises the suspicion of historians because it hints at an a priori pattern in which history is organized. However, the other side of the dilemma is the question of whether disqualifying hindsight amounts to disqualifying history itself. Limiting oneself to recording events as they were "contemporaneously perceived" amounts to effacing the specific historicity of the past. It renders the *pastness* of the past, its position in time, a coincidental, external fact. It makes the past a sort of present that only coincidentally is positioned in another time. In this case, historical knowledge in itself has no uniqueness in relation to other disciplines of the knowledge of man—it is simply a sociology, anthropology, or economics of the past. Thus, the upsetting dilemma that Graham actually presents is the choice between, on the one hand, giving up on history as a special form and special object of knowledge, and on the other, affirming history together with a certain teleological form that accompanies it.

This dilemma is underlined by various attempts to rescue history that encircle this problematic coincidence of history and teleology. On the one hand, White suggests that history, as a discipline, "which is in bad shape today," should revive itself by forsaking its presumption to objectivity and retreating to its literary origins.[30] That is to say, White suggests saving the shape of history but at the expense of the object of historical knowledge. Since stories cannot be true, White suggests that we keep the stories and renounce their claim to represent reality. Again, the shadow of teleology can be seen to motivate this suggestion: the fact that a story has an ending, a closure, points to the sense in which any story is teleological.

The same threat can be discerned in a contrasting defense of history that insists on its truth value. Leon Goldstein defends history through its unique technique:

> History is a technical discipline in the sense that it uses methods which are peculiarly its own. History is a way of knowing, not a mode of discourse; and the proper point of departure of a critical philosophy of history is not the finished product of historical writing but that way of knowing and its technique.[31]

Unlike White, Goldstein insists on the truth value of historical knowledge. But in a way, Goldstein saves the object of historical knowledge at the expense of its shape. For Goldstein the question of the philosophy of history is: How is it possible to discover things about the past? But in his dismissal of the peculiarity of "the finished product of historical writing," he gives up the possibility that the knowledge of the past has a distinct form.

Can there be a third possibility? Teleology does indeed represent one of the most basic ideological distortions of the view of the past, namely, the idea that all history is aimed toward our present state. Yet a teleological form should not always be a result of an epistemological distortion. When a retrospective view exposes a real feature of the object of its gaze, then the teleological form is grounded in reality.

The theoretical ground for this possibility is most clearly formulated by Žižek in what he terms "the fundamental dimension of ideology," which is a misrecognition that is not simply an epistemological distortion but has an ontological status.

> [I]deology is not simply a "false consciousness," an illusory representation of reality, it is rather this reality itself which is already to be conceived as "ideological"—*"ideological" is a social reality whose very existence implies the non-knowledge of its participants as to its essence*—that is, the social effectivity, the very reproduction of which implies that the individuals "do not know what they are doing."[32]

This notion of misrecognition as part of social reality can serve as the theoretical ground for the ontological status of the advantage of hindsight. If misrecognition is inherent in social reality itself, then its exposure can occur only at a later time and, thus, appear in the form of teleology. The posterior recognition appears in this case as a narrative where the ending is inscribed, in its absence, in the beginning. Or in other words, it appears as a narrative where the ending completes or explicates the beginning. In the present case, capitalism exposes the fact that the Calvinists, in some sense, were already referring to money when they were relating to God.

Of course, there is no historical law that dictates that misrecognition must indeed become explicit. That is to say, there is no law of history that motivates a teleological progress. But the idea of misrecognition as a form of social reality points to things that if indeed they become explicit, their explication of necessity wears a form of revelation in time. It points to things that can appear only in a teleological form. One can indeed speculate about misrecognition that persists in its misrecognised form; however, the ontological status of this possibility is dubious, like Kant's thing-in-itself.

Teleology is unacceptable today, among other reasons, because of the religious overtones associated with it. It hints at an all-knowing observer of history or at an a-historical entity holding the telos of history. However, this rejection points to the reason why a certain teleological form is actually acceptable. Rather than being guided by the image of an a-historical, all-knowing observer of history, a teleological form can be guided by its conceptual twin, namely, historical non-knowledge.

This twist is suggested in Žižek's defense of Hegel against the common accusation of his thought as a teleological philosophy of history. This common accusation finds the Hegelian telos in the notion of the absolute subject that emerges at the end of history and reconciles the antagonism between the historical subjects and the social substance. Žižek's correction to this view is that "*there simply is no such 'absolute subject'*" and the Hegelian subject is "*nothing but* the very movement of unilateral self-deception."[33] In a way, what Žižek develops here is a teleological form with no telos, where non-knowledge marks historical existence as such.

The shift between all-knowledge and non-knowledge involves a change in the conception of the historical object. A comparison with the simplest positivist form of the history of science, as a continuous progress toward better understanding, can clarify the difference. In this conception, the physical object can serve as the horizon of teleological progress. One can claim, for example, that the Greeks did not know about the molecular composition of water but with the passage time, humanity discovered it.

Even if this type of non-knowledge can be viewed in some sense as real, it certainly cannot be viewed as historical. There can be no historical meaning to the fact that the Greeks did not know the molecular composition of water; there can be no way to attribute an effect to this non-knowledge within its own time. The only way to say something meaningful about it is by inserting (explicitly or implicitly) our own knowledgeable vantage point into the subject—that is, by speaking of it from within the teleological framework. Thus, in this case adherence to teleology indeed excludes history.

However, regarding social objects, the picture must change radically. In the case of social objects like money, non-knowledge cannot be anchored in the physical externality of the object. Rather, the misrecognition of the object is to be conceived of as constitutive to the object itself. If people misunderstand money, then their non-knowledge of it is part of the way it functions as money. In this sense, non-knowledge does become a real historical fact—a fact that might indeed be visible only in retrospect, but nevertheless is effective within its own time. Thus, in this case we find a dimension of a necessary identification of history and teleology, a certain necessary teleological form of history. The basic term to describe this teleological form would be *cunning* or *deceit*. In this form, that which eventually appears was originally a blind spot around whose absence the social reality of the past was organized. Yet it is still teleological in its form precisely because it shows how a present was already implicit in the past.

There is one more important difference in this notion of a necessary teleological form. A teleological form without a telos implies a notion of history that links a moment of revelation with its opposite, in the form of a certain effacement. If non-knowledge is a condition of social reality as such, as something is revealed, something else must slip away from our sight. If non-knowledge is not related to an external reality but is constitutive to social reality, then the moment of its explication can never be complete because it changes the picture itself, the object of knowledge. While the teleological moment is that of explication, its complementary proper historical one is that of effacement or amnesia. That is precisely the full description of Weber's narrative. The historical movement is that of an effacement of cause: the movement culminates in the modern capitalist entrepreneur who no longer knows why he acts as he does. But this movement is at the same time of a teleological form if we recall that the capitalist's conduct explicates or reveals a secret of his religious antecedents.

The Concept of History and the History of the Concept

The theoretical grounds for this twofold movement of teleological-explication and historical-amnesia are presented explicitly in Marx's *Grundrisse*. The following, probably Marx's bluntest declaration of a teleological point of view, appears in the 1857 introduction.

> Human anatomy contains a key to the anatomy of the ape. The intimations of higher development among the subordinate animal species, however, can be understood only after the higher development is already

known. The bourgeois economy thus supplies the key to the ancient, etc. But not at all in the manner of those economists who smudge over all historical differences and see bourgeois relations in all forms of society. One can understand tribute, tithe, etc., if one is acquainted with ground rent. But one must not identify them.[34]

Note that the notion of teleology here is not the commonplace notion of it as a law of history or even as a historical necessity.[35] It is located, rather, in the realm of understanding: "bourgeois economy supplies the key to the ancient . . ." The present explains the past. Yet its positioning in the realm of understanding does not undermine its status of real teleology—that is, it does not make of it merely a feature of the historical perspective, of historical knowledge. This is particularly apparent in *Grundrisse* because there Marx goes to great lengths to present understanding and knowledge as real historical facts. A closer look at his deliberation reveals that this conception of understanding as a historical fact actually rests on the assumption that the lack of understanding is a real historical fact—indeed, a key fact in a given historical reality.

Such a notion of non-knowledge as a historical fact is hinted at in the text preceding that famous anatomy metaphor, in which Marx discusses Adam Smith's discovery of labor *as such* as the source of wealth—an immense step forward in relation to the former economic schools that tried to situate the source of wealth in specific kinds of labor.

How difficult and great was this transition may be seen from how Adam Smith himself, from time to time, still falls back into the Physiocratic system. Now, it might seem that all that had been achieved [by Smith] was to discover the abstract expression for the simplest and most ancient relation in which human beings—in whatever form of society—play the role of producers. This is correct in one respect. Not in another. Indifference towards any specific kind of labor presupposes a very developed totality of real kinds of labor, of which no single one is any longer predominant. As a rule, the most general abstractions arise only in the midst of the richest possible concrete development, where one thing appears as common to many, to all. Then it ceases to be thinkable in a particular form alone. On the other side, this abstraction of labor as such is not merely the mental product of a concrete totality of labors. Indifference towards specific labors corresponds to a form of society in which individuals can with ease transfer from one labor to another, and where the specific kind is a matter of chance for them, hence of indifference. Not only the category, labor, but labor in reality has here become the means of creating wealth in general, and has ceased to be organically linked with particular individuals in any specific form.[36]

At first glace the historical role of understanding seems to be formulated in a positive manner. Smith discovered the concept of labor as such, of abstract labor or labor in general, when abstract labor appeared also in reality, most particularly in the form of wage labor: labor that is interchangeable in relation to the laborer, external to his personality and life course, and so on. The appearance of this abstract concept thus marks a certain historical organization of society, where "individuals can with ease transfer from one labor to another, and where the specific kind is a matter of chance for them."

But no less important is the designation of the historicity of pre-capitalist economy through a notion of a limit to understanding. That is what Marx refers to when he points our attention to the difficulty of Smith's discovery. Whereas capitalist economy is characterized by the emergence of the abstract category of labor, in both thought and practice, feudal economy is characterized by the absence of this category. Prior to Smith, labor was unthinkable independently of the laborer. In abstract, theoretical terms, labor can be seen as the source of value even in relation to feudal economy. But this means that the specific historical description of feudal economy comprises of the fact that the category of labor was unthinkable during that period. The *natural* relation of a person to his occupation can be seen as reflecting the absence of the category of labor from both thought and action. In this sense a certain absence can be seen as an organizing principle of feudal economy.

Yet this is not the whole picture. The later appearance of the abstract category, in both thought and action, is not a simple moment of discovery of a hidden foundation. It is not progress toward greater transparency because it has in itself a blinding effect. The explicit appearance of the category blinds us from understanding the difficulties that Smith had to overcome to arrive at it. That is to say, it obscures from us the unique historicity of the past prior to it. Before its appearance, it is unthinkable yet after its appearance, its absence is unthinkable. In a way, Smith's historicity consists of the difficulty he has in constructing a concept of labor as such, while our historicity consists of the difficulty we have of observing Smith's difficulty. History is eventually conceived of as a shift of impossibilities. This is no mere witticism. This double blindness is fundamental to what Marx argued, namely, the idea that the abstract category is intertwined with history. In the following he formulates this more explicitly:

> This example of labor shows strikingly how even the most abstract categories, despite their validity—precisely because of their abstractness—for all epochs, are nevertheless, in the specific character of this abstraction, themselves likewise a product of historic relations, and posses their full validity only for and within these relations.[37]

The abstract category is intertwined with history in a perplexing manner. It is valid in some sense for all epochs precisely because it is abstract, yet it is fully valid in relation to a specific historical economic organization in which it has become materialized, embedded in concrete social reality. The first question refers to the *abstract*, partial validity of the category prior to its materialization. In what way is it valid for a social reality that precedes its materialization?

An answer to this is that the specific historicity of such a time can be viewed as the different ways in which the abstract category is *not* fulfilled. Labor can be seen as the source of wealth in any society if we see it as an analytic category. But the specific historicity of a pre-capitalist social organization is defined by the absence of this category in economic practice—that is, by the manner one's *labor* is inseparable from one's way of life, social position, and so on.

The second question is: What happens after the emergence of the abstract category? The point is that this emergence is not just a moment of revelation of a previously hidden condition but is by the same token a moment of obfuscation. Precisely because it is abstractly valid for all epochs, it obscures the difference between capitalist and pre-capitalist societies. In other words, its abstractness hides its own specific historicity. It is one of the categories that tempt the economists to "smudge over all historical differences and see bourgeois relations in all forms of society." Its appearance effaces the historicity of the past as an economy to which it was valid only in the abstract. And by effacing the historicity of the past, it effaces its own historicity.

The historical movement displayed by this is, again, twofold and similar to the twofold movement of teleological-explication and historical-amnesia we found in Weber. In the teleological moment, a secret of any economy hitherto becomes explicit and embedded in economic practices. But this teleological moment is supplemented by the historical moment of effacement: as the secret becomes explicated, it effaces its own historicity. The abstract category explicates a secret that is valid for all economies, yet its appearance is not a movement toward transparency because this appearance is in itself an immense historical change.

Two Forms of A-historicity

When Marx writes that the abstract category is valid for all epochs, he clearly invokes a certain notion of a-historicity. However, it is certainly not a naive notion of the a-historical constant that remains the same through the ages. Rather, Marx invokes the a-historical dimension that in some remarkable way is intimately related to change. According to Marx, the fact that an abstract and the a-historical category become explicit is itself a major historical change.

Žižek's idea of the impossible-real as an a-historical condition of history provides a good formulation for an understanding of the form of a-historicity that Marx alludes to. In the naive form, a-historicity refers to the constant that accompanies the change of historical forms and lies beyond them. By contrast, in referring to the a-historical with the Lacanian term of *impossible-real*, Žižek enables us to conceive of the a-historical in a way that does not view it as an unchanging kernel that always exists. Rather, his conception suggests that the a-historical kernel is something that never really exists—it is an organizing principle that can be discerned through the manner in which history outlines its absence. This type of a-historical kernel is what can never be fully present but is discernible in the change between historical moments.

These two forms of a-historicity can be described in simple, schematic terms. The most basic change of a historical form forces us to acknowledge an equivalence between two forms A and B that can be denoted A = B. For example, in ancient times sheep had a function similar to that of coins today (sheep = coins). The simplest way to account for this historical identity is by using a third, unchanging element C, which is valid for both A and B (thus, sheep are equivalent to coins because both are forms of means of exchange). This, of course, is the definition of a-historicity as simple persistence, as a constant that lies behind change. It provides a way to account for historical change, but it does so at the expense of relegating historical knowledge to a marginal status because it maintains that both A and B are but ephemeral forms of the unchanging C.

Is there an alternative way to account for the identity A = B? We can actually see it as a basic form of historical identity if we maintain it without the constant C. In this alternative, it is precisely the difference between A and B that allows each to explicate the other. It is because A is *not* B that the statement A = B is indeed meaningful. The example of labor, as Marx says, shows this strikingly. It is because the craft of a feudal artisan is not, or not yet, labor (not external and independent, etc.) that the historical identification between them teaches us something about both of them.

This is precisely what Marx says when he writes "one can understand tribute, tithe, etc., if one is acquainted with ground rent. But one must not identify them." By maintaining the difference between tribute and ground rent, these two historical forms of exploitation can shed light on each other. Tribute, which relates to direct, feudal social relations between people, demonstrates that impersonal ground rent is actually a relation of exploitation. And vice versa: ground rent demonstrates that the feudal relation of direct social domination is actually a method of making profit. What should be noted is that this alternative way to account for the identity A = B is the one that attributes primary status to history because it is the horizon that allows their identification. In this alternative, the formula A = B simply articulates the identity of the historical thing. That is to say, in this alternative, the formula A = B is that which fully reveals what A and B really are. In other words, the two approaches to a-historicity are distinguished by their relation to difference. While the first approach uses the a-historical constant to explain historical difference, in the second approach it is the difference that explains. The difference between A and B explains what both A and B are.

This is precisely the reading I propose for Weber's narrative, in which the Protestant ethic explains capitalist spirit and vice versa. The religious ethic exposes the pattern of an alien, inhuman imperative at work in cold, rational capitalism (it shows that, in a sense, capitalism is still religious). The capitalist spirit shows that the Protestant ethic was from the beginning economic (i.e., that this religious imperative was related to money from the start). And most important, in this view, desire for money fills the place of the a-historical kernel that never fully exists. Desire for money is the kernel, which in no moment is fully articulated, yet informs the narrative as a whole.

Historical Ontology

Shell remarks on a Heraclitean notion of transformation in Marx's thought: "Both Marx and Heraclitus focus on money not as fetishized form but as the activity of transformation."[38] This should be understood as a basic formulation of the historical ontology that characterizes Marx's thought. It suggests that money is a thing whose very identity is most intimately related to change. Money is what it is insofar as it changes its form.

At this point, we can present equivalent formulations for this historical ontology. First, historical ontology is supported by the priority of difference over identity. That the difference between two historical forms, A and B, explains what both really are means that the narrative of the change from A to B is logically prior to both. Second, the priority of difference over identity is associated with an ontological status of lack. The transformation between two historical moments, A and B, can explain what both moments really are when each of them by itself is, in a sense, partial. Third, these two features account for the ontological status of the advantage of hindsight and with it, for a teleological form as a necessary component of history. Finally, all these features eventually support a basic requirement, namely, a way to attribute ontological status to a historical narrative.

This last point clarifies the theoretical need of such ontology. It can be clarified again vis-à-vis White. What White's argument successfully demonstrated is that to assign a truth value to narratives, we cannot stop short of formulating a comprehensive historical ontology. What he proved is that there is no way to compose a single, truthful narrative out of the endless repository of historical facts that the historian has at his or her disposal. But this does not necessarily mean that there is no truth in narratives. What it does imply is that if we wish to hold onto the truth of narratives, we must reconsider what we mean by facts. If we put the ontological priority on facts—discrete, atomic, synchronic facts—then, indeed, we would not be able to assign truth value to narratives.

To maintain a sense of reality for narratives, we must assign the ontological priority to the narrative over the discrete facts. In other words, we should consider seriously the series of equivalent formulations of historical ontology: that a fact receives its meaning only through other facts and that social reality does not consist of facts alone. For example, social reality comprises also what Ricoeur termed "traces," which strictly speaking are not facts but should be conceived of as traces of something that is absent, that is, as material embodiments of lack.[39] In short, reaffirming a narrative amounts to considering how it is negatively inscribed on the world of facts.

One may still be skeptical as to the possibility of arriving at the correct historical narrative. In this respect White's argument seems most convincing: How can we construct a single narrative out of the immense knowledge we have of the past? But this doubt belongs to a question of technique and should not be confused with the philosophical question of history. Perhaps we cannot construct a fully authoritative narrative. Actually, it is most probable that we cannot. But this doubt applies in the same way to facts. We can never come up with a fully authoritative fact either.

The Iron Cage Revisited

The philosophical questions of history are most relevant in relation to the broad shape that Weber assigns to his narrative. This shape is informed alongside the metaphor of the iron cage by the ideas of rationalization and disenchantment, which refer to a spread of a cold, calculating, utilitarian mindset. The emphasis that Weber puts on these ideas reflects his insistence on the causal direction of history as it highlights the movement away from a source and the corresponding historical moment of change. Although these are certainly central components of the narrative in any reading, the emphasis on them reflects the suppression of the complementary movement of explication of the source and the corresponding moment of persistence.

The idea of disenchantment, taken on its own, reflects mainly the sentimental view of the pre-capitalist societies. This view sneaks, from time to time, into Weber's text when he imagines the bewilderment that a pre-capitalist person would have felt in the face of the conduct of a capitalist entrepreneur. Regardless of this sentimental motive, it is doubtful whether disenchantment can be taken seriously as a theoretical concept. It seems much more reasonable to maintain that any social organization must be involved with a certain form of *enchantment*—that a social organization can never be fully transparent to its subjects. More specifically, looking at contemporary capitalism, it seems almost absurd to think of it in terms of disenchanted reality.

Although production may be rationalized in some senses, one need only look briefly at the sphere of consumption to see how economic reality is still enchanted. For example, consider the craze for Apple touch screen products.

Doesn't the secret of their popularity reside in the way they are immediately enchanting? The same goes for the idea of rationalization. The important point in Weber's thesis is that it acknowledges a dimension of irrationality that accompanies the spreading of the instrumental rationality of capitalism. However, the true force of the thesis lies in the possibility of conceiving of this irrationality not simply as a residue but as a necessary supplement of capitalist rationality—indeed, as the obverse of rationality.

The dilemma regarding the correct way to frame Weber's narrative can be brought to bear on basic questions in the growing discipline of the sociology of money. A central approach of this new discipline is to pose an opposition to the economic conception of money as a-historical, homogeneous, and as an abstract means—a conception that serves the rational, utilitarian, economic frame of mind. Some sociologists instead suggest to study empirically the historically changing practices of the use of money under the assumption that money is what people do with money. Although the background for this line of critique is understandable, it raises a basic question of categorization: Is its ideal a sociological, non-economic knowledge of money, or can it offer an alternative economic conception of money?

To see that these are not empty, semantic distinctions, we can look at the work of one of the most impressive representatives of this sociological approach to money. In her book *The Social Meaning of Money*, Viviana Zelizer provides a huge number of examples of monetary practices in areas that for a strict economic view would seem marginal. She examines historically money gifts, charity money, money exchanges among married couples, and other monetary practices. The marginality of these money exchanges serves her argument because Zelizer strives to demonstrate the need to think of different *moneys* instead of the singular, homogeneous, abstract money of economic thought. For this reason, it is perfectly legitimate to study "everyday money" instead of focusing solely on money in business transactions.

Consider one small example Zelizer brings. She describes the gradual development of the phenomenon of money gifts in the twentieth-century United States. She focuses on the extent to which the money gift was circumscribed and the changing social customs that led to the lifting of the restrictions of who could give it to whom and under what circumstances, as well as how the obstacles that prohibited it were overcome.[40] An interesting case is the question of a money gift from a man to a woman. When money gifts first became acceptable in America, it was still understood that it was inappropriate for a boy to give such a gift to a girl. The obscene logic behind this prohibition is clear, but one should note its economic nature: such a gift raises the question of what was given in return. This observation is certainly meaningful, but the question is: What exactly is its meaning?

This micro practice is presented by Zelizer as an example of the power of resistance of social practices to the corroding, flattening influence of economic considerations. Social practices resist the cold, calculating spirit embedded in money. They color and shape money instead of being colored and shaped by it. Nevertheless, this very same situation can be interpreted in diametrically opposite terms. This example actually indicates the spread of the economic point of view. When a money gift from a boy to a girl is prohibited, their relations are ipso facto defined in monetary terms (i.e., this is a situation when a money gift is not appropriate). Money as a threatening potential is part of the background that defines their social relation.

What can mislead us to see here a point of the resistance of social practices to the cold and flattening power of money is the economic misconception of money as inherently involved with calculating, utilitarian rationality. But what Weber reminds us is that money is strictly irrational—not only in the marginal case of the practices of money gifts, but also in its most familiar economic role, namely, in the practices of the capitalist entrepreneur. What Zelizer's example proves is not necessarily the need of a sociological reply to economics, but perhaps the need of an alternative economic thought.

An anecdote that Hart recounts sheds a different light on Zelizer's example. He recalls a Ghanaian student who said that in his country "it was common for a boy, after sleeping with a girl he has met at a party, to leave some money as a gift and token of esteem." Such an act would naturally appear obscene to Westerners who "think that including money in a transaction makes a huge difference to its social significance." Indeed, once the Ghanaian student had done the same with a visiting American student; "the resulting explosion was gigantic—'Do you imagine that I am a prostitute?' and so on."[41]

The point is that we can read the examples of Hart and Zelizer not just as exemplifying the diversity of social money practices. Rather, when the examples are read side by side, they seem to illustrate different stages in a development of the logic of money. The remarkable point is that the young Ghanaian who can give a money gift to a woman he has slept with represents a social reality that is still less immersed in capitalism. That is to say, whereas for the Ghanaian, money is still, more or less, an ordinary object, for the American couples that Zelizer studied, money acquires a special (and in a sense sacred, taboo) status. It is because the boy can give the girl, as a gift, any object *but* money that we can say that money has penetrated more deeply the social framework of their relationship. Zelizer's argument actually demonstrates the eroticization of money in capitalism. To recall a term from the previous chapter, the gift that the American boy gives to his girlfriend is *non-money*—an object that in that form precisely partakes in the reality of money.

The conjunction of these two couples highlights a paradoxical defining feature of capitalism. We are accustomed to saying that in capitalism anything can be bought with money. But the strange fact is that in traditional societies, the purchase of a wife is done explicitly and quite ordinarily and does not seem to carry a traumatic nature. It is in capitalism that this practice carries an obscene nature and, therefore, is avoided or bypassed or kept at some distance (e.g., through the engagement-ring industry).

It is precisely this obscene nature of the notion of marriage as an economic transaction that characterizes the ascent of money in capitalism. It marks the manner that spheres of social and cultural interactions become colored by money. The obscenity of this notion can be read as symptomatic to the libidinal character that money acquires. In this sense it is wrong to conceive of capitalism as a social reality in which everything can be sold and bought. Chapter 5 explores at length the idea that capitalism is actually involved with the rise of the notion of what money cannot buy.

Indeed, the historical perspective highlights the limitation of the sociological approach that views the social practices of money through an opposition between economy and society. History provides a background in which Zelizer's argument seems to turn against itself. At the micro level her book indeed provides many examples of socially constructed money, but eventually these examples, taken together, form a narrative of an ever expanding articulation of an economic logic. History as a unique form of knowledge escapes both the economic thought and Zelizer's view.

The story of the *gifting* of money is a good example of this. It begins with the money gift being a problem, an improper act, and advances through different practices that gradually legitimated it throughout the beginning of the twentieth century. These practices took the effect of personalizing the money gift against the impersonal nature of money itself, and they proceeded mainly through certain limitations set on the indefinite potential of money. Thus, for example, in the initial stages, the money gift was made possible by designating a specific purpose for the money given (e.g., for buying books, for future education, for furniture).

However, one should ask whether the full meaning of this practice is revealed at a later stage when it is institutionalized in the practice of commercial gift certificates. These still carry a *personal* face, but there is nothing in them that is really counter-economic. They directly serve the most basic practical economic goals of business: increasing sales, advancing payments, and creating a captured clientele. We can refer to this commercial appropriation of the money gift, borrowing from Marx a description of the expansion of the capitalist mode of production. When it reaches new lands, capitalism changes them "without apparently attacking the mode of production itself." Production goes on in traditional ways, yet the crucial but invisible change has already taken place as the sale of the product has become the main interest.[42]

In the same spirit we can say that when a money gift is prohibited between a pair, this relationship is already an economic one. The change is still invisible, yet the relationship is already inserted within an economic frame of thought, and the road is paved for its complete incorporation in the economy in the form of the birthday gift certificate.

Can gift certificates be understood by orthodox economics? Most certainly, they cannot. Viewed from the perspective of the individual, a gift certificate is a form of waste. Because it sets an artificial constraint on money, in the framework of orthodox economics, the gift certificate forces the individual away from his or her order of preferences. That is to say, it forces the consumer to acquire less utility from the same amount of money, or to spend more money for an equivalent utility (in simple language, it forces the individual to buy things that he or she does not really need, things he or she would not buy had the gift been in the *real* money form). This is an important point. The gift certificate passes as personal because it is strictly speaking wasteful. And waste is not a non-economic concept. It is prima facie an economic concept, yet it is inconceivable in orthodox economic terms. Accounting for it does not require a sociological explanation but a different economic theory, such as found, as we shall see, in Veblen's thought.

The fact that economics fails to understand such a basic business practice is indicative of the type of knowledge that the gifting of money requires. It requires notions that surpass the opposition between rationality and irrationality. The business practice of issuing gift certificates is a basic means of rational profit maximization (with its irrational kernel of profit for its own sake). However, in this case it is clear that the obverse of this rational drive is an irrational form of consumption (irrational in the very same terms that render the mirroring business conduct rational). But this calls for a generalization. Isn't it reasonable, not to say necessary, that the business drive for profit for its own sake should be involved with a sort of irrational consumption?

The example that opens Zelizer's book strengthens this argument. It is the practice of earmarking money, designating sums of money to specific purposes (such as *coal money*), sometimes by physically marking it. This is probably the most direct example of how social practices detract money from its homogeneity. Again, this practice represents a diversion from the model of economic rationality (the economic subject handles his or her expenses wholesale, without the aid of tricks to artificially self-restrain one's self).

Yet again, this irrational practice can be seen as a rational reaction to the surge of the consumer economy and the peculiar difficulties it puts on handling budget affairs. For this reason it would be absurd to conclude that the person who earmarks money is not an economic subject. This person is the archetype of the principal economic subject of the last century: the consumer. What these examples expose is the absurdity of the very idea of economic rationality, which can be maintained by limiting the gaze to production and profit making, at the expense of omitting consumption and the waste related to it. It is absurd precisely in relation to the real and unique characteristic of the subject matter of economic study, namely, the fact that a dollar received in one place is exactly a dollar paid in another.

Evidence that this absurdity calls for an economic reply—a heterodox one, to be sure—is that there was a time when such questions could be posed within the discipline. A prominent example is Wesley C. Mitchell, a student of Veblen, who was the president of the American Economic Association in 1923–24, but today is unknown to most economists. Mitchell pointed precisely to the gap between the rationality of production and the irrationality of consumption in his famous article "The Backward Art of Spending Money." The article begins with a puzzle: Why does the art of spending money lag behind the art of making money? Knowledge about making money is systematically accumulated, distributed, and practiced whereas knowledge about spending money remains incidental. That an economist could have asked such a question seems remarkable enough and indicative of the narrowing of the economic horizon entailed with the crystallization of orthodox theory.

Mitchell's answer to the riddle is even more interesting because it points to the institution of the family as the cause of the gap between rational making money and irrational spending money. The process of the rationalization of the economy involved the transfer of production from the family to a bigger impersonal organ, namely, the business enterprise, which proved vastly more efficient as an economic unit. However, because of our instinctual love for the family, we have kept consumption within its bounds. "And so long as the family remains the most important unit for spending money, so long will the art of spending money lag behind the art of making money."[43] Not only does this economic view encompass both rationality and irrationality in money, it ties the gap between them to the ubiquitous institution of the family.

Mitchell's explanation represents a slight deviation from the framework of institutional economics as it was elaborated by his teacher Veblen. Mitchell explains an economic phenomenon (patterns of consumption) by an ostensibly non-economic institution (family). Veblen, as we shall see, tended to an opposite line of thought. He typically provided economic explanations for social, ostensibly non-economic institutions (the sub-title of *The Theory of the Leisure Class* declares that it is "an economic study of institutions"). Following through this logic produces a somewhat different formulation of Mitchell's argument, which seems warranted by the apparent increase of the gap between rational production and irrational consumption. During the almost 100 years that have passed since Mitchell wrote his article, consumption has seemed to develop from being less rational or non-rational to being simply irrational. We can speculate how Veblen would have formulated the argument: there are many explanations for the institution of the family; however, the economic explanation is that the family is required for maintaining the necessary gap between rational making of money and irrational spending. This is clarified in the next chapter.

Chapter 5

THE ECONOMIC SUBLIME
The Fantastic Colors of Money

In their well-known work *The World of Goods*, Mary Douglas and Baron Isherwood attempt to sketch an anthropological approach to consumption. This attempt deserves careful attention for two reasons. One, it illuminates an extraordinary blind spot of economic thought, namely, its inability to explain consumption, that is, to answer what seems a most basic question—"why people want goods."[1] Two, Douglas and Isherwood's work is even more important because of the failure of their attempt to provide a complementary anthropological answer to the question. A careful reading of their work suggests that instead of a cultural supplement to the weakness of economics, what is needed is a fundamentally different economic approach. Briefly, what is needed is not an approach that views culture as a supplement to the economy, but rather one that seeks the hidden economy of culture.

To fill the peculiar economic lacuna regarding consumption, Douglas and Isherwood propose an approach in which goods are seen as meaningful objects and not just as objects of utility. To chart the realm of this anthropological approach, the authors draw a boundary between consumption and the market: consumption starts where the market ends. The difference between the two is that in contrast to economic action, consumption is not a "compelled" action. Thus, the realm of consumption is marked by the notion of "certain things that cannot be sold or bought."

To clarify the nature of this boundary, Douglas and Isherwood recount an old story:

Apparently, some fabled New York hostess in the 1890s, worrying how to surpass her rival who habitually gave each guest a rich jewel, was worried even more by their derision when, her turn having come, she folded a crisp $100 bill in each napkin.[2]

The interesting point is that more than exemplifying the boundary, the story actually shows how this boundary is traversed. It does indeed suggest two realms: the private sphere of consumption, marked by freedom and cultural meanings (hospitality, gifts, social ties), which contrasts with the sphere of the market, which is distinguished by utility considerations, calculating economic thought, and business transactions. The difference between these two spheres is demonstrated by the misguided effort to purchase something that belongs to the first realm, for example, appreciation, respect, or social esteem, as if it belongs to the market place. Thus, the boundary is indeed maintained in the fable together with a notion of things that money cannot buy. However, accepting the distinction literally, as Douglas and Isherwood seem to do, leads to spoiling the joke altogether.

The vulgar mistake of the hostess is funny not because it is silly but rather because it stands in a complex relation to the correct manner of her rival. The vulgar money gift is not simply the opposite of the rich jewel but also of its hidden principle. It spells out explicitly a dirty principle on whose secrecy rests the nobility of its mirror image. The jewel itself is an item that is as close as any item can be to money. It embodies and signifies monetary value without actually being money. It is a form of *minimal difference* from money. This difference is the way it is desired in a context where money repels. The vulgar mistake of the hostess actually unearths the hidden economy of the allegedly non-economic sphere of social consumption.

In other words, the force of the anecdote is that it presents the category of things that money cannot buy as an economic category. This category, signaled in the anecdote by the more elegant and successful hostess, is far from being opposed to the realm of economy. After all, she did not win the invaluable respect of her guests, for example, by amicable conduct and a generosity of spirit but with a rich jewel. Thus, things that money cannot buy point to a unique economy, set in an intricate relation to our notions of the calculating economy. What money buys and what it cannot buy point to two types of economy, which are simultaneously external and internal to each other, just as the vulgar hostess remains outside the circle of social appreciation, yet exposes the embarrassing hidden principle of this circle.

The point is actually almost trivial: "things that money cannot buy" cannot signify a realm that is indifferent to economy. Rather, this category is the most basic economic signification of a sphere that is ostensibly beyond economy. It

refers, indeed, to noble, sublime qualities, but it gives them an economic definition: things that money cannot buy. It is not non-economic in the way, for
example, that noble thoughts or friendship can be beyond economy. Rather, it
is the economic formulation of things that do not appear as directly economic:
appreciation, respect, social ties. In other words, it is the economic sublime.

However, the boundary that Douglas and Isherwood outline does indeed
refer to a theoretical weakness of economic theory when it comes to consumption. Orthodox economics is indeed limited to the utilitarian, calculating sphere of things that money can buy. However, what the joke shows
against that argument is that this weakness should be corrected by an alternative economic knowledge: beyond utility calculations, we do not necessarily
find a sphere free of calculation but in this case, a sphere governed by a necessarily hidden calculation.

This boundary has much to do with the desire for money. Indeed the gift
of a jewel embodies desire entangled with monetary value. Its minimal difference from money, the inherent threat of becoming disgusting by revealing its
invisible logic, its location beyond the sphere of utility calculations—all these
illustrate again the complex, traumatic nature of the desire for money. However, we should not look only at the jewel but also at the topology of money
in which it is positioned. This topology suggests a more general formulation,
namely, that the desire for money is articulated with the category of what
money cannot buy.

A reward of this order is often invoked to explain the pursuit of wealth
that exceeds apparent utility. Adam Smith formulated this in his *Theory of
Moral Sentiments*: "For to what purpose is all the toil and bustle of this world?
What is the end of avarice and ambition, of the pursuit of wealth, of power,
and pre-eminence?" As these are not explained by the need to supply the ne-
cessities of life, Smith concludes the real reason is "To be observed, to be
attended to, to be taken notice of with sympathy, complacency, and approbation."[3] How should we understand these colloquial excuses for the insatiable
appetite for wealth? They should not be taken literally, of course, as real benefits that are acquired with wealth and motivate its acquisition.

The point of this chapter is that we should not dismiss them as mere illusions either. What this chapter suggests is that the economic context confers
a dimension of reality on them. In the economic context we can see the illusory benefits—"To be observed, to be attended to, to be taken notice of with

sympathy, complacency, and approbation"—as manifestations of the category of what money cannot buy, that is necessarily entangled with the desire for money. Their economic reality is, strictly speaking, the desire for money. This point was already foretold in the previous chapter in relation to Weber's thesis: an unconditional desire for money, the desire for money in itself and not merely for the things it can buy, is by necessity entangled with the order of what money cannot buy.

A crucial point is that this category is most visible today not in relation to capitalist entrepreneurs or to profits. Rather, its most typical manifestation is in the sphere of consumption. For example, Eva Illouz, in *Consuming the Romantic Utopia*, shows how our most basic images of romance are shaped by the discourse of advertising. Romance—perhaps the prototypical representation of the category of what money cannot buy—is not simply opposed to the sphere of the economy but is subsumed by it. In modern capitalism, romance is embedded in a consumerist cosmos (consumerist language, goods, imagery, etc.).[4] Illouz invokes the need in a "political economy of romance."[5] This chapter suggests a general framework that can address this need by viewing what money cannot buy as a fundamental economic category. It suggests that this category should be explored in some sense as an economic term and not simply by forgoing the economic point of view.

Can the category of what money cannot buy be conceived of as a real economic category? This chapter shows that it can be posed as the theoretical axis of Veblen's early work, culminating in *The Theory of the Leisure Class*. This category may appear vague and resistant to conceptualization. Yet Veblen's work shows how to put it within a meticulous economic analysis of institutions. Furthermore, his work shows how this category is relevant not only for extreme forms of economic conduct, as those of the wealthy, but how it penetrates the economy as a whole. Indeed, in some sense what money cannot buy can be seen as the primary economic category in Veblen's thought since from the outset, what is at stake in the economy according to him is not subsistence but social comparison and competition.

Reading through Economic Misunderstanding

The best way to present the radical nature of Veblen's thought is to start from the way his work is misunderstood by economists on the rare occasions that they refer to him. I start with what seems to be a simple, straightforward summary of Veblen's approach in one recent reformulation of his work by two economists. In the first words of their article in *The American Economic Review*, Laurie Simon Bagwell and B. Douglas Bernheim explain that Veblen argued that "wealthy individuals often consume highly conspicuous goods and services in order to advertise their wealth, thereby achieving greater social status."[6]

At first glance, this may seem a pretty accurate rendition of Veblen's main line of thought. Veblen does indeed stress the importance of status in certain economic behaviors, and how such status is inherently connected with the conspicuous nature of these behaviors—conspicuous waste, conspicuous nonproductive leisure, and more. Expensive and conspicuous goods are indeed consumed as a means of displaying their owner's wealth; as Veblen writes "in order to gain and to hold the esteem of men it is not sufficient merely to possess wealth or power. The wealth or power must be put in evidence, for esteem is awarded only on evidence".[7]

So what is the source of discrepancy of this economic formulation with Veblen's thought? It lies in the deep-rooted adherence by economists of methodological individualism, which leads them to explain any economic act by the utility it holds for the various individual actors. Of course, conspicuous commodities are actually defined as possessing a component of non-utility, but the Veblen-minded economist solves this problem with a substitute for utility: status. With normal commodities, one obtains utility, and from conspicuously non-utilizable commodities, one acquires status. In this way Veblen's cosmos is incorporated wholesale into the economic frame of mind.[8]

A closer look reveals that this formulation of Veblen's theory in terms of utility-seeking individuals omits the very core of his work. The term *status* does appear frequently in *The Theory of the Leisure Class*; however, in the book, status is not something that one has in this or that measure. Rather, Veblen uses the term *status* in a manner closer to its original meaning, relating to law. Of the ninety occurrences of the term in the book, we find it most often in expressions such as "regime of status" (17), "relations of status" (15), and similar expressions ("system of status," "law of status," "code of status," or "stage of status"), which refer mainly to social organizations or to historical stages (to be precise, Veblen characterizes our own urban civilization as a phase of a decay of the regime of status). Only occasionally does Veblen use status in expressions such as "personal status" or "superior status" (3 times each), which may be understood as implying a personal quality that may be achieved in greater or lesser degrees. Instead, status refers mainly to a special type of co-ercion that characterizes certain societies. Thus, while the economic reading understands status as a special hidden utility that explains apparent waste, Veblen refers to status as a system or an unwritten law that enforces waste.

The examples that underline in the most explicit way the mismatch of the economic reading of Veblen are those that are most easily labeled satiri-cal. Thus, Veblen writes of "certain Polynesian chiefs, who, under the stress of good form, preferred to starve rather than carry their food to their mouths with their own hands" and recalls a tale of a king who was burned to death because there was no servant in attendance to shift his seat away from the fire.[9] Both examples demonstrate the logic of conspicuous leisure. The rulers have enough power that they do not need to bring food to their mouths or move their chairs with their own hands. However, in both these cases, the economic utilitarian reading arrives at an absurdity. It would be ridiculous to say that the chiefs and the king acquired higher social status by dying due to their insis-tence on refraining from the most mundane efforts.

One may dismiss these examples as exaggerated or even as purely fictional. Yet this should not undermine their importance. Even as fiction, they con-form to the basic logic of Veblen's argument; and as exaggerated, they articu-late this logic in the fullest manner. What is exaggerated is a basic economic principle of Veblen, namely, the force that status exerts on the individual, and the foreignness of this force to the individual's point of view, marked, in each case, by the horrible death to which it leads.

Of course, there are formulations of Veblen that may seem to support the economic interpretation of *The Theory of the Leisure Class* in terms of social gains achieved by conspicuous behavior. For example, the expression "ability to pay" that recurs throughout the book may indeed seem more *economic* in the standard use of the term. Thus we read that "the chief use of servants is the evidence they afford of the master's ability to pay." Because of this peculiar eco-nomic function, there arises a class of servants whose duties become increas-ingly scant, allegedly in opposition to any economic logic. Of course, the logic behind it is that in their doing nothing, the servants demonstrate their master's wealth—not only has he servants that work in his place, he also has servants who are idle in his place (what Veblen terms "vicarious leisure").[10]

Despite the calculating flavor of this example, hidden within it is the same logic as in the pathological cases of the king and the chiefs. We can observe this if we note what is often omitted from accounts of Veblen. After elaborating the economic explanation of various practices, Veblen usually adds a remark, stating that this explanation is different from the way the agent itself perceives his conduct. The agent does not conceive of his own act in its economic meaning, but the economic cause is always mediated through some *noble* third term, such as honor, decorum, and so forth.

Thus, in the example of the personal servants, Veblen indeed explains that it is a

> serious grievance if a gentleman's butler [. . .] performs his duties [. . .] in such unformed style as to suggest that his habitual occupation may be ploughing or sheepherding.

However, he immediately qualifies this by stating that

> [W]hat has just been said might be taken to imply that the offense of an under-trained servant lies in a direct suggestion of inexpensiveness or of usefulness. Such, of course, is not the case. The connection is much less immediate. What happens here is what happens generally. Whatever approves itself to us on any ground at the outset presently comes to appeal to us as a gratifying thing in itself; it comes to rest in our habits of thought as substantially right.

This addition brings the more common example of the personal servant closer in its structure to the allegedly satirical examples of the king and the chiefs. Both share the same notion of the economic cause as foreign to the agent's point of view.

This similarity is far from being coincidental. In truth, the economic cause is necessarily absent in the Veblenian framework. One can notice that in some simple cases, its absence becomes almost tautological. Consider, for example, the claim that the prestige of classical learning, of knowledge of "the dead languages . . . of correct spelling; of syntax and prosody" lies eventually in their being time consuming and unproductive.

The argument here is that ordinary abstinence from work does not leave any material evidence. And this is precisely the advantage of a massive investment of energy in explicitly unproductive efforts such as the study of Latin. However, in this case we can see why the economic cause is necessarily hidden. There can be various reasons that a gentleman gives as to why he studies Latin. He might say that it is a language of culture, of religion, or of philosophy. He might even say that it is challenging or prestigious. All these explanations might have a measure of truth in them. But they are not the economic explanation (they may be closer in type to psychological or sociological explanations). There is one explanation that is analytically impossible for the agent to recount, and this is by definition the economic one: I invest such efforts in an unproductive task because it is demanding and unproductive.

One might suspect the analytical nature that this argument eventually assumes or ask what rescues it from mere tautology. The answer is that for Veblen's arguments to have any meaning at all, they must rely on an economic cause that is constitutively absent. His explanations are aimed at what we usually conceive of as cultural practices and objects—things such as dress, household practices, manners, or standards of beauty, to name just a few.

However, Veblen does not aim to reduce culture to its economic explanation. Rather his theory assigns a relative autonomy to the realm of culture precisely because it keeps a distance between culture and its economic explanation. For example, in relation to dress, Veblen writes that "the marks of expensiveness come to be accepted as beautiful features of the expensive articles." However, following the pattern we have already noted, he immediately adds that this is not "pure make believe" and comments that "we readily, and for the most part with utter sincerity, find those things pleasing that are in vogue."

The off-hand formulation of the addition should not mislead us. It is actually a necessary part of the argument. For the adjective *beautiful* to have any meaning at all in this context, it must be separated somehow from its economic explanation. If expensiveness is a principle of beauty, it must be a hidden principle. The economic cause is by necessity absent, but this also means that in this framework, beauty is not just an epiphenomenon but holds a semi-autonomous reality of its own.

Why was this basic principle of Veblen ignored by his interpreters mainly in economics? The reason is that the idea of the absent economic cause is related to a whole array of shifts in relation to orthodox economics. To fully grasp Veblen's theory, we must go through the whole multi-dimensional shift that it produces. One such shift is easily discerned. Veblen does not formulate a predictive theory but an interpretative one. Unlike orthodox economics, he does not purport to elaborate a full explanation for human action. He does not elaborate a mechanism that determines human decision making. Instead, his thought provides a context of interpretation of human action—an economic context.

The example of beauty perfectly demonstrates this difference. What he explains is the hidden grammar of beauty. He explains why certain things are beautiful (to be more precise—he exposes only one factor that determines things as beautiful, what he calls "pecuniary beauty"). Indeed, beauty belongs to an environment in which human action takes place, and it can effect human action but unlike the economic concepts of utility and preferences, it is not supposed to determine human action.

Veblen inquires not only into the beauty of objects but also into the historical standard of the beauty of women. This standard, he claims, depends on the economic role of the wife within the household. In archaic economies where the role of the wife is to work for her household, the ideal of beauty would be the "robust, large-limbed woman." By contrast, in more developed economies where women have become vicarious consumers of leisure for their husbands, the standard of beauty changes as to imply the woman's inability to work: the romantic ideal of beauty dwells on "the delicacy of the hands and feet, the slender figure," and especially "the slender waist," which is "attenuated to a degree that implies extreme debility."[11]

Note that the economic reading of Veblen again would be perfectly absurd here. Paraphrasing Bagwell and Bernheim, it would say that an individual marries a conspicuously unproductive wife to advertise his wealth and gain social status. This, of course, would omit from the picture the very phenomenon that Veblen sets out to explain: the historical standard of beauty. He does not purport to explain why an individual man marries an individual woman. Part of the answer is the obvious one: because he finds her beautiful. What Veblen explains is part of the hidden logic of beauty—insofar as there is such logic and insofar as it is economic in kind.

This shift from predictive to interpretative theory is involved with three additional fundamental shifts. It is conceptually linked to the fact that Veblen's theory provides a concept of waste (in contrast to orthodox economics for which waste is ontologically impossible), that it is a historical theory (in contrast to the deeply a-historical nature of orthodox economics), and that it incorporates a notion of the sublime (i.e., it treats the notion of what money cannot buy as an economic category—not as defining the outer limit of the economy but as the economic definition of the sublime). A full description of

Veblen's thought requires the comprehension of these three shifts together, as well as their interconnections.

To put it in a somewhat condensed form: Veblen's thought is historical in that it deals with institutions, that is to say, with a certain form of persistence. A minimal characterization of institutionalized practices is that they persist beyond the meanings or explanations that individuals may have of them. In relation to practices of the display of wealth, the outcome of this form of persistence is twofold. On the one hand, the display of wealth is produced without hidden utility and for that reason, it is a pure form of waste. On the other hand, from the perspective of the agent, the practice of display is experienced as belonging to the sphere of the sublime, of that which upsets utility calculations, of that which money cannot buy. That is the recurring pattern of the argument of Veblen. Something, a certain object or practice, necessitates an investment of unproductive effort. However, it enters the economy of display once it becomes appreciated for itself, apart from its economic meaning.[12]

The case of manners perfectly exemplifies this tripartite shift in the fundamentals of economic thought. Veblen acknowledges several historical, sociological, and anthropological layers that are present in manners: manners can be seen as signs of good will as well as residues of gestures of dominance and subservience. All these explanations are valid in their respective contexts. However, the economic explanation of manners is indifferent to the meanings that manners may carry. It refers to their persistence as time-consuming, non-productive practices. This persistence takes place insofar as manners become appreciated for their own sake. They persist because they are associated with the power or wealth of those who can afford to invest the efforts necessary for meticulous manners. But this form of persistence means nothing except that from an economic perspective, manners embody waste while from the perspective of the agents, manners appear sublime. That is how Veblen describes their persistence:

> [D]eviations from the code of decorum have become intrinsically odious to all men, and good breeding is, in everyday apprehension [. . .] an integral feature of the worthy human soul.[13]

Nothing less: "integral feature of the worthy human soul."

To return to the Polynesian chiefs who preferred to starve rather than transport food to their mouths with their own hands: what is brought to the extreme in this satirical example is the absence of the economic cause and its replacement with a sublime injunction. For the chief himself it is not the economic cause that drives him to death.

> It is true, this conduct may have been due, at least in part, to an excessive sanctity or taboo attaching to the chief's person. The taboo would have been communicated by the contact of his hands, and so would have made anything touched by him unfit for human food. But the taboo is itself a derivative of the unworthiness or moral incompatibility of labor.[14]

Here we can see the need for a careful reading of Veblen. The passage might be read as if the economic cause is missing only by chance ("this conduct may have been due at least in part"). But behind this cautious formulation stands a necessity, namely, that the economic cause cannot function unless it is masked—and in this case masked behind the harsh form of taboo. This, again, is almost a tautological claim. A more precise formulation would say that the radical externality of the economic cause is nothing but a harsh form of taboo. In other words, the taboo is the trace in experience of the absent economic cause.[15]

We can summarize the economic misunderstanding of Veblen. In general, the economic reading aims at bracketing the realm of appearances, of cultural illusions, and of *spiritual* things that constantly emerge in Veblen's text to arrive at the level of solid economic reality. The economic reading brackets away factors such as beauty, religious taboo, or sanctity that recur again and again throughout the text to arrive at the basic transaction: acts of alleged waste are actually aimed at the purchase of social status. In truth Veblen is interested in the opposite argument. He studies the unique reality of appearances and cultural illusions such as beauty, sanctity, honor, or religious taboo and sees irreducible waste as that which confers reality on them.

Waste and the Sublime

When reading *The Theory of the Leisure Class* one cannot avoid noticing the recurrence of objects of analysis that can typically be categorized as things that money cannot buy: the sanctity of the taboo in the case of the Polynesian chiefs; manners as a feature of a "worthy human soul"; the beauty of women; and the case of non-productive servants, whose function Veblen characterizes as "spiritual rather than mechanical."[16] This recurrence is not coincidental. Veblen's theory can be read as an economic theory of things that money cannot buy—a theory that takes this category seriously as a real economic category.

To notice the pivotal function of this category in Veblen's thought, we should look at its most extreme manifestation, namely, the analysis of religious practices.[17] Veblen points, for example, to the allegedly simple fact that "the local sanctuary is more ornate, more conspicuously wasteful in its architecture and decoration than the dwelling-houses of the congregation" and, furthermore, that this splendor "contributes little, if anything, to the physical comfort of the members." This combination makes it a paradigmatic example of *vicarious consumption*—a term designating the economic way of increasing consumption by the aid of delegates. In its standard use in the book, vicarious consumption refers to people who consume leisure at the expense of the head of the household: personal servants, wives, guests. The religious example is a point of exception where all agents are vicarious consumers, who consume in place of their divinity. Thus, "the principle of conspicuous waste has colored the worshipers' notions of the divinity and of the relation in which the human subject stands to him."

At first glance this statement can be read as a claim about the influence of economic things on culture: religious imagery has been penetrated by economic language. Man imagines his God in images inspired by his earthly reality, including his economic reality. However, to this we should add the more troubling idea, namely, that the economic sphere includes, to begin with, elements that can articulate even the religious sublime. God can be an economic agent in Veblen's theory because from the outset, his thought allocates a primary place in the economy to the sublime. A certain form of the sublime emerges wherever the economic cause is repressed and replaced by a third element (beauty, decorum, worthy human soul, religious imperative).

This third element appears as sublime precisely because it replaces the economic cause and therefore appears as that which upsets utility calculations. This ultimately settles the place of the category of things that money cannot buy in Veblen's theory. This category signals the conceptual conjunction between waste and the sublime. From the perspective of the subject, this category refers to the sublime, to that which can exert a categorical injunction that suspends all calculation. However, from an impersonal, economic perspective, this same category is the description of waste: what money cannot buy refers to a thing or a practice that necessitates expenditure with no compensation.

These abstract formulations of the uniqueness of Veblen's theory demonstrate his potential relevance to contemporary consumer society. The phenomenon of the leisure class in Veblen's sense, with its thick social fabric, has become marginal in contemporary economic reality. However, Veblen's thought is essential for us because his analysis of the leisure class introduces an economic framework that ties together elements that are foreign to orthodox economics: the reality of appearances and cultural illusions, waste, the sublime, and what money cannot buy. These have survived beyond the specific social phenomenon of the leisure class, and they now permeate the sphere of consumption as a whole as a single look at a commercial break on TV would confirm. In a superficial reading, most advertising involves the category of what money cannot buy through images of different types of the sublime attached to the most mundane goods.

Naturally, economists can dismiss these images as trifling illusions, as fanciful exaggerations that are not to be taken seriously, as devoid of economic significance. The truth is that economics has no tools to treat these images other than as mere illusions. But the question that remains is whether by ignoring the images of advertising, economics forfeits its ability to deal with consumption as a whole. Veblen, by contrast, provides us with a way to attribute economic reality to this imagery.

An Economic Theory of Consumption

In *No Logo*, Naomi Klein refers, with some hesitation, to a "spiritual" element of the modern brand name. In contrast with the traditional product, the "selling of the brand [. . .] acquired an extra component that can only be described as spiritual."[18] What Veblen teaches is that the hesitation is unwarranted. The spiritual carries a mark of illusion, yet what Veblen shows is how economic reality can be attributed to cultural illusions. According to this line of thought, it is the economic point of view that shows a brand name as truly spiritual. Thus Veblen provides us with a key to understanding brand names that evades the thought of economists. Although he wrote before their institutionalization, Veblen already noted a basic feature of the economy of brand names. He encodes this feature in the distinction he draws between the "honorific element" and the "element of brute efficiency," which he claims characterizes modern goods:

> [T]here are today no goods supplied in any trade which do not contain the honorific element in greater or less degree. Any consumer who might,

Diogenes-like, insist on the elimination of all honorific or wasteful elements from his consumption, would be unable to supply his most trivial
wants in the modern market.[19]

In a sense this is prophetic. The parallel paradox of consumer economy is that
today one cannot satisfy one's most basic needs without buying brand names
despite the fact that as symbolic objects, brand names cannot be conceived
solely in terms of needs but comprise an element that surpasses needs. We
satisfy our needs by things produced for aims other than needs. Veblen's reference to an honorific element points to the theoretical solution to this paradox.
Usually we conceive of honor as an interpersonal relation. But when *all* objects comprise an honorific element, this sense of the term becomes meaningless. It is meaningful not when an object induces an honorific relation with
other people, but when the object comes in place of an absent interpersonal
relation. When the honorific element, so to speak, is imbued in the object, it
embodies honor that can no longer be experienced as an interpersonal relation. Parents who face the demands of children to buy trendy brand names
know this very well. Seldom does the brand confer honor. Usually it enables
the child to avoid the embarrassment of not owning the item.

   To better understand this, we must look at a parallel to the Marxist concept of fetishism that Veblen develops. This parallel is visible in Veblen's
analysis of the way conspicuous consumption replaces conspicuous leisure as
the dominant display of wealth. Despite his popular identification with the
concept of status, Veblen actually sees his time as an era of the decay of the
"regime of status."[20] In this regime of status, wealth is displayed not just by
material possessions (conspicuous consumption) but by the whole conduct
and social life of the individual person (conspicuous leisure). An individual's
manners, education, servants, parties hosted—all display the liberation from
the need to occupy oneself in productive labor.

   Veblen is well aware of the decay of manners in his time but unlike the
standard gentlemen critics of the phenomenon, Veblen sees an economic
cause for it. His explanation is that conspicuous leisure is more serviceable in
traditional communities, where the relevant social sphere consists of acquain-
tances and neighbors, to whom the elaborate conduct of conspicuous leisure
can be addressed. In the modern and anonymous urban society, the situation
is quite different. Here the addressees of display consist of total strangers and

alienated neighbors. In such contexts it is clear that possessions, and not social conduct, are the more efficient way to display wealth. Thus possession of conspicuous goods becomes "an ordinary means of decency."[21]

In cultural terms, the replacement of conspicuous leisure by conspicuous consumption represents a transition from the image of old money to that of new money. Conspicuous leisure explains one unchanging characteristic of the long-lasting cultural trope of old money, namely, its inimitability. Jean Moliere's *The Bourgeois Gentleman*, to name a classic representation of this theme, draws its comic effect from the failed attempts of Mr. Jourdain, the son of a rich merchant, to learn the ways of aristocracy (dance, music, fencing, clothing). Veblen provides the economic key to this theme. In a regime of status, informed by conspicuous leisure, the conduct of aristocracy is by definition inimitable. It is based on gestures whose function is to display leisure and thus by necessity require an investment of effort through time. The shift to conspicuous consumption in urban industrial societies is a shift of emphasis to the culture of new money, which requires no effort, but only possessions, for the display of wealth and power.

The novelty of Veblen's idea emerges if we foster, to its paradoxical conclusions, the notion that the object of conspicuous consumption is addressed to strangers. That is, if we adopt it together with the impossibility engrained in it: strangers cannot be impressed or, at least, one can hardly experience the impression one leaves on strangers.

This detachment from the level of experience links Veblen's view of conspicuous consumption with Marx's fetishism. As with Marx's notion of fetishism, relations between people are replaced here by things. And, moreover, things in both cases occupy that aspect of social life that cannot be fully subjectivized. Note that this replacement again touches the radical kernel of Veblen's thought. The relation of esteem between specific people is replaced with a relation with indefinite others. But for this replacement to take place, from the beginning the relation of esteem must not have been simply a pure interpersonal relation. Veblen is well aware of this as he claims that the esteem of others is an element in a person's relation to oneself:

[T]he usual basis of self-respect is the respect accorded by one's neighbours. Only individuals with an aberrant temperament can in the long run retain their self-esteem in the face of the disesteem of their fellows.[22]

Setting aside the sense of psychological intuition, one can identify in this formulation a notion of the social, not as merely interpersonal but as grounded upon a split within the economic subject.

The social is situated in the subject's relation to self as it is mediated through others. But what is more important is that in the context of Veblen's theory of conspicuous consumption, it becomes not just a theory of the subject but also a theory of the economic object. In this view the object embodies the split in the subject: it stands in the place of the subject's relation to self through the abstract other. This is Veblen's way to account for the social nature of property: the relation of private property consists not only of a person and an object but also of society as it is represented in the object.

This claim again displays Veblen's distance from orthodox economic thought. In the economic understanding of Veblen, the object of conspicuous consumption grants the individual some advantage in relations with others (status). But the idea of the object as addressed to strangers suggests that it is actually the other way around. The object that appears to represent the subject for society is, in fact, an invidious representative of society in the intimate space of the subject.

Commodity as One's Relation to Oneself

This status of the object is exemplified in two symmetrical patterns of car commercials. Many car commercials revolve around the gaze of other people at one's new car. However, this gaze is often set within two parallel patterns that transpose it in two mirroring ways. In the first pattern, the gaze is asymmetric—the driver does not return a gaze to the envious gazes at the car. In the second pattern, the gaze is indeed returned, but in various ways we learn that the car itself is a fake.

An example of the first category is a commercial for Peugeot 307, which begins with a series of scenes in streets filled with invisible cars (we can see the people riding in the cars as if the cars are perfectly transparent). No car is actually seen until a 307 enters the frame and cruises between the invisible vehicles, its own driver perfectly hidden behind the dark windows. The transparency of all the surrounding cars represents the fact that the gaze of all the envious watchers is not being returned by the driver of the 307.

In another commercial of this type, the owner of a Peugeot 307 confronts a series of minor accidents that jeopardize the integrity of his new car, but the people suspected of causing these accidents have their gazes turned elsewhere, as if unaware of his presence (e.g., the bar at the parking gate goes down too soon and hits his roof top but as he turns to look at the booth, we see the operator engrossed in his newspaper).

Finally, a perfect example of this pattern is a Peugeot 307 commercial that demonstrates the car's spaciousness by depicting it as unrealistically huge, as high as a small building. The clip comprises a sequence of gazes: we see the passers-by look up in wonder at the huge car as it travels slowly through the streets; then, we see the car from their point of view. The driver himself is left unseen, but his gaze is represented as we see what he looks at: big advertising boards, tall monuments, and the upper floors of buildings. This composition of gazes emphasizes the one absent gaze around which the commercial is organized, namely, the returning gaze from the driver to the passers-by who look up in wonder at the car. This absence poses a challenge: if what the commercial is promoting is the promise that *everyone will look up at you*, then why is this social situation left unacknowledged?

This challenge is highlighted by the second pattern of commercials, where the gaze of others is acknowledged, but the price for it is that the car itself is unreal. An example of this second type is a commercial for Renault Clio where a young man on a scooter feels constantly ignored. Stopping at a red light, he notices two young women looking seductively at him but then understands that they literally see through him as they flirt with a Clio driver who stopped by his side. In the final scene of the clip, we see him in a new Clio, exchanging gazes with another young woman at a street light, but then we find out that his car is actually made of cardboard that he cut from an advertising board. Similarly, in a commercial for Peugeot 206, we see a young person in India smashing his car until it has the general shape of a 206. In the final scene, we see him cruise the streets in his ridiculously remodeled car, exchanging voluptuous gazes with young girls.

Taken together, these two symmetric patterns perfectly demonstrate the relation of the object to disavowed social relations. The object stands for the social that cannot be reduced to interpersonal relations. If the car is real, it cannot partake in an interpersonal interaction; if an interpersonal interaction occurs, the car is not real.

We should not miss the haunting dimension of the social as it appears in these commercials. Their organizing principle and their twisted promise is *you will be looked at without you noticing it*. It is a principle we usually attribute to social discipline rather than to consumption. But this is a logical outcome of Veblen's idea of the object of display addressed to strangers. Since strangers cannot be addressed, the real meaning of the display is its opposite: observation. The object of display is in truth a representative of the gaze of society upon us. It is no coincidence that the huge 307 ends with an image of surveillance. The absent gaze—the returning gaze from the driver to the passers-by—is indirectly represented in the commercial by a substitute. The last thing that we see the driver view is an advertising board with a big photo of a feminine face that appears to stare directly at him.

Symbol as Thing

There is a decisive proof that shows that Veblen would have understood brand names better than modern economists do. *The Theory of the Leisure Class* displays Veblen's awareness of a basic feature of brand name economy that orthodox economics cannot digest. Recalling Chapter 3, the basic misunderstanding of economics in relation to brand names is its inability to account for the possibility of a symbol becoming a thing. As Sowell put it, brand names are a "way of economizing on scarce knowledge,"[23] in which the symbol attests to the quality of the thing. As I argued in the previous chapter, this explanation is actually built upon an ignorance of the peculiar reality of the brand name. In a typical brand name, the symbol does not testify to the quality of the product but, rather, is a part of the product itself.

Veblen does not write about brands, but his whole system in *The Theory of the Leisure Class* displays awareness of a similar reversal in which the symbol itself replaces that which it came to symbolize.

> Decorum set out with being symbol and pantomime and with having utility only as an exponent of the facts and qualities symbolised; but it presently suffered the transmutation which commonly passes over symbolical facts in human intercourse. Manners presently came, in popular apprehension, to be possessed of a substantial utility in themselves; they acquired a sacramental character, in great measure independent of the facts which they originally prefigured.[24]

Again, one has to bracket the tone of popular psychology in the above quotation to see its theoretical core. This is actually a proposition that explicates the ontology of economic entities in Veblen's conspicuous economy. A symbol—any product or practice that testifies to wealth, leisure, and so on—becomes an economic entity only when it substantializes into a thing of its own merit. This reversal is valid for all the examples Veblen uses in *The Theory of the Leisure Class.*

Thus Veblen's thought is in fact based on the blind spot of orthodox economic thought in relation to the modern consumption economy. It is no accident, then, that his thought remains undigested by economics. Thus, the same Sowell summarizes a lexical entry on Veblen with a disparaging note: "It is difficult to see how economics as it exists today is any different from what it would have been had there been no Thorstein Veblen. Still, he had his time in the sun."[25] Factually, of course this is true. Yet this proposition can register not just Veblen's marginality in economics but also the inability of orthodox economics to come to terms with the fundamentals of Veblen's thought.

Veblenian Theory of the Brand

Veblen can actually provide us with a new way to theorize brand names. His method is best portrayed by reference to two other ways that I would term, somewhat simplistically, as economic and post-modernist. Post-modernist explanations of brand names are those based on the idea that in contemporary culture, images and symbols have taken on a life of their own. The key is Baudrillard's concept of simulacra and the hyper-real, which refers to a reality in which simulations exist and proliferate independently, without reference to prior, pre-symbolic, reality.

In this framework we can insert also the brand name: a symbol that is sold and bought for its own sake, without referring to a prior, *real* utility. A closer look at this conception explains why economics rejects it. The terminology of simulacra tends to the boundless reproduction and multiplication of signs and symbols. But for that very reason, a simulacrum cannot be conceived of as a commodity. It lacks the basic trait that makes something into an economic entity: because it is effortlessly reproducible, it cannot be conceived through the notion of scarcity, which is so central to economics. It is for that reason that economics automatically turns to find a real trait beyond the symbol—to see the symbol as attesting to the quality of the thing, as in Sowell's explanation.

At first glance it may appear as if these are the only two possibilities: the brand is either the symbol or the reality to which the symbol refers. Veblen's theory of "symbolical facts" suggests a third option, that of the real symbol.

In his thought, we find the idea that there is a level of reality beyond the symbol, but this reality is not utility, which allegedly explains the cost of the symbol, but rather it is the cost itself. That is what lies at the heart of Veblen's theory: a notion of a costly symbol, that is, of a symbol that cannot be indefinitely reproduced because it is costly. The symbolical facts he analyzes are all costly but can become economic entities insofar as their symbol does not refer directly to its cost.

Adapting this idea to the realm of brand names, we can see in it an option that combines elements from both the post-modernist and the economic approaches. With the former it shares the idea that the brand item is fundamentally symbolic, that is, that it consists of symbols that do not refer to a prior level of reality. With the latter it shares the need to indicate the manner in which the reproduction of symbols is limited or, in other words, to point out the parallel to the *material substance* with regard to brand names. In strict opposition to this economic approach, the Veblenian framework suggests that the dimension of real qualities beyond the symbol is not the properties of the product but its price. Thus, it places the brand name at the center of an anti-utilitarian view based on a concept of waste. It suggests that what guarantees the authenticity of the brand symbol and limits its reproducibility includes, among other things, its price. And price, being a quality of the thing, signifies a dimension of pure waste.

At this stage we can finally account for the function of the pervasive imagery of the sublime in the contemporary consumer economy. The Veblenian outlook identifies the sublime as the other side of waste. A thing is genuinely wasteful insofar as it appears sublime. Maybe this is the deep-seated reason why advertising, as the scene where brand names are actually produced, is suffused with images of the sublime. The prolific advertising line of Stella Artois beer perfectly demonstrates this connection between waste and the sublime. These commercials display the irrational efforts and losses people are willing to endure to enjoy their Artois.

In one commercial a bartender in a train disconnects his restaurant wagon from the rest of the train for the purpose of perfectly pouring a glass of Artois for a customer. In another commercial a dyspeptic writer enters a bar to celebrate finishing a novel, but his money suffices only for a regular beer and not for an Artois. So he pays the bartender with the manuscript he came to celebrate (we understand this after the fact when we see the eupeptic, silly-looking barman signing the book in a bookstore). Yet another commercial discloses explicitly the economy of the whole line: two bank robbers let their sack of banknotes burn to ashes rather than extinguish the fire with the glasses of Artois that they poured to celebrate the successful robbery.

What is the logic alluded to in these commercials? A superficial reading would claim: to demonstrate the better quality of Stella Artois, the commercials show the efforts people make to have it. The problem with this superficial interpretation is that it rests on equivalence (better quality demands a higher price, as the recurring slogan says: *perfection has its price*); however, the rigid pattern of these commercials resides in the way they escape any equivalence. They are built around a series of upset equivalencies: on the one hand, Stella Artois is better than other beers and thus more expensive; on the other hand, the experience of the beer is of an incomparably higher worth than its price. In other words, the commercials state: Artois is expensive (in relation to other beers) because it is cheap (in relation to its own quality).

Veblen's thought provides an economic logic that is appropriate to this paradoxical formula. Artois commercials illustrate the category of what money cannot buy, exemplified most explicitly by the image of burning money. The commercials associate waste and the sublime in two complementary ways, one symbolic and one real. On the symbolic level, this association is the explicit content of the commercials: some sublime quality or an extraordinary event (the perfect way to serve a beer, the life work of an agonizing writer) upsets all calculation and justifies a grand gesture of waste (disconnecting the wagon, giving up the fruits of a life's work). Indeed, it is the grand gesture of waste that portrays the events and actions as sublime (the successful robbery becomes a noble achievement when it justifies the annihilation of the thing robbed).

This symbolic depiction of waste is complemented by a real sense of waste if we take into account the commercials aim to transform the price of Artois into its unique quality. This is actually the correct way to read the recurrent slogan of perfection has its price. It is not that one pays more for good beer, but rather that expensiveness is part of the experience. It is, so to speak, what gives the beer its taste. The price is not paid for the supreme qualities of the beer but is itself the epitome of its supreme quality.

It is this effect of the commercials that can explain the strange fact that the price occupies such a strategic position in this line of advertising. In a naive conception of advertising, price is what should eventually be suppressed:

because advertisers aim to manipulate us to part from our money, it seems they should convince us that an item has superb qualities. Here the procedure is reversed. What the commercials suggest is: pay the unjustifiably high price and, thus, you will know that you celebrate an extraordinary moment. This is the reason why the commercials are constructed mainly out of acts of exchange. They do not really represent a suspension of economic calculation. Rather, they represent an economy of radically upset equivalencies, centered on the notion of buying what money cannot buy.

Further evidence in favor of this interpretation is found in a new and minimalist line of commercials of Artois. These commercials do not contain a narrative but comprise a single gesture accompanied by the famous slogan. For example, a bottle of Artois stands on a table; a white-gloved hand enters the frame and gives the bottle a slight turn to achieve a perfectly straight position; then, the old slogan appears: *perfection has its price*. The point in these commercials is that what makes the beer perfect is something foreign to the immediate experience of drinking beer. It is found in doing it *correctly*—in the ritualistic form of consuming the beer (which includes the correct way to put it on the table, etc.). The point is that by being merely slight modifications, these gestures represent an infinite progression into an unreachable end (there is always one more slight correction to improve the experience).

The Veblenian perspective introduced here enables us to point to a concrete equivalent to this unreachable end, that is, the price mentioned in conjunction with the corrective gesture. Strictly speaking, price cannot be a part of the experience and, therefore, occupies the same structural place as the correct manner represented in the commercials as a horizon that is radically external to the immediate experience of beer yet that gives it its meaning. On a more abstract level, we can formulate thusly: in Veblen's thought the economy of display is actually defined by its externality to the sphere of experience (the economic cause is the one that the actor cannot recount as an explanation of his act). Thus, the slight gesture that points to an unreachable end can be understood as actually pointing to waste as the ultimate economic, impersonal cause of consumption.

Veblen and Marx: Money Old and New

John Patrick Diggins finds a fundamental contrast between Marx and Veblen. Veblen, he claims, could indeed sympathize with Marx's moral indignation toward capitalism. According to Diggins, Veblen was also perhaps "the only

American social scientist of the nineteenth century who was intellectually pre-pared to challenge the economic theories of Karl Marx on their own terms." Yet despite this intellectual and critical proximity, Diggins sees a fundamental dis-parity between their respective theories of the nature of history. Veblen, Diggins claims, could not accept Marx's Hegelian conception of history: "Veblen and Marx subscribed to two contrasting philosophies of history, the Darwinian and the Dialectical."[26] Veblen indeed promoted an evolutionary approach to the economy. But the intriguing point is that by incorporating symbols, or what he called symbolical facts, in his evolutionary view, he actually arrived at a concep-tion of history much closer to Marx than may appear at first sight.

This proximity becomes apparent if we set aside the different grand nar-ratives of both thinkers and focus instead on a prior philosophical question regarding history: the question of historicity. When it comes to history as a narrative, Veblen and Marx seem to focus their attention on different aspects of economy and history: Veblen constructs a grand conjectural narrative that stretches from prehistoric humankind to the present, organized according to some basic principles of the articulation of power relations through symbolic modes of consumption.

Marx, by contrast, elaborated a narrative of narrower time spans and focused on the organization of production. However, with regard to both thinkers, the grand narratives of economy imply notions of the historicity of economic entities, of their being embedded in history and of the way history is embedded in them. To be sure, this is what is at stake in Veblen's idea of in-stitutional economy. Institution does not refer simply to persistence over time but also to persistence as a specific mode of existence to things whose mode of being is institutional. At this preliminary question of historicity, we find a surprising proximity between Marx and Veblen.

We should recall Marx's argument against the economists; that for them, "there has been history, but there is no longer any."[27] This should be read not just negatively as a critique of a mistake, but also positively as pointing to the form of historicity of economic things. Social relations persist through eco-nomic things precisely by their appearance of having no past. This is the idea in Žižek's reading of fetishism in terms of repression: fetishism explains how the relations of feudal domination persist in free, capitalist societies as they are mediated through *things*, commodities. A thing perpetuates social relations by appearing as a-historical, as merely a thing.[28]

Note, first, that Veblen is immune to a Marxist critique of the a-historical form of economic thought. Veblen's thought is motivated by the way history *still is*. His theory consists in seeing the economic present as a historical time, laden with residues of the past, that can be traced in the smallest gestures that comprise its social fabric (in manners, fashion, religion, taste, social interactions, etc.). Furthermore, in Veblen's thought the economic is the pure form of the historical as the presence in absence of the past. The economic interpretation of practices, rather than sociological and anthropological explanations, presents them in their most strange facet, in a form most alien to agents, and in this sense as historical. At the heart of this historical view lies the same principle we found in Marx, namely, historicity as effacement of history. Veblen does not provide an explicit formulation of this notion of historicity, yet we can detect it in what at first sight appears as a psychological principle that is quite central to Veblen's argument: what he terms "mental substitution."

Note the function of this substitution in relation to the concept of leisure that is so central to Veblen's thought. From ancient times, he notes, a degree of leisure and exemption from productive work has been considered "as a prerequisite to a worthy or beautiful, or even a blameless, human life." This subjective value may appear as directly related to leisure, but it is actually "secondary and derivative." It is in part "the result of a mental substitution." That is to say, "the performance of labor has been accepted as a conventional evidence of inferior force; therefore it comes itself, by a mental short-cut, to be regarded as intrinsically base."[29]

Productive labor—which from a straightforward evolutionary view must have filled a central role in the life of the species—was relegated to inferiors and thus became an evidence of inferiority, and as such "intrinsically base." One should not be misled by the psychological tone of this formulation. What lies at its heart is a conceptual relation between economy and historical persistence. In this relation, a thing becomes an economic entity precisely because it persists through effacement.

Leisure in the naive sense of the term would be conceived of as a non-economic thing, as the opposite of economy. It can be considered in the realm of economy when it acquires a mandatory form—when one is obliged to display one's leisure and, therefore, toils in a host of explicitly non-productive efforts that enable this display. In this situation leisure is no longer the opposite of labor but becomes a specific type of labor. Note that here Veblen reproduces exactly Marx's recipe for historicizing the economy. An entity becomes an economic thing when it persists without its cause, when its absence of history becomes its positive property, in the shape of some sublime quality.

The apparent gap that separates Veblen and Marx results in part from the fact that they apply this basic formula of the historicity of the economy to two different, even if interpenetrating, spheres: to production and to profit making, in Marx; and to consumption and waste, in Veblen. That their views should be seen as complementary can be evidenced by the fact that they relate to the two major forms of entanglement of money with time. While Veblen can be considered the theorist of old money par excellence, Marx is the theorist of new money. But both of these *temporalities* of money refer to its social nature, and both are based on historicity as an effacement of history.

In Marx the social nature of money is grounded on its being ontologically new, as demonstrated in the previous chapters. To summarize: the misanthropic, anti-social nature of money, identified with the cultural imagery of new money, results from the absence of use value being its positive quality. It is this type of absence-as-positive quality that explains, for example, the inhuman form of capital as a movement essentially alien to any human goal. But this idea of the absence of qualities as a positive quality can be eventually sustained against the background of history as the horizon of radical absence. What sustains money in its unique position is its *mysterious nature*, which is a code name for the way it traverses time without an explanation for its unique position—that its persistence is entailed with its absence of past.

In Veblen we can find a mirror image of this idea if we read his thought as an exploration of the culture of old money. Old money practices also are sustained by a form of persistence involved with a certain effacement of the past. But in this case what is effaced is the monetary aspect itself. The unique social nature of old money consists of the way it appears unrelated to money. An expensive thing or practice can appear beautiful, noble, or sublime insofar as it does not appear as simply expensive.

A perfect illustration of this relation of old money to money can be found in one of the classical literary depictions of the topic, Edith Wharton's *House of Mirth*. In the same scene in the novel where we learn that the Bart family has gone bankrupt, we also learn that the protagonist Lily Bart has exquisite taste in flowers. Lily likes to have flowers in the house at all times, and the flowers that she likes are always of the most expensive kind. However,

Wharton immediately adds that Lily knows nothing of such earthly matters as the price of flowers.

This is the position of old money: naturally choosing the most expensive commodity without being aware of its price. In relation to theory, this reflects the semi-autonomous status that the practices of the leisure class hold by necessity as conspicuous things that are appreciated as inherently noble. This detachment from the economic significance of things is a condition of their existence. Returning to literature, this necessary, semi-autonomous status of the practices of leisure tells us why Lily Bart is the prototypical representative of old money. Its full literary figuration is not a wealthy, old money person, but the person who has lost his (and, more often, her) money yet retained an exquisite taste that requires wealth.

In *The House of Mirth,* this is the key to the narrative. The father of the family makes only a short appearance in the novel. He enters to tell his wife and daughter that financially they are broke, and a few pages later he dies, leaving the two women with the task of finding a rich match for Lily, who would support their way of life. The novel progresses through a sequence of failed attempts to find such a match. Beyond the psychological explanation for the way that the beautiful Lily half-consciously sabotages these attempts is a structural necessity. The notion of old money cannot stand the exposure of the implicit monetary character of the prospective marriage: exchanging beauty and long-nurtured elegance for financial security.

At the end of the novel after a long process of deterioration, Lily finds herself in a situation where she must actually work for a living. As she is completely unqualified for work and humiliated by the need to work, she puts an end to her life, not in a very dramatic way but quite passively, just like Veblen's Polynesian chiefs, who preferred to starve rather than carry their food to their mouths with their own hands.

Economy, the Obverse of History

This shared notion of historicity is the key to the fact that despite the ostensibly wide gap in their theoretical interests, Veblen and Marx actually share a similar economic ontology, radically foreign to contemporary orthodox economics. The first component of this ontology is a direct counterpart of Veblen's and Marx's notion of historicity. The idea of economic entities as constituted by historical repression implies the notion of economy as an *other scene*: a context defined by an absent cause, a context in which the meaning of action is alien to the perspective of the agent.

In Marx we find this notion of economy already in the distinction between use value and exchange value. Use value describes the thing as it appears in common experience but, eventually, its economic destiny is governed by considerations of exchange value that are alien to its use value. The first four chapters of *Capital* can be read as a conceptual-historical analysis of how this initial gap unfolds to encompass the whole of the capitalist economy: it is the key to the foreignness of money—for example, as an object that carries alienation and spreads with social alienation—and consequently this foreignness of money is the key to its turning into capital as embodying a drive resistant to subjectivization.

In Veblen we can construct this conceptual connection from his view of institutions:

> Institutions are products of the past process, are adapted to past circumstances, and are therefore never in full accord with the requirements of the present.[30]

This is not an empirical observation regarding social institutions but can be read as the definition of the form of institutional persistence. Institutions are by definition never in accord with their time. That which is in full accord with its time needs neither history nor institutionalization. This is the key to the inability of orthodox economics to deal with both history and institutions. This dis-accord to the present is not some *noise* that should be reduced but comprises the very substance that Veblen explores. Economy occupies this dimension of dis-accord in its pure form.

Recall the analysis of manners. For example, whereas an anthropological explanation focuses on the element of positive continuity and on the measure institutions are still in accord with the level of experience as meaningful gestures, an economic explanation focuses on pure institutional preservation as it is entailed with the idea of absent cause and with viewing manners as a meaningless, time-consuming code of behavior.

A perfect example of the immanent relation between economy and history is found in one of Veblen's marvelous concepts, namely, the idea of *vicarious leisure*. Veblen looks at the effort that housewives and servants invest in explicitly futile actions, such as hosting according to the correct manner. These actions, he writes, might simply seem as "wasted effort." Yet the term *vicarious leisure* has "the advantage of indicating the line of derivation of these domestic offices, as well as of neatly suggesting the substantial economic ground of their utility" (i.e., the utility of a display of wealth through the consumption of leisure).[31]

First, note that the designation of the historical dimension ("line of derivation") is at the same time a designation of the economic cause. And second, this shift of focus to the historical-economic dimension involves an overturning in relation to the accepted meaning of the thing explained: what appears as an effort (the drudgery of servants and housewives) is revealed to be a form of leisure (the leisure of the master of the house). Notice that this institutional shift in the view enables an economization of leisure. First, it enables one to answer a direct economic question: What is the labor that personal servants are paid for? Second, it enables a view of leisure as an economic magnitude in the sense of an organ that runs through a system. With the term *vicarious leisure*, we see how leisure can be exchanged, transferred, and infinitely increased—just like money.

Consumption as Production

This last transformation, which turns leisure into a form of labor, reveals one more affinity of Veblen to Marx. Marx's focus on production does not entail a disregard of consumption. Rather, it is a position that views production as the ultimate theoretical perspective for explaining economic phenomena, including consumption. Thus, in *Grundrisse*, Marx stresses that only consumption completes the process of production, that is, makes the thing produced into an item of use. To recall a quote from the previous chapter: "The product only obtains its 'last finish' in consumption. A railway on which no trains run [. . .] is a railway only [in potentiality], and not in reality."[32] In *Capital* such Hegelian formulations are absent, but the incorporation of consumption as a distinct moment of production is folded inside the concept of surplus value. We can speak of surplus value only when we conceive of the laborer's consumption in terms of the reproduction of the labor force—that is, by expanding the perspective of production to cover economy as a whole.

The same topology is visible in Veblen's view of leisure, not just as the opposite of labor but also as a specific type of labor. The concept that best captures this idea is the concept that came to define Veblen's later work, namely, the *instinct of workmanship*. At first glance, this concept might seem to be one that is the most distant from the economics of leisure and waste. That is how it first appears in *The Theory of the Leisure Class*:

> [Man] is an agent seeking in every act the accomplishment of some concrete, objective, impersonal end. By force of his being such an agent he is possessed of a taste for effective work, and a distaste for futile effort. He has a sense of the merit of serviceability or efficiency and of the demerit of futility, waste, or incapacity. This aptitude or propensity may be called the instinct of workmanship.[33]

This invocation of instinct displays Veblen's Darwinist orientation. However, it also shows why we should not take his commitment to evolution at face value. The strange point is that by committing to evolution as a necessary theoretical framework, Veblen arrives at a species of history.

The point is that the *instinct of workmanship* is not posited as a biological determinant or as having substantial content. Unlike evolutionary biology, this instinct is not related to specific habits and capabilities that are accounted for by the demands of survival. Rather, Veblen uses the evolutionary horizon as the background of a problem that calls for a solution. His typical question is this: Assuming the need of survival, how is it that humankind has come to *dislike* work? This is the starting point of an early article by Veblen, "The Instinct of Workmanship and the Irksomeness of Labor." It begins with the question of how could the assumption of economics that "[m]an *instinctively* revolts at effort that goes to supply the means of life" be settled with the need of the race to develop habits of survival.[34]

The answer Veblen provides in this article prefigures the type of argumentation that he later uses in *The Theory of the Leisure Class*. In the article Veblen provides a conjectural narrative of transformation wherein competitive and invidious sociability leads to a shift in the manifestation of this instinct so that productive work is eventually assigned to the weak and avoidance from it becomes prized. At this stage we can already figure out how commitment to an evolutionary thought leads Veblen to a theory of history. By incorporating also *symbolical facts*, as the identification of certain labors with the weak, in an evolutionary framework, Veblen fundamentally divorces humankind from nature and posits it in a state of constant disaccord with its surroundings.

The full importance of this principle of thought seems to be realized in the context of *The Theory of the Leisure Class*. The instinct is posited here as objective and impersonal yet without holding any determinate biological content. Its objectivity is an aspect of the radical externality of the economic perspective. It is not revealed through certain unchanging habits of the human animal. Rather, it is retroactively constituted through the fact of change. The ultimate meaning of this instinct is that with the progress of civilization, humanity does not turn to leisure in its narrow sense, as opposed to labor, but directs its excesses to the occurrence of leisure as a form of labor.

Dispossession and Ownership

A further disagreement that Diggins finds in Veblen and Marx relates to their respective theories of the source of ownership. Veblen, he claims, was more informed of anthropological findings, and he had perhaps a keener grasp of the problem of private property. In addition, he claims, Veblen's belief in science and the theory of biological evolution made him hostile to Hegelian-Marxist categories of understanding. Thus, in contrast with the Marxist view of alienation as the source of private property, Veblen sees women as the original form of property: the beginning of ownership is located, according to him, in the captivity of women following conflicts between archaic hordes. Again, this dissimilarity obscures a deeper affinity of Veblen and Marx.

Indeed Veblen provides a conjectured historical narrative of the beginning of ownership, whereas Marx's analysis of the relation between alienation and private property is mainly conceptual. However, a closer look at Veblen's historical narrative reveals within it the very conceptual kernel that Marx explicitly formulates: both thinkers recognize a need to include a certain form of dispossession as a necessary moment in ownership. Marx states this more explicitly when he argues that in contrast to commonsense, we should see alienation as prior to private property. As noted in Chapter 1, this idea is formulated by Marx as a logical inference: "if the product of the labor does not belong to the worker [. . .] this is only possible in that it belongs to another man."[35] In other words, "not belonging to someone else" is seen as logically prior to belonging to someone. This relation is brought to an extreme in Marx's claim, in his "Comments on James Mill," of how private property eventually alienates also its proprietor: "we ourselves are excluded from true property because our property excludes other men."[36]

This last remark brings us directly to Veblen. Why does he come up with his speculation about captive women as the original form of property? The background for it is his insistence on conceiving of property as always social—not a social institution that somehow springs from mere individualist possession of things. And in this essentially social framework of thought about property, women can serve as an original form precisely because they cannot be simply possessed.

Consider the theory, presented in an early article of Veblen's entitled "The Beginning of Ownership." Veblen's point of reference is the Lockean notion that ownership is based on productive work: a person creates a thing and the thing becomes his property. In reference to this age-old story, Veblen notes that the idea of an individual producer cannot but be a fiction, a projection of our own concepts of private property unto the past. Any form of production, he claims, is always social. Furthermore, ownership cannot originate from a direct relation of a person to an object. Regarding the savage, Veblen writes:

> [T]he relation of any individual to his personal effects is conceived to be of a more intimate kind than that of ownership simply. Ownership is too external and colorless a term to describe the fact.[37]

For the savage, his effects seem to him to be part of his own person.

This claim can be formulated using a distinction between ownership and possession. In modern legal terms possession is a weaker relationship than ownership. However, there is a sense in which it can be seen the other way around. Ownership can be seen as weaker in the sense that it is socially mediated and not an intimate, immediate relation to an object—different from primitive possession, where a thing can be included within the "quasi-personal fringe of facts and objects," which includes man's shadow, his name, as well as his personal effects. (In this terminology we would say that the youth fashion of displaying the logo of underwear represents a widening of the logic of ownership, which dispossesses the individual from his most intimate belongings. Even their underwear is not immediately theirs.)

So how does ownership emerge out of this immediate primitive possession? Veblen locates its origin, and actually the origin of economy itself, outside the realm of production and sustenance. Veblen finds ownership in the barbarian culture of fight, coercion, and seizure. It begins with women being taken captive. These women "serve the purpose of trophies very effectually," and they become "insignia of [their captor's] prowess." Later, this first form of ownership, of people, extends to things—the objects that the woman captive produces. Beyond the specifics of this barbarian story, its crucial point is the reason why women break the circle of intimate, immediate possession: "These captives continue to be obviously distinct from their captor in point of individuality, and so are not readily brought in under the quasi-personal fringe."[38] That is, the first form of property emerges with the object that cannot be had, cannot be directly possessed. In this way, Veblen's concept of ownership reproduces the two elements of Marx's concept: private property is in the first place *not of others* (women as insignia of prowess, addressed to others), and it is marked by an element of disowning its owner (women that cannot be had).

Erotic Economy

Naturally, one can dismiss Veblen's speculation about the origin of private property in the ownership of women just as easily as today we dismiss its Lockean double that grounds property in labor. However, there is a crucial difference between the two. The Lockean narrative fully deserves the designation of myth in that it projects the present into a lost past and, thus, brings about a naturalization of the present. It finds in the past the image of an archaic man, who already possesses a fully developed, modern idea of private property. Veblen's narrative, be it true or false, can be considered a historical one, in that it performs the opposite procedure: it finds in the past a radically foreign reality that can serve as a starting point to denaturalize the present. It names as an original form what to our eyes appears as a perversion of ownership—ownership of people as prior to ownership of things. Its test, therefore, is not simply in finding historical or pre-historical evidence that support it. It should be tested against the present according to the way it enables us to find in our own institution of property vestiges of this foreign past. That is what Veblen does in *The Theory of the Leisure Class* where he points to so many traces of the barbarian past in the most refined circles of aristocratic culture.

The book recurrently turns to the economic role of the woman in the household: the way the wife consumes in place of her husband, the head of the household; the way her conspicuous leisure is shown to function as a mechanism to increase the husband's consumption of leisure. However, the best evidence for the persistence of the connection between women and property is found, not in the aristocratic edge of the economic spectrum but in its opposite, in poor households that complete the circle, where the wife embodies dispossession as the most persistent characteristic of property. In those families, "there is assuredly no conscious attempt at ostensible leisure," yet "decency still requires the wife to consume some goods conspicuously for the reputability of the household and its head."

> [A]s the latter-day outcome of this evolution of an archaic institution, the wife, who was at the outset the drudge and chattel of the man, both in fact and in theory [. . .] has become the ceremonial consumer of goods which he produces. But she still quite unmistakably remains his chattel in theory; for the habitual rendering of vicarious leisure and consumption is the abiding mark of the unfree servant.[39]

Theory survives the fact. This is a good description of institutional history. In fact, it seems that the wife is now the opposite of property because she spends in spite of the household's apparent material deprivation. Yet this is the evidence that she embodies the institutional kernel of ownership, that is, that element in it that contrasts our conceptions of ownership, that moment that persists in opposition to our conceptions.

To put it bluntly: the man who has close to nothing still has his wife to disown him. Her small gesture of waste is the last remnant of property the household still clings to. Whereas some might see this argument as a chauvinist fantasy, Veblen is actually a radical feminist because he sees private property, the most ubiquitous, and seemingly neutral, social institution as gendered. His thought implies that feminism cannot stop short of a critique of the institution of private property.

Is this speculation relevant to the contemporary consumer economy? To see how, we should turn our gaze from real families to the role of women in the phantasmatic scene of consumption in advertising. The blunt fact is that in advertising, a woman, much more than a man, can still appear as the equivalent of a product. A commercial for Jaguar cars perfectly demonstrates this. The advertisement is constructed around the adjective *gorgeous* that accompanies a series of scenes that alternates between images of enchanting, gorgeous young women (at a fancy dinner party, on a yacht, in bed, etc.) and briefer images focused on Jaguar cars. An announcer reads lines that accompany the images and refer to the absolute uniqueness of the women (or cars): "Gorgeous demands your immediate attention. Gorgeous makes effort look effortless. Gorgeous stays up late and still looks gorgeous. Gorgeous has no love for logic, gorgeous loves fast. Everyone cares what gorgeous says [. . .]

Gorgeous can't be ordinary even if it tries [. . .] Gorgeous doesn't care what others are doing. Gorgeous was born that way."

We are well inside the aristocratic imagery of old money: the inimitable quality, the irresistible overpowering beauty, the *natural* feel of elegance. Simplistic as it may seem, perhaps this commercial should not be explained along the lines of manipulation, as unconsciously persuading the consumer: *buy the car and you shall get the girl* (that is how Seth Stevenson contemptuously interpreted it in *Slate*).[40] One problem in this line of interpretation is that it is mediated through an idiot consumer who believes that buying the car would bring him the girl. (Although it might be correct to say that as consumers we are idiots in some way or another, summoning the idiot as mediating the *message* is a poor interpretative technique.)

A different interpretation would say that the young women appear in the commercial as unreachable. They mark the unreachable element in the Jaguar luxury car, which makes it a supreme form of private property. That is, rather than signifying *buy the car and you will get the girl*, the women in the commercial signify *even if you buy the car you cannot really have it*.

This interpretation is actually almost tautological. The advertising formula of associating a car and a girl is based on the assumption that it is impossible to sell an expensive car simply by offering its properties as a car. Something must be added that surpasses its car-properties. Thus the girl signifies that which one does not acquire simply in having the car. But that is another way of saying that the women in the commercial mark the element of dispossession within ownership.

The formula of advertising a car by directly associating it with a woman is now rarely used in such a blunt manner as in the Jaguar commercial. It is no accident that it resurfaces in the context of luxury amidst images of aristocratic social life. That is perhaps the central point of Veblen's book: in an economic context, the fact that something appears as refined culture means that its barbaric kernel is no longer directly visible. The refined culture of high society is nothing but the form of persistence through repression of the barbaric kernel of direct power relations.

The Double Fantasy of the Prostitute

The triangle of woman-ownership-dispossession can further be situated within a peculiar phantasmatic construct that surrounds the most explicit form of woman as property, namely the prostitute. Kitschy representations of the prostitute often include a surprising fantasy: one can either have sex with the prostitute without paying or pay without having sex. This double construct is perfectly exemplified in Billy Wilder's *Irma La Douce*. The protagonist Nestor (Jack Lemmon) is a hapless Parisian cop who is fired and then accidentally defeats a pimp in a fistfight in a bar. Consequently, the beautiful prostitute Irma (Shirley MacLaine) falls in his arms and, seemingly against his will, she makes him her new pimp and takes him into her bed and home, where they live like a romantic bourgeois couple.

This is the first half of the fantasy—sleeping with the prostitute without paying—but it does not stop here. Soon enough Nestor becomes jealous of Irma's clients. To keep them away, he secretly starts working at night as a hauler in the market to maintain their household. But the money he earns must enter the account through Irma, whose self-identity is centered on supporting her man. Therefore, he impersonates an impotent English lord who pays generously for her company, without even touching her, and thus frees her from the need to see real clients. He becomes so exhausted from his secret life that he is too tired to have sex with Irma as Nestor. This twist completes the first phantasmatic construct with the other half: paying the prostitute without sleeping with her.

Obviously the psychoanalytic Madonna-whore duality has much to do with this fantasy. The prostitute who does not take money embodies the two poles of this duality in one person: she is the despised woman, the whore, and yet since offering herself for free is the ultimate gift, she embodies also a character of maternal compassion. However, what this psychoanalytic framework does not explain is the central place of money in the fantasy. All the characters' positions and their interrelation are defined through exchanges and money (who can give money to whom and who cannot; what can be given instead of money, etc.).

This function of money has no clear explanation in the psychoanalytic framework because in Freud's elaboration of this duality, the whore is not necessarily a prostitute but simply a despicable woman.[41] An image of a prostitute as an emblem for a wretched woman is simply taken for granted by him. However, it is at this level of obvious truths, of the mute presence of property relations within gender relations that Veblen's institutional economics can shed light. From this perspective the truly obscene aspect of the film is revealed when it is viewed not as a fantasy about women and sex but as an erotic fantasy about private property.

A version of Veblen's notion of primitive ownership surfaces in the first half of the fantasy. Sleeping with the prostitute without paying puts her in the position that Veblen ascribed to captive women, namely, as a mark of distinction of one man in comparison with others. Furthermore, while the first half of the fantasy articulates the primitive layer of direct ownership of women, the second half represents its repressed, refined double. Here the gendered property relation appears in the image of a woman that cannot be had—the chaste prostitute who is paid for not having sex.

A more artistic treatment of this kitschy theme is found in a play *The Whore from Ohio* by the prominent, late Israeli playwright Hanoch Levin. The old beggar Hoybitter dreams of having sex with the prostitute Bronatzatzky for his seventieth birthday. He pays her but fails to accomplish the act. Later she comes to his room and pretends to confess her great love for him. Now his desire is aroused, but the prostitute takes advantage of the situation and runs off with his treasured life savings.

The play's title refers to an interesting interlude that transposes the scenario into an explicit fantasy. Hoybitter's son, the beggar Hoymar, tries to persuade his father to give up his lascivious dreams and concentrate on activities more appropriate to his age like going to the synagogue and praying. The father, in reply, starts to recount aloud a detailed fantasy that gradually grips his son. It is the fantasy about the whore from Ohio who is so rich that she doesn't need men, and the most they can hope for is to stand by the gate of her estate and look at the post box and "rub" until the huge, black guard comes to throw them away like a floor rag. The whore who is too rich to need clients is the ultimate representation of wealth as an impersonal social reality.

Levin's play is important in the way it steps out of the kitschy fantasy of the goodhearted whore. When Bronatzatzky the prostitute deceitfully confesses her love for Hoybitter in order to steal his money, she allows Levin to unravel the economic infrastructure of the fantasy. The play shows how love is actually produced by the fantasy's avoidance of the exchange of sex for money. It points our attention to the weird positioning of Wilder's fantasy: the movie is located in the marginal social scene of crime and prostitution in Paris, but the love story of Irma and Nestor is actually steeped in a comfortable, almost lustless bourgeois form, centered in the domestic life of the couple, their room, their double bed, and their strolls in the park.

History as a Sub-species of Evolution

Veblen's Darwinian tendency is often mentioned.[42] Veblen was also a self-proclaimed evolutionist, and one of his early criticisms of economics was that it is not an evolutionary science.[43] However, as contemporary economists adopt—sometimes unknowingly—evolutionary lines of thought, an opportunity arises to re-inspect Veblen's alleged Darwinian approach. The striking feature is that as economists implement evolutionary thinking, they actually highlight the principal difference of Veblen's thought from orthodox economics. A stark similarity between economics and evolutionary thought is found in the resemblance of the relatively new economic concept of *signaling* to the evolutionary concept of *handicap principle*. We consider both concepts.

The concept of signaling refers to qualities that are economically valued not for themselves but as signals of other qualities. In the article that eventually brought the concept to the center of attention, Michael Spence introduces signaling through the problematic situation of the job market, where employers take risks when hiring people whose capabilities they cannot be sure of. Spence points to a mechanism that allows *signals*, such as education, to attest to the capabilities of a prospective employee, without being directly related to those capabilities.

At the heart of these mechanisms lies the notion of a costly, unproductive signal. For such signals to function, it must be that "the costs of signaling are negatively correlated with productive capability."[44] That is to say, if a certain signal, such as education, would entail a higher cost from less capable people, then incapable people would not bother to achieve it in the first place. In such a situation, it is likely that a candidate who holds the appropriate credentials is also a capable person, even if his or her education appears irrelevant to the job. Even if the education does not contribute to the person's professional capabilities, the fact that one had bothered to accomplish it signals that he or she already has these capabilities.

The interesting thing is that this argument is independently yet exactly reproduced in the field of evolutionary biology in Amotz Zahavi's handicap principle (published only two years after Spence's article). The most famous example of this principle is the peacock's tail. Why does the male peacock have such a magnificent and awkward tail that seriously harms its capability to evade predators? The answer according to the handicap principle is that the peacock has a heavy and conspicuous tail to display its capability to lift such a heavy tail—that is, to attest to its strength. This indeed harms his chances of escaping predators, but it enhances his charm for female peacocks, programmed in an evolutionary manner to seek a strong mate.[45]

The basic principle is identical in both the economic and the evolutionary mechanisms. Something enters the sphere of the sign only insofar as it is costly and in a way superfluous. To function as a signal, the education must be costly without improving the capabilities of the worker just as the tail harms the functioning of the peacock. This redundancy or arbitrariness of the signal suggests that we are dealing here with a biological theory of the sign. And indeed the strongest similarity between the theories is that both eventually produce a *veritable sign*—a sign that cannot deceive, a sign that necessarily attests to the presence of the thing signified.

Naturally, this is also the reason why these theories cannot account for the human sign, which essentially is related to a possibility of deception. We should note that this eventual inadequacy of the economic and evolutionary theories for the understanding of the human sign is not coincidental. We have already encountered it twice in this book, namely, in Adam Smith's conception of the coin symbol and in the conception of the brand name in contemporary economics. Both are aimed at producing a symbol as material, infallible evidence for something else and for that reason, both eventually overlook the unique reality of the objects concerned. In a sense, what economics fails to see is the dynamic in which the veritable sign by necessity eventually deceives: because the symbol is a veritable sign, it can eventually (or perhaps even right at the beginning) replace that which it was meant to attest to.

This dynamic, which is alien to both evolutionary biology and to economics, is central to Veblen. Note that at first glance, *The Theory of the Leisure Class* seems to foretell the basic argument of signaling and the handicap principle. Like Spence and Zahavi, Veblen develops a notion of costly, superfluous, veritable signs, which materially attest to wealth and leisure (knowledge of Latin cannot be achieved without considerable investment of effort and, thus, infallibly attests to leisure).

However, what differentiates Veblen's symbols from the veritable signs of economics and evolutionary biology is precisely their detachment from a goal. All the objects and practices that he analyzes are material evidence of wealth and leisure, but they truly become symbols when they do not signify wealth and leisure but are related to something else that is noble or sublime. Man repeats the costly gestures of the peacock without any advantage because these gestures have come to be valued for themselves.

This difference can be formulated very simply as: the handicap principle can indeed explain why the peacock's tail is heavy and conspicuous, but it cannot explain why it is beautiful. Evolutionary biologists would rightly remark that beauty is not a biological fact. But this is actually the uniqueness of Veblen's thought. In what he studies, beauty does carry a reality of its own, irreducible to the economic function that explains it. There is no sense in claiming that the female peacock sees the male's tail as beautiful. But Veblen's economy of display takes effect only if certain things genuinely look beautiful to people. And it is this partly autonomous reality of beauty that diverts conspicuous practices from being merely goal-oriented.

A good formulation for the *human difference* that Veblen stumbles upon when he attempts to apply evolutionary thought to humankind is found in Žižek's *The Parallax View*. The human being behaves as an animal but with the difference of *fully assuming* this animal role, not just performing it.

> The ultimate lesson of psychoanalysis is that human life is never "just life": humans are not simply alive, they are possessed by the strange drive to enjoy life in excess, passionately attached to a surplus which sticks out and derails the ordinary run of things.[46]

This is exactly the relation between the animal and the human surplus. The peacock's tail is actually nothing extraordinary but simply part of the normal run of things, in contrast to what the human being perceives as beautiful, which in its extreme form derails behavior from strictly functional terms. The interesting thing is that Žižek does not locate this surplus in a specific human advantage over the animal, in its being of a higher order than an animal, but rather in man's being, in a way, more animal than animal. Thus he locates the specific human impulse not in desire but in what is often considered its biological counterpart, namely, in drive.

> The paradox here is that the specifically human dimension—drive as opposed to desire—emerges precisely when what was originally a mere by-product is elevated into an autonomous aim: man is not more "reflexive" than an animal; on the contrary, man perceives as a direct goal what, for an animal, has no intrinsic value. In short, the zero-degree of "human-

ization" is not a further "mediation" of animal activity, its reinscription as a subordinated moment of a higher totality (for example, we eat and procreate in order to develop a higher spiritual potential), but the radical narrowing of focus, the elevation of a minor activity into an end in itself. We become "human" when we get caught into a closed, self-propelling loop of repeating the same gesture and finding satisfaction in it.[47]

We can find here a good formulation of the reason why Veblen's adherence to Darwinism eventually leads to a determination of the peculiar human realm of economy and history. The realm of history does not emerge through a simple dismissal of evolution but by folding into it. Costly signs, which could have been subject to evolutionary explanation, become the subject matter of institutional persistence and a historical mode of existence when they are no longer by-products but "elevated into an autonomous aim." This reading situates the sphere of historicity not in a simple contrast to evolution but as a sub-species of evolution. It can be traced in the opening lines of *The Theory of the Leisure Class*: "The upper classes are by custom exempt or excluded from industrial occupations, and are reserved for certain employments to which a degree of honour attaches."[48]

From a mechanistic perspective there is a certain redundancy in this sentence. Veblen does not refer here simply to the organization of labor and consumption between classes in an analogy, for example, to the organization of a lion pride—who does what and who gets what. He adds to this mechanistic description the redundant notion of *honor*. Of course, this addition is actually the central theme of the book. And the point is that this honor is not an additional advantage of the upper classes, aside from their preferred occupations, but a burden they carry, which converts their mechanical advantages from rights to duties: they are not simply entitled to leisure; they must at all costs perform and display their leisure—no matter how much work this requires of them.

Cautious Thoughts about Grand Narratives

Veblen's *The Theory of the Leisure Class* is not usually read as a monetary theory. In fact, the noun *money* appears only once throughout the work, in one of the last pages of the book, and, even then, it is a part of the expression "waste of money," which denotes exactly the money practices that economics cannot formalize (the words *cash* and *currency* also appear only once each). It would thus appear as a linguistic peculiarity that the related adjective *pecuniary* is one of the most frequent words in the book. It appears 285 times and qualifies a long list of things and practices: pecuniary reputability, pecuniary culture, pecuniary emulation, pecuniary comparison with other men, pecuniary standard of living, pecuniary canons of taste, pecuniary beauty, pecuniary decency, to name just a few. Taken seriously, this peculiarity suggests a theoretical perspective that crosses the distinction between money and things. Conspicuous things are, so to speak, the adjectives of money, its visible aspect. Or vice versa: money is an essentially hidden principle that governs the visibility of economic things.

To read Veblen's thesis as a monetary theory, we must recall that for him ownership is fundamentally a social, competitive relation, based on "invidious comparison." In a way, Veblen inverts the common logical order: things-private property-wealth (that is to say, people make things into their property, and property that is relatively big is wealth). Instead, he posits wealth as the inner principle of property. Property as a social institution is always about having more. An object (or a person) assumes the position of property as it fills the function of a display of excess toward others. In its essence, private property is luxury. The fact that today we also handle subsistence through private property only reflects the fact that this institution has spread to cover so many things in our world. This fact characterizes "a community where nearly all goods are private property."[49] From this perspective, the economic predicament is not simply scarcity but the fact that we satisfy needs with objects of luxury.

In a sense, this conception of ownership is a mirror image of the Marxian distinction between use value and exchange value. Common to Marx and Veblen is the idea that the economic function of a thing is determined not by its inherent qualities, but by its place in a system of objects. Exchange value is determined by a relation of one object to another object, which is essentially indifferent to the object's self-qualities.

In Veblen, similarly, an object's function as private property is determined by its relation to other objects of property. However, the similarity does not stop there. Just as this basic matrix leads Marx to elaborate the concept of capital in terms of an insatiable drive for abstract value, foreign to subjectivity and indifferent to use value, it leads Veblen to point to a parallel insatiable drive in relation to consumption:

> In the nature of the case, the desire for wealth can scarcely be satiated in any individual instance, and evidently a satiation of the average or general desire for wealth is out of the question. However widely, or equally, or "fairly" it may be distributed, no general increase of the community's wealth can make any approach to satiating this need, the ground of which is the desire of every one to excel every one else in the accumulation of goods.[50]

In Marx's concept of capital, money is a hidden principle that determines the fate of things while being indifferent to their very thingness. Things are produced or made obsolete in accordance with a drive for pure quantitative increase.

Veblen unearths a similar principle in relation to consumption. An insatiable aspect, alien to the thingness of things, governs their consumption. Money can be seen as the internal principle of consumption because it is strictly quantitative, and it has sense only in a comparative social setting—only as *more than others have*. Veblen's concept of ownership as a social institution comprises a monetary logic that predates money.

We should recall Marx's comment from the beginning of this book that greed is impossible without money since "all other kinds of accumulation and of mania for accumulation appear as primitive, restricted by needs on the one hand and by the restricted nature of products on the other."[51] This remark contrasts things and money according to the respective ways they are desired. While money can be desired indefinitely, the desire for things is restricted by their thingness. Following this logic, Veblen shows us how things can be desired *as money*, that is to say, how they can be desired indefinitely. A Patek Philippe wristwatch that costs two million dollars proves that even things can be desired beyond any limit.

Taken together, Marx and Veblen can provide us with a possible outline for a grand narrative of money as an object of desire, which should be taken with the same caution that any grand narrative warrants. In reading Marx we see how money carries with it a drive that consumes the whole economy. As an object assumes the place of money, it detaches itself from the circle of things and becomes a no-thing, which, precisely through the desire that attaches to it, annuls the thingness of all things. Under its governance all things become by-products of its endless drive of increase.

Veblen provides us with a possible complementary narrative. In Veblen's version, the principle of insatiable growth pre-exists money. The drive to *have more* is not a product of money but defines the institution of private property. The grand history he proposes is the expansion of the institution of ownership to subsume larger portions of social life. Yet these two narratives are complementary, and the differences between them result from their different perspectives and different subject matter. To begin with, Marx refers to production, whereas Veblen refers to consumption. But they also differ with reference to their perspectives on power. Whereas Marx studies how money and commodities encode power relations, Veblen explores the articulation of power: the shift between power and symbolization. Finally, whereas Marx studies the effects of money on social reality, Veblen studies practices and things that are sustained in a necessary distance from their monetary principle.

Perhaps the narrative of money could be organized around the way it is entangled with the category of what money cannot buy. Some contemporary anthropological work enables us to confer concrete content to this abstract formulation. Graeber, for example, turns to forms of *primitive* money to formulate an alternative to mainstream accounts of the origin of money. Money, he claims, originates outside the economy of subsistence of everyday life, in "transactions that economists don't like to talk about," such as marriage settlements, penalties, and blood feuds. He finds money that is reserved for such transactions, which he terms "human economy," in economies that predate the state and the market—such as that of the Iroquois or the Tiv of central Nigeria. Following the work of Philippe Rospabé, he claims that primitive money was not used for settling debts but, to the contrary, as a "way of recognizing the existence of debts that cannot possibly be paid."[52]

Exchanges of things used to satisfy daily needs are final and leave no debt behind, whereas exchanges in the realm of human economy are characterized as an ongoing obligation, an unresolvable debt. In these types of exchange, one finds specific and highly prestigious currencies that are exempt from market exchange. For the Tiv, for example, brass rods can be used to acquire a wife in an exception to the marriage rules, where only another woman can be given in exchange for a woman (a man marries his sister to the brother of the woman he wishes to marry). An important point is that because acquiring a wife in exchange for currency remains a somewhat illegitimate way, this exchange is never complete, and the husband must keep paying off the guardian of his wife forever. In this case money is entangled explicitly with what it cannot buy.

It may seem doubtful in what sense this type of social currency fully deserves the title of money. In a retrospective view, it lacks the basic feature of money as a universal means of exchange, as an object that can be exchanged for any other object. But it has the potential of becoming money, and the focal point of Graeber's view is the disastrous consequences of the realization of this potential in the encounter of human economies with developed commercial economies in the Atlantic slave trade. In the contact with European commerce, the currencies that were excluded from market exchange soon became subsumed by it and played a part in brutal enslavement.

With this transformation special currencies come closer to being money. But it can also be claimed that by becoming money, they incorporate in a market economy the category of what money cannot buy. The *noble* connotations that this notion usually carries should not mislead us. That is what Veblen taught us, that what money cannot buy is entangled with power relations and, by extension, with brute force. It appears noble to the same extent that it obscures its barbaric origin. The blood-soaked form that this connection assumed in the case of the slave trade can be seen as reflecting the swiftness of the transformation as a result of an encounter with external economies.

Graeber's narrative may seem untypical as it relates to what may appear as esoteric forms of money at a historical moment when modern money was already half-formed. But a certain parallel to it in a more euro-centric historical account of money can be found in Erica Schoenberger's broad perspective on the value of gold. In contrast to the orthodox narratives, Schoenberger claims that gold does not originate as a means of market exchange. It begins as a marker of social standing and power. Its use is reserved for higher classes, where it circulates as gifts conferring and acknowledging honor (and again, its noble nature should not mask the fact that its production demanded extraordinary social costs).

Gold gradually becomes a means of exchange when broader social circles adopt it because of the prestige attached to it. In ancient Greece, for example, this happens when emerging city-states coin gold in an attempt to gain power vis-à-vis the landed aristocracy: "the gold coins of Athens made a very public statement about where political decisions, security, and justice were now to be found."[53] The general outlines of the process are similar to Graeber's account. Gold assumes its place in a monetary economy from without, by carrying prestige that attached to it because of its being exempt from ordinary market transactions. Gold assumes its central role because of its relation to what cannot be sold and bought.

The question that these anthropological observations raise is the question of the present. It is the question of whether, and in what manner, the origin of money outside the economy of daily subsistence is still effective in contemporary monetary economies. Needless to say, the calculating mind of economic thought has little to do with the category of what money cannot buy. From this perspective, whatever the origins of money are, its current function is of a rational means of measuring value and storing value. But Marx, Weber, and Veblen show us the ongoing presence of this category in capitalist economies.

Recall the beginning of this book. Marx actually traces this category in the basic structure of monetary economies. The fact that money can appropriate any other good is the one thing we know for sure about such economies—if we deduct the metaphysical, neoclassical assumption of utility. This situation can be interpreted in two ways. In the orthodox view, the fact that money can buy anything signals it as means. Marx suggests otherwise, that its meaning is that money is "the object most worth possessing." It means, strictly speaking, that money is better than what money can buy, but another way to put it is that money is entangled with what money cannot buy. That is what signals money as an object of desire. The decision between these two interpretations of the basic structure of a monetary economy is informed by the concept of capital.

Marx's concept of capital can be seen as a further elaboration of his basic insight about money, as evidence in favor of his early intuition. Capital, in this view, exists insofar as desire for money annuls the wishes for all other goods. In theory, the orthodox view that money is but means with which we acquire things could have been valid. Maybe there could be an economy where money is strictly the means for purchasing goods. But this would surely not be a capitalist economy.

At this point we can notice an affinity between Marx and Weber in contrast to the common notion of an opposition between them, crudely presented as an opposition between materialism and idealism. Whereas Marx points to the category of what money cannot buy from a formal analysis of money and capital, Weber provides a sharp phenomenological exploration of it in the connection between capitalist conduct and the religious dogma of salvation. Both share the notion that capitalist conduct is entangled with active renunciation of ordinary aims. Both share the understanding that the capitalist is not simply a person who wants more money but that his money-conduct is aimed at more *than* money. Marx did not pursue this phenomenological aspect of capital, yet we can find some references to it in his early work in the chapter about money in the *Economic and Philosophic Manuscripts*: "I *am* ugly, but I can buy the *most beautiful* woman. Which means to say that I am not *ugly*, for the effect of *ugliness*, its repelling power, is destroyed by money."[54]

Finally, in Veblen's thought we find a supplement to this capitalist drive in the sphere of consumption. In the economy of display, things assume their position insofar as they also transcend ordinary use and stand for the category of what money cannot buy, as it is outlined in the association between waste and the sublime. This spilling over of the logic of money into commodities can be referred to the basic Marxist formula of a monetary economy. If money is worth more than anything it can buy, things assume a pecuniary status, to use Veblen's terminology, insofar as they represent what money cannot buy. The fact that today even the most basic merchandise incorporates images of what money cannot buy reflects the extent to which our economy has been monetized, given to the alien logic of money.

Critical approaches to the economy sometimes use this category as a moral and political anchor. There are some things, we are told, like health, education, or happiness that money cannot buy. A basic moral problem of the contemporary economy is that it commoditizes a growing number of these. The demands to liberate such spheres from commodification are shared by most critical perspectives on the economy, but its common formulation may be mistaken. It is futile to say that there are some things that money should not buy because, in a way, economy was always about things that money cannot buy. And it seems that this recognition points to the need of a more radical critique of economy and economics.

NOTES

Introduction

1. Andy Warhol, *The Philosophy of Andy Warhol (From A to B and Back Again)* (Orlando, FL: Harcourt, 1975), p. 77. One can add one more colloquial explanation for Gates's conduct, namely, that he wants to be the ultimate winner—somewhat like a sportsman—and arrive at the top of the list of the richest people on earth. This explanation comes closer to the truth of the desire for money, but it does so at the price of dispensing with an assumption of economics called methodological individualism. Wishing to be the richest person on earth means that one's desires are not simply one's own, that other people, the whole world in fact, are present within one's desires.

2. Ingham 2000, p. 17.

3. Defoe 1936, p. 68.

4. Veblen2007, p. 16.

5. Marx 1971, p. 190.

6. Žižek 1992, p. 5.

Chapter 1

1. Ingham 1996.

2. Marx 1973, p. 163.

3. R. H. Frank 1999, p. 16.

4. That economics does hold a worldview underlines its theoretical weakness in relation to all other sciences of humankind. Unlike academics in all other disciplines of the social sciences and humanities, economists no longer argue about the fundamentals of their field: about what is money, what are commodities, what is an economic action—indeed, what is an economy. Far from being a sign of progress, this unparalleled agreement points to the presence of ideological layers within the basic theoretical assumptions of the discipline.

5. Friedman 1992, p. 10.

6. Friedman's view represents the metallist conception, which sees money as an outcome of market activity. The major alternative conception of money in economic discourse, called chartalism, sees money as a creation of the state. The debate between them entails many theoretical and ideological issues. However, chartalism shares the same distinction—that the demand for money, in contrast to the demand for com-

modities, needs explanation. Thus Abba Lerner writes that "the modern state can make anything it chooses generally acceptable as money" by accepting it for tax settlement (Lerner 1947, p. 313). As for Friedman, the fact that people accept money appears to require explanation; moreover, here it is grounded on what for the citizen appears as a sort of punishment.

7. Douglas and Isherwood 1979, p. 3.

8. When J. R. Hicks wonders at the marginal utility of money, he naturally determines that

[a] preference for holding money instead of spending it on consumption goods presents no serious difficulty, for it is obviously the ordinary case of a preference for future satisfactions over present. (Hicks 1935, p. 5)

In any case, the utility of money is derived from things—whether present or future ones. Hicks also asks why people hold cash rather than holding their reserves in interest-bearing financial assets, and his answer has to do with uncertainty and preference of liquidity. What should be noted is that this whole line of inquiry has nothing to do with greed precisely because of the marginal framework. Economists can inquire only after the residue: what part of their wealth people would prefer to keep; at what point would they stop consuming, etc. This residual nature is alien to our notion of greed as a desire that transcends any limit.

9. *The Financial Crisis Inquiry Commission Report* (FCIC), p. xxii. I thank Robert Wosnitzer for pointing out this peculiarity to me.

10. Hayek 1962, pp. 66–67.

11. Ibid., p. 67.

12. In the case of utility, it seems particularly productive to study the concept in light of its later development. Gary Becker won a Nobel Prize for conceiving what has come to be known as *economic imperialism*, which refers to the application of economic methods to phenomena that are not directly economic, such as crime, the household, and others. He applies a utilitarian perspective to questions such as: Is smoking a *rational addiction*? and When is suicide rational? What is important to note is that the expansion of the utilitarian view to encompass ostensibly non-economic phenomena is a logical implication of the neoclassical idea of marginalism. In neoclassical economic thought utility is not a property of things. Rather, it encodes information about all possible courses of action of an agent. The utility of a certain good is meaningful only in relation to all the other goods we could have purchased in its place. For that reason, for utility to have meaning at all, everything must be included within its view.

13. Keynes 1952, p. 329.

14. Ibid., p. 330.

15. Friedman 1970.

16. Marx 1976, p. 92.

17. Ibid. 1975, p. 375.

18. As Gogol's police inspector, who was "a great patron of all arts and manufactures," but for a bribe preferred a bank note to anything else, says:

There can be nothing better than it—it doesn't ask for food, it doesn't take much space, it'll always fit into a pocket, and if you drop it, it won't break.(Nikolai Gogol, "The Nose," in *The Overcoat and Other Short Stories* [Mineola, NY: Dover Publications, 1992], p. 69).

19. Lacan 1977, p. 287.

20. Marx 1976, p. 252.

21. Ibid., pp. 244–245.

22. Ibid., p. 252.

23. Ibid., p. 247.

24. Norris 1900, p. 359.

25. FCIC 2011, p. 6.

26. Galbraith 1961, p. 18.

27. There was a time when economics could consider the opposition between money and things. The institutional economist Wesley Mitchell touches on this in his article "Making Goods and Making Money" (1950), which presents the primacy of the art of making money over that of making goods. His simple claim is that whereas economics deals with both, in the contemporary economy the considerations of making money are superior. Within the current framework of methodological individualism, such a distinction cannot be made. The ideological layer of orthodox economics emerges in its basic assumption that the ordinary way to make money is to make good things that appeal to the utilitarian individual.

28. Marx 1973, p. 147.

29. FCIC, p. 4.

30. Ibid., p. 6.

31. Marx 1973, p. 163.

32. Greenspan and Kennedy, 2007.

33. Simmel 1978, p. 247.

34. Ibid., p. 228.

35. Keynes 1952, p. 326.

36. Veblen 2007, pp. 22–23.

37. Graeber 2011, p. 94.

38. Veblen 1898b.

39. One can get a sense of the entanglement of scarcity and abundance from a visit with a toddler to a candy store. The abundance of choices that characterize the contemporary consumer economy is directly experienced as a frustrating scarcity. A choice entails giving up so many others—much more than, e.g., forty years ago.

40. Searle 1995, p. 1.

41. Ibid., p. 46.

42. Ibid., p. 47.

43. Ibid., p. 47.

44. Ibid., p. 43.

45. Ibid., p. 7.

46. Ibid., p. 39.

47. Marx 1976, pp. 164–165.

48. Marx 1971, pp. 134–135.

49. Ibid., pp. 165–166.

50. Žižek 2011, p. 222.

51. Marx 1971, 135.

52. Wood writes that "there are strong reasons to doubt there could be [a 'theory of alienation'] worth exploring," (Wood 1981, p. 4).

53. Ibid., p. 5.

54. Marx 1971, p. 143.

55. Ibid., pp. 137, 140–141.

56. Ibid., p. 136.

57. Ibid.

58. Ibid., p. 137.

59. Hegel 1991, p. 81.

60. Marx 1971, p.135.

61. Ibid. 1976, p. 165.

62. Locke 1823, pp. 116–117.

63. Ibid., p. 118.

64. Marx 1971, pp. 141–142.

65. Žižek 1997, p. 107.

66. Maybe this is the basic reason why supermarkets put effort into keeping the shelves full at all times, as if no object is ever taken off the shelf.

67. We can think of a parallel political example when the statue of a despot is toppled during a revolution. The cathartic thrill that accompanies such incidents testifies that they are not only symbolic events in the fall of a regime but have real effects in hastening its demise. But such events are real not because the statues stimulated awe in the people. Rather, in their massive inert presence, the statues served as material evidence that everybody is afraid of harming them.

68. See Margaret Thatcher Foundation, http://www.margaretthatcher.org/document/106689.

69. Braudel 1980, pp. 84–85.

70. Bennett 2010, p. 2.

71. Ibid., p. 5.

72. Marx 1976, p. 163.

73. Žižek 1989, p. 34.

74. Tversky and Kahneman 1981, p. 457. This experiment has acquired a legendary status, to the extent that it is quite hard to actually find it. It is mentioned numerous times, without exact reference, and in many different versions: some speak of pens and fancy suits; others mention coats, cars, and toys, and all with a variety of prices. It seems that calculating minds derive some pleasure in repeating that a $5 saving is a $5 saving in any circumstances. So maybe it is worth dwelling on this. An alternative explanation of the results is that selling for $15 something that can be sold for $10 appears simply as unfair. And acting in the name of a general principle of fairness, even if the act is unlikely to have significant effect, is actually related to rationality in the broad sense of the term.

75. The most telling fact about economics' narrow concept of rationality is that the discipline was shaken by the discovery that people would not drive five minutes to save $5. Yet it never bothered economists that people dedicate their lives to non-utilitarian goals such as joining a communist party or a green movement, and so forth.

76. Not all the claims of behavioral economics are related to utility. Among the

other popular research themes, there are many experiments that show that people do not handle risk and probability in a rational way. But again, there is a wide difference between the claim that ordinary people do not master mathematics, and in some cases even apparently simple mathematics, and the claim that people are irrational.

77. Ariely 2008, p.219.

78. In a sense, the ultimate deceit of behavioral economics is its insistence on conducting its clever experiments despite the fact that they are closer in nature to thought experiments. Most people, excepting obstinate economists, would easily guess their outcomes (that is actually a tautology, since many such experiments are conducted through questionnaires, asking people what they would do in certain circumstances). By conferring an empirical nature on its findings, behavioral economics strengthens the impression that its results are related to real people more than to economic thought. In fact, the only thing that can legitimately be thought to be empirically tested here is economic thought itself.

79. Appadurai 1986, p. 5.

80. Freud 1905, p. 149.

81. Butler 1987, p. 24.

82. Marx 1976, pp. 256–257.

83. Ibid. 1992, p. 423.

84. Ibid., p. 422.

85. Similarly, Jane Austen understood that the thought of possible money has a distinct sense of reality, superior to the sense of reality of money itself. In the opening chapters of *Sense and Sensibility*, through a long conversation with his wife, John Dashwood betrays the promise he made to his father that he would assist his three half-sisters after his father's death. After basking in his generous, initial decision to give each sister a thousand pounds, he gradually decreases the sum until, with the active encouragement of his wife, he settles on restricting his help to "acts of assistance and kindness" such as "looking out for a comfortable small house for them, helping them to move their things, and sending them presents of fish and game" (Austen 1994, pp. 10–11). What motivates this passage is precisely the reality effect of the thought of giving money. Dashwood feels sufficiently generous for having made the decision to give away some of his money that he can immediately forgo his generosity and, with a clear conscience, replace it with a more modest gift. One may wonder whether we find here a contradiction to Kant's claim, in his refutation of the ontological proof of the existence of God, that "a hundred real thalers do not contain the least coin more than a hundred possible thalers." There is a sense in which the opposite is true: the possible money is more real than the real money.

86. Quoted by Martin Nicolaus in his foreword to Marx's *Grundrisse*, p.11.

87. Dickens, *David Copperfield*, p. 259.

88. Ibid., p. 366.

89. Marx 1971, p. 201.

Chapter 2

1. Dickens 1994, *Hard Times*, p. 1.

2. Nussbaum 1995.

3. Dickens, *Hard Times*, pp. 5–6.

4. Ibid., p. 6.

5. Marx 1977, p. 85.

6. Becker 1992.

7. The tactlessness of this statement suffices to suggest otherwise. If people were indeed tireless utility-calculation machines, such a statement would not appear blunt. Of course, Becker can invoke some kind of unconscious utility mechanism constantly at work behind our emotional and social life. It is doubtful, however, whether this unconscious utility calculator is still compatible with the economic concept of human beings.

8. Dickens, *Hard Times*, p. 63.

9. Ibid.

10. Ingham 1996.

11. Smith 1904, pp. 24–25.

12. Only a few hold onto a belief in the truth of this narrative. Yet it keeps recurring as a fiction that nonetheless helps demonstrate what is a monetary economy (e.g., by comparing it to barter economy). Most symptomatic to this story's status is the attempt to treat it as *conjectural history*: demonstrating how under certain assumptions of rationality, the story could have happened *without* committing to the claim that this indeed proves that it happened (see Dowd 2000). By undermining its truth value, this last view actually emphasizes the story's relevance to economic thought. What it claims is that even if the story did not take place, it should have.

13. Marx 1976, pp. 148–151.

14. Searle 1995, p. 40.

15. Dickens, *Hard Times*, pp. 150–151.

16. Ibid.

17. Radford 1945.

18. Adam Smith 1904, pp. 25–26.

19. McCallum 1989, p. 17.

20. Dickens, *Hard Times*, pp. 14–15.

21. Dickens, *Hard Times*, p. 25

22. Žižek 1989, pp. 47–53.

23. A concrete example of this abstract connection is to be found in Michel Foucault's analysis of the spread of the neo-liberal doctrine in Germany after the Second World War. Basing the state's legitimacy as much as possible on free market mechanisms had the effect of detaching the state from its Nazi past. When Ludwig Erhard states that "we must free the economy from state control [because] only a state that establishes both the freedom and responsibility of the citizens can legitimately speak in the name of the people," he is practically saying, according to Foucault, that "the National Socialist state, which violated these rights, was not, could not be seen retrospectively as having exercised its sovereignty legitimately. That is to say [...] the Germans cannot be held responsible for what was done in the legislative or regulatory framework of Nazism" (Foucault 2008, p. 82). There could theoretically be other ways to legitimate the new German state in opposition to the Nazi state. But the economy provided a way to do it from scratch, without any political content for the new state but the economy. Economy provided, in other words, a way of practically obliterating the past.

24. McLuhan 1964, p. 9.

25. Marx 1976, p. 182.

26. Giddens 1990, pp. 21–24.

27. Marx 1976, p. 164.

28. Ibid., pp. 149–150.

29. Marx 1975, p. 113.

30. White 1978, pp. 82–99.

31. Ibid., pp. 89–90.

32. In this discussion, one should not confuse the ontological question with the question of historical technique. One can doubt whether historians can reach the true narrative, but this doubt conveys nothing unique in relation to the discipline of historiography. Behind it is a more fundamental question: In what sense can narratives have a truth value? It is this latter question that informs this discussion.

33. Marx 1976, pp. 180–181.

34. Shell 1978, p. 57.

35. Marx 1976, p. 187.

36. Ibid., p. 255.

37. Hart 2001, pp. 16–17.

38. Žižek 1989, pp. 24–25.

39. Ricoeur 1984, pp. 5–15.

40. Ferenczi 1976, p. 86.

41. Marx 1976, p. 161.

42. Akerlof 1970, p. 489.

43. The cynicism of the economic outlook goes deeper than that and is marvelously entangled with the economic object. It is not necessary to hold that a specific seller is a liar; in an economic view, it is enough that he is *statistically* a liar to cause a reduction in the price. But then, because the price is reduced from the outset, even if the seller is an honest person, doesn't an incentive exist to lie anyway—just to compensate for the reduction that was made to begin with?

Chapter 3

1. Friedman 1992, pp. 3–7.

2. Marx 1973, p. 151.

3. Ingham 2000.

4. Marx 1976, pp. 188–189, n.1.

5. Marx 1973, pp. 168–169.

6. Marx 1973, pp. 155–156.

7. A. Smith 1904, p. 28.

8. Friedman 1992, pp. 259–260.

9. Simmel 1978, p. 178.

10. Hart 1986.

11. Marx 1971, p.201.

12. In a personal conversation Daniel Matiuk noted the peculiar status that gold assumes in this respect at times of financial uncertainty. During times of crisis, the price of gold rises as people turn to what traditionally appears to be a solid asset. The irony is that the material status of this gold is dubitable: hardly anyone actually

touches it and, moreover, it's more likely to be a fund that replicates the price of gold. What people buy, in truth, is more a *simulation* of gold than a material substance. In one sense, the rush for gold during a crisis affirms Friedman's argument that market mechanisms eventually force governments to manage money properly. However, the simulative nature of this rush marks that a return to gold is impossible. Yet it also underlines the need to consider the materiality of non-material money.

13. Benjamin Klein, "Brand Names," *The Concise Encyclopedia of Economics,* 2008, http://www.econlib.org/library/ENC/BrandNames.html.

14. Sowell 2000, p. 318.

15. Naomi Klein 1999, p. 21.

16. In general the phenomenon of brand names should be considered in historical terms even though today brand names are created from scratch, without having a past. The emergence of the brand name is entangled with a retroactive understanding. Brand names fully assume their role in the economy when manufacturers gradually acknowledge that what they sell is the brand rather than the product. Klein writes: "It took several decades for the manufacturing world to adjust to this shift. It clung to the idea that its core business was still production and that branding was an important add-on." (Naomi Klein 1999, p. 23) As in the shift to symbolic money, this retroactive understanding is the necessary shape of the historical transition from products to brands. In a world where people buy bread, or think that they buy bread, one cannot sell a symbol of bread.

17. We should recall Jean Baudrillard's thought experiment in *The System of Objects*, where he wondered what would happen if all the symbols, advertisements, and logos that embellish our cities would suddenly be replaced by one meaningless signifier "GARAP": "A pure signifier, having no referent, signifying only itself, it is read, discussed, interpreted in a vacuum, signified despite itself—in short, consumed qua sign" (Baudrillard 2005, pp. 197–198). What this thought experiment captures is the way that the specific meanings of all new commercial symbols are indifferent to their economic functioning. Moreover, it suggests that their very opaqueness, meaninglessness, and strangeness account for their being economic objects. In retrospect we can see this thought experiment as a step in Baudrillard's intellectual route that led him away from Marxism into his own wild brand of post-modernism. GARAP, allegedly, pointed to the autonomous sphere of signs, detached from material reality. But this step could just as easily lead in the opposite direction, to a reformulation of materialist categories rather than to a rejection of them: the opaque GARAP can be understood as an illustration of the peculiar materiality of the symbol—through its resistance, the symbol acquires the qualities of a thing.

18. N. Klein 1999, p. 22.

19. Foster 2005, p. 8.

20. Marx 1975, p. 375.

21. Marx 1976, p. 161.

22. Krugman 2013.

23. Marx 1976, p. 247.

24. Preferences are a more elegant way for economics to use the idea of utility. An agent's preferences define what he will do at any moment with his free resources,

e.g., at what moment he will stop purchasing bread and buy butter instead. Economic theory shows that the two concepts are logically equivalent: a person's preferences imply a utility function that can be assigned to different objects. Currently, economists seem to prefer the concept of preferences, perhaps because it avoids the metaphysical awkwardness of utility. It seems as if preferences necessitate no assumption of a further magnitude behind people's choices and focus only on actual choices. Yet, because these concepts are equivalent, the concept of preferences simply shifts the philosophical problem of the concept of utility. In the case of preferences, the problem is the necessary assumption of counterfactuals: an action has economic meaning only if it can be considered against a whole sphere of choices not taken. The statement *I want some bread* has no sense from an economic perspective unless it is formulated *I want bread more than I want candy*. Needless to say that the ideological layer of economic theory surfaces here again in the form of *compulsory freedom*: because economics conceives of human action in terms of choice, it cannot in principle conceive of un-free action. With typical academic honesty, Becker states that from an economic perspective even death is voluntary:

According to the economic approach, therefore *most* (if not all!) deaths are to some extent "suicides" in the sense that they could have been postponed if more resources had been invested in prolonging life. (Becker 1976, p. 10)

25. Ibid., p. 5.

26. Žižek 1997, p.7.

27. Foster 2005, p. 11.

28. Marx 1971, p. 134.

29. Debord 2006, p. 8.

30. Jhally 1990, pp. 83–90.

31. Dayan 2009.

32. Boorstin 1963, p. 67.

33. Couldry 2003, pp. 47–48.

34. Ibid. 2004, p. 63.

35. In a similar vein Michael Schudson presented advertising as "capitalist realism"—a parallel to the communist official art form of *socialist realism*. Schudson argued that apart from selling specific products, advertising promotes capitalism itself: it shows consumption, in general, as a consummation of human life. It is capitalism's way of saying to itself "I love you." (Schudson 1986, p. 232.)

36. Baudrillard traces a similar difference within the *real* shopping experience in relation to the visions of abundance in big department stores:

There is something more in this piling high than the quantity of products: the manifest presence of surplus, the magical, definitive negation of scarcity [. . . .] We find here the fervid hope that there should be not enough, but too much—and too much for everyone: by buying a piece of this land, you acquire the crumbling pyramid of oysters, meats, pears or tinned asparagus. You buy the part for the whole.

What should be added to this description is that in buying *the part for the whole*, we pay for what we cannot have. We buy a small piece of abundance, which loses this aura precisely because we buy it.

37. Debord 2006, p. 16.

38. Fleetwood 2000, p. 189.

39. Kennedy 2000, p. 196.

40. Ibid., p. 205.

41. Ibid., p. 206.

42. Ibid.

43. An early crucial insight regarding the theoretical need in a concept of consumption work was made by Baudrillard in *The Consumer Society*. Baudrillard does not explicitly use the concept, but its contours are portrayed in his overall attempt to explain consumption as a function of production. Consumer society, according to him, is the last stage of a process of increasing rationalization of production. Consumer society emerges as the means to absorb the increasing productivity capacity: "[the order of production] produces needs, the system of needs, demand/productive force as a rationalized, integrated, controlled whole" (Baudrillard 1998, p. 76).

44. Naomi Klein quotes a senior advertising manager as stating, in the language of the market, the idea that branding is essential for profits. When a backlash against the trend of brands arose at the end of the 1980s, Graham H. Phillips of Ogilvy & Mather warned executives against the severe consequences of cutting down on advertising:

I doubt that many of you would welcome a commodity marketplace in which one competed solely on price, promotion and trade deals, all of which can easily be duplicated by competition, leading to ever-decreasing profits, decay and eventual bankruptcy. (N. Klein 1999, p. 14)

45. One must read the first pages of *The General Theory of Employment, Interest and Money* to see the trouble Keynes takes to prove—in 1935, mind you!—that there can be unemployment. From the premise of neoclassical economics, unemployment can be conceived only as voluntary—workers refuse to endure the disutility of work at the current level of wages (simply put, they are not unemployed; they want more money). Since then, economics began to understand that there can be unemployment, but it is important to note that economics understands unemployment through macroeconomic theory, which in contrast to the utilitarian framework of microeconomics, has no clear philosophy. As Paul Krugman notes, microeconomics is a field that "operates by fairly strict intellectual rules" whereas macroeconomics is traditionally "full of ad hoc assumptions that, in the jargon of the field, are not 'derived from microfoundations'" (Krugman 1994, p. 51). It is clear what the perceived logical order of priority is here. Microeconomics always has the upper hand because it has a philosophy. One cannot avoid the suspicion that the sweeping victory of neo-liberalism owes something to the fact that it has a coherent, even if counterfactual, philosophy.

46. Baudrillard 1998, p. 31.

47. Marx 1992, p. 422.

48. Foster 2005, p. 12.

Chapter 4

1. Krugman 1996.

2. Weber 1958, p. 53.

3. Ibid., pp. 48–49.

4. Ibid., p. 51.

5. Callon 1998a.

6. Weber 1958, p. 49.

7. Schumpeter 1981, pp. 320–321.

8. MacIntyre 1962, p. 50.

9. Weber 1958, p. 49.

10. It is important to recall here Shell's elaboration of the complex function of sight and invisibility in the economic thought and fantasies of ancient Greece. Sight and invisibility explicitly combine in the figure of Gyges, the first tyrant and the first minter, as recounted by Herodotus (Shell 1978, pp. 11–62). Shell tracks the transformation and insistence of this conceptual couple in Plato's *Republic*. This *archeology* of the money thought suggests that money is intertwined with the omniscient gaze from its inception.

11. Weber 1958, p. 117.

12. Ibid., p. 172.

13. Ibid., pp. 115.

14. Ibid., pp. 113–114.

15. Ibid., p. 70.

16. Marcel Mauss opens his essay "The Gift" with an enigma:

In primitive or archaic types of society what is the principle whereby the gift received has to be repaid? What force is there in the thing given which compels the recipient to make a return? (Mauss 1967, p. 1)

This formulation of the question opens the way for an answer in terms of the primitive's absurd beliefs: tales of spirits that reside in objects, etc. What should be added is that we no longer ask: *What force is there in money that compels the shopkeeper to give us a commodity in return?* Adjoining these two questions works both ways. It presents the archaic replies in terms of spirits as fundamentally partial explanations masking the fact of economy. Once the question is asked, answers are always given, but this is precisely their status. On the other hand, turning our gaze to ourselves, we should consider the possibility that in a way, we believe that there is a spirit residing in money.

17. Veblen 1985, pp. 184–185.

18. Weber 1958, p. 55.

19. Marx 1975, p. 113.

20. Weber 1958, pp. 71–72.

21. Butler, Laclau, and Žižek 2000, p. 214.

22. Shell 1982, pp. 47–83.

23. Žižek 2006, p. 17.

24. Weber 1958, p. 175.

25. Freud 1908c, p. 221.

26. Ibid. 1933, p. 149.

27. Weber 1958, p. 54.

28. Appadurai 2011, p. 524.

29. Graham 1997, p. 33.

30. White 1978, p. 99.

31. Goldstein 1976, p. xix.

32. Žižek 1989, p.21.

33. Ibid. 1999, pp. 76–77.

34. Marx 1973, p. 105.

35. Again, it is easy to reject teleology due to its implying a certain grand scheme of history. This is the way Karl Löwith attempts to undermine Marx's conception of history in his *Meaning in History* (Löwith 1949)—by presenting this conception as based on a religious and eschatological view of an eternal struggle between the forces of light and darkness. The point is that any conception of grand history can be easily presented as arbitrary. But in Marx's thought such a conception is supported by a logically prior consideration of historicity.

36. Marx 1973, p. 104.

37. Ibid., p. 105.

38. Shell 1978, p. 58.

39. Ricoeur 1984, pp. 5–15.

40. Zelizer 1997, pp.71–118.

41. Hart 2005, p. 165.

42. Marx 1992, pp. 119–120.

43. Mitchell 1950, p. 6.

Chapter 5

1. Douglas and Isherwood 1996, p. 3.

2. Ibid., p. 38.

3. A. Smith 1966, pp. 70–71.

4. Illouz 1997, pp. 112–120.

5. Ibid., pp. 66–76.

6. Bagwell and Bernheim 1996, p. 349.

7. Veblen 2007, p. 27.

8. This movement of incorporation-sterilization can already be felt in the accepted economic term that appears in the title of Bagwell and Bernheim's article: "Veblen effects." This term suggests that Veblen pointed to a certain peculiarity within the standard economic behaviors and thus avoids the possibility of seeing him as outlining an alternative economic knowledge.

9. Veblen 2007, pp.32–33.

10. Ibid., pp. 44–45.

11. Ibid., p. 98.

12. In a similar vein, E. Ray Canterbery writes against the crude economic reduction of conspicuous consumption to the drive to buy expensive goods. He points to the marvelous example of F. Scott Fitzgerald's *The Great Gatsby*, where Jay Gatsby's vulgar conspicuous temptation of Daisy eventually fails because she cannot leave the trappings of the old aristocracy: "As in Veblen's [*Theory of the Leisure Class*], the cultural illusions are more important than wealth or money for Fitzgerald's central characters" (Canterbery 1998, p. 143). This suggests a good way to describe Veblen's work: it is an analysis of the economic reality of *cultural illusions* (manners, beauty, honor, religion, etc.). Veblen actually shows that cultural illusions are real economic phenomena.

13. Veblen 2007,p. 36.

14. Ibid., pp. 32–33.

15. Kenneth Burke famously described Veblen's work as "satire-masked-as-science." It could equally well be described the other way around, as science masked as satire. The real troubling possibility is the identification of both terms, in a science that is immanently satirical. This possibility arises out of Veblen's conception of the economic cause as foreign to the individual's point of view. Because of its externality, the articulation of this cause has an effect similar to the Brechtian effect where a character in a play articulates explicitly his *objective* social role. (Kenneth Burke, 1950. *A Rhetoric of Motives*. Berkeley: University of California Press, p. 132.)

16. Veblen 2007, p. 44.

17. Ibid., pp. 80–83.

18. N. Klein 1999, p. 21.

19. Veblen 2007, pp. 104–5.

20. Ibid., p. 35.

21. Ibid., p. 60.

22. Ibid., p. 25.

23. Sowell 2000.

24. Veblen 2007, p. 36.

25. Sowell 1987, p. 800.

26. Diggins 1999, pp. 43–48.

27. Marx 1975, p. 113.

28. Žižek 1989, pp. 24–25.

29. Veblen 2007, p. 30.

30. Ibid., pp. 126–127.

31. Ibid., p. 43.

32. Marx 1973, p. 91.

33. Veblen 2007, p. 16.

34. Ibid. 1898a, p. 187.

35. Marx 1971, pp. 141–142.

36. Ibid., p. 201.

37. Veblen 1898b, p. 355.

38. Ibid., p. 364.

39. Ibid. 2007, p. 58.

40. Available from http://www.slate.com/articles/business/ad_report_card/2005/12/gorgeous_drop_dead.html.

41. In "A Special Type of Object-Choice," Freud explains why for some men a prostitute-like woman is a "love object of the highest degree." But in the English translation, James Strachey remarks that "The German *Dirne* [...] is not well rendered by 'prostitute,' which in English lays too much stress on the monetary side of the relation" (Freud 1910, p. 167).

42. See, e.g., Hodgson 2003.

43. Veblen 1898c.

44. Spence 1973, p. 358.

45. Zahavi 1975.

46. Žižek 2006, p. 62.

47. Ibid., pp. 62–63.
48. Veblen 2007, p. 7.
49. Ibid., pp. 22–23.
50. Ibid., p. 26
51. Marx 1973, p. 163.
52. Graeber 2011, pp. 132–133.
53. Schoenberger 2011, p.11.
54. Marx 1975, p. 377.

BIBLIOGRAPHY

Akerlof, George A. 1970. "The Market for 'Lemons': Quality Uncertainty and the Market Mechanism." *The Quarterly Journal of Economics* 84, no.3: pp. 488–500.

Althusser, Louis. 1971. *Essays on Ideology*. London: Verso.

————. 1979. *Reading Capital*. London: Verso.

Appadurai, Arjun (ed.). 1986. *The Social Life of Things: Commodities in Cultural Perspective*. Cambridge: Cambridge University Press.

————. 2011. "The Ghost in the Financial Machine." *Public Culture* 23, no. 3.

Ariely, Dan. 2008. *Predictably Irrational: The Hidden Forces that Shape Our Decisions*. New York: Harper Collins.

Austen, Jane. 1994. *Sense and Sensibility*. Reading, Berkshire:Penguin.

Bagwell, Laurie Simon, and B. Douglas Bernheim. 1996. "Veblen Effects in a Theory of Conspicuous Consumption." *The American Economic Review* 86, no. 3.

Balibar, Etienne. 1995. *The Philosophy of Marx*. London: Verso.

Baudrillard, Jean. 1998. *The Consumer Society: Myths and Structures*. London: Sage Publications.

————. 2005. *The System of Objects*. London: Verso.

Becker, Gary S. 1976. *The Economic Approach to Human Behavior*. Chicago: University of Chicago Press.

————. "The Economic Way of Looking at Life." Nobel Lecture, December 9, 1992. http://www.nobelprize.org/nobel_prizes/economics/laureates/1992/becker-lecture.pdf.

Bennett, Jane. 2010. *Vibrant Matter: A Political Ecology of Things*. Durham, NC: Duke University Press.

Boorstin, Daniel J. 1963. *The Image or What Happened to the American Dream*. Harmondsworth, Middlesex: Penguin.

Braudel, Fernand. 1980. *On History*. Chicago: University of Chicago Press.

Broda, Philippe. 1998. "Veblen and the Vanishing of the 'Leisure Class.'" In Warren J. Samuels (ed.), *The Founding of Institutional Economics*. London: Routledge.

Butler, Judith. 1987. *Subjects of Desire: Hegelian Reflections in Twentieth-Century France*. New York: Columbia University Press.

Butler, Judith, Ernesto Laclau, and Slavoj Žižek. 2000. *Contingency, Hegemony, Universality: Contemporary Dialogues on the Left*. London: Verso.

Callon, Michel. 1998a. "An Essay on Framing and Overflowing: Economic Externalities Revisited by Sociology." In Michel Callon (ed.), *The Laws of the Markets*. Oxford: Blackwell Publishers/The Sociological Review, pp. 244–269.

———. 1998b. "Introduction: The Embeddedness of Economic Markets in Economics." In Michel Callon (ed.), *The Laws of the Markets*. Oxford: Blackwell Publishers/The Sociological Review, pp. 1–57.

Canterbery, E. Ray. 1998. "*The Theory of the Leisure Class* and the Theory of Demand." In Warren J. Samuels (ed.), *The Founding of Institutional Economics*. London: Routledge.

Collingwood, R. G. 1956. *The Idea of History*. New York: Oxford University Press.

Couldry, Nick. 2003. *Media Rituals: A Critical Approach*. London: Routledge.

———. 2004. "Teaching Us to Fake It: The Ritualized Norms of Television's 'Reality' Games." In Laurie Ouellette and Susan Murray (eds.), *Reality TV: Remaking Television Culture*. New York: New York University Press, pp. 57–74.

Cross, Gary. 1993. *Time and Money: The Making of Consumer Culture*. London: Routledge.

Davidson, Paul. 1978. *Money and the Real World*. London: Macmillan.

Dayan, Daniel. 2009. "Sharing and Showing: Television as Monstration." In *The End of Television? Its Impact on the World (So Far)*. *The Annals of the American Academy of Political and Social Sciences* 625 (September): pp. 19–31.

Debord, Guy. 2006. *Society of the Spectacle*. London: Rebel Press.

Defoe, Daniel. 1936. *Robinson Crusoe*. London: Collins' Clear-Type Press.

Dickens, Charles. 1994. *David Copperfield*. London: Penguin.

———. 1994. *Hard Times*. London: Penguin.

Diggins, John Patrick. 1999. *Thorstein Veblen: Theorist of the Leisure Class*. Princeton, NJ: Princeton University Press.

Douglas, Mary, and Baron Isherwood. 1996. *The World of Goods: Towards an Anthropology of Consumption*. 2nd ed. London: Routledge.

Dowd, Kevin. 2000. "The Invisible Hand and the Evolution of the Monetary System" in John Smithin (ed.), *What Is Money?* London: Routledge, pp. 139–156.

Ferenczi, Sándor. 1976. "The Ontogenesis of the Interest in Money." In Ernest Borneman (ed.), *The Psychoanalysis of Money*. New York: Urizen Books.

Ferguson, Niall. 2008. *The Ascent of Money: A Financial History of the World*. New York: Penguin.

The Financial Crisis Inquiry Commission. 2011. *The Financial Crisis Inquiry Report (FCIC)*. Washington, DC: U.S. Government Printing Office. http://www.gpo.gov/fdsys/pkg/GPO-FCIC/pdf/GPO-FCIC.pdf

Fleetwood, Steve. 2000. "Marxist Theory of Money." In John Smithin (ed.), *What Is Money?* London: Routledge, pp. 174–193.

Foley, Duncan K. 1986. *Understanding Capital: Marx's Economic Theory*. Cambridge, MA: Harvard University Press.

Foster, Robert J. 2005. "Commodity Futures: Labour, Love and Value." *Anthropology Today* 21, no. 4.

Foucault, Michel. 2008. *The Birth of Biopolitics: Lectures at the College de France, 1978–79*. New York: Palgrave Macmillan.

Frank, Robert H. 1999. *Luxury Fever: Why Money Fails to Satisfy in an Era of Excess.* New York: The Free Press.

Frank, Thomas. 1997. *The Conquest of Cool: Business Culture, Counterculture, and the Rise of Hip Consumerism.* Chicago: The University of Chicago Press.

Freud, Sigmund. 1905. "Three Essays on the Theory of Sexuality." *SE* 7, pp. 123–243.

———. 1908a. "Character and Anal Erotism." *SE* 7: pp. 167–175.

———. 1908b. "Hysterical Phantasies and Their Relation to Bisexuality." *Penguin Freud Library* 10: pp. 83–94.

———. 1908c. "On the Sexual Theories of Children." *SE* 9: pp. 205–226.

———. 1910. "A Special Type of Choice of Object Made by Men (Contributions to the Psychology of Love I)." *SE* 11: pp. 163–175.

———. 1933. "New Introductory Lectures on Psychoanalysis." *Penguin Freud Library* 2.

Friedman, Milton. 1970. "The Social Responsibility of Business Is to Increase Its Profits." *The New York Times Magazine* (September 13): p. SM17.

———. 1992. *Money Mischief: Episodes in Monetary History.* New York: Harcourt Brace Jovanovich.

Galbraith, John Kenneth. 1961. *The Great Crash 1929.* Boston: Houghton Mifflin.

Giddens, Anthony. 1990. *The Consequences of Modernity.* Stanford, CA: Stanford University Press.

Goldstein, Leon. 1976. *Historical Knowing.* Austin: University of Texas Press.

Graeber, David. 2011. *Debt: The First 5,000 Years.* Brooklyn, NY: Melvillehouse.

Graham, Gordon. 1997. *The Shape of the Past: A Philosophical Approach to History.* Oxford: Oxford University Press.

Greenspan, Alan and James Kennedy. March 2007. "Sources and Uses of Equity Extracted from Homes." Federal Reserve Working Paper 2007–20, Divisions of Research & Statistics and Monetary Affairs, Federal Reserve Board, Washington, DC. http://www.federalreserve.gov/pubs/feds/2007/200720/200720pap.pdf.

Harford, Tim. 2008. *The Logic of Life: The Rational Economics of an Irrational World.* New York: Random House.

Hart, Keith. 1986. "Heads or Tails? Two Sides of the Coin." *Man,* New Series 21, no. 4: pp. 637–656.

———. 2001. *Money in an Unequal World.* New York: Texere.

———. 2005. "Money: One Anthropologist's View." In J. Carrier (ed.), *Handbook of Economic Anthropology.* Cornwall: Edward Elgar.

Harvey, David. 1990. *Condition of Postmodernity: An Inquiry into the Origins of Cultural Change.* Oxford: Blackwell.

Hawthorne, Nathaniel. 1917. *A Wonder Book and Tangle Wood Tales.* New York: J.M. Dent & Sons.

Hayek, F. A., 1962, *The Road to Serfdom.* London: Routledge.

Hegel, G. W. F. 1991. *Elements of the Philosophy of Right.* Cambridge: Cambridge University Press.

Hicks, J. R. 1935. "A Suggestion for Simplifying the Theory of Money." *Economica,* New Series 2, no. 5: pp. 1–19.

Hodgson, Geoffrey M. 2000. "What Is the Essence of Institutional Economics?" *Journal of Economic Issues* 34, no. 2: pp. 317–329.

————. 2003. "Darwinism and Institutional Economics." *Journal of Economic Issues* 37, no. 1: pp. 85–97.

Illouz, Eva. 1997. *Consuming the Romantic Utopia: Love and the Cultural Contradictions of Capitalism*. Berkeley and Los Angeles: University of California Press.

Ingham, Geoffrey. 1996. "Money Is a Social Relation." *Review of Social Economy* 54, no. 4: pp. 507–529.

————. 2000. "'Babylonian Madness': On the Historical and Sociological Origins of Money." In John Smithin (ed.), *What Is Money?* London: Routledge, pp. 16–41.

Jameson, Frederic. 1992. *Postmodernism, or the Cultural Logic of Late Capitalism*. Durham, NC: Duke University Press.

Jhally, Sut. 1990. *The Codes of Advertising*. London: Routledge.

Kennedy, Peter. 2000. "A Marxist Account of the Relationship between Commodity Money and Symbolic Money in the Context of Contemporary Capitalist Development." In John Smithin (ed.), *What Is Money?* London: Routledge, pp. 194–216.

Keynes, John Maynard. 1936. *The General Theory of Employment, Interest and Money*. London: Macmillan.

————. 1952. "Economic Possibilities for Our Grandchildren." In *Essays in Persuasion*. London: Rupert Hart-Davis.

————. 1965. *A Treatise on Money*, Vol. 1: *The Pure Theory of Money*. London: Macmillan.

Klein, Benjamin. 2008. "Brand Names," *The Concise Encyclopedia of Economics*. http://www.econlib.org/library/ENC/BrandNames.html. Accessed July 30, 2013.

Klein, Naomi. 1999. *No Logo*. New York: Picador USA.

Korten, David C. 2001. *When Corporations Rule the World*. San Francisco: Kumarian Press and Berrett-Koehler.

Krugman, Paul. 1994. *Peddling Prosperity: Economic Sense and Nonsense in the Age of Diminished Expectations*. New York: W.W. Norton.

————. 1996. "The Gold Bug Variations: The Gold Standard—and the Men Who Love It." In Slate, November 23. http://www.slate.com/articles/business/the_dismal_science/1996/11/the_gold_bug_variations.html.

————. 2013. "Profits without Production." *The New York Times* (June 20, p. A23). www.nytimes.com/2013/06/21/opinion/krugman-profits-without-production.html.

Lacan, Jacques. 1977. *Écrits: A Selection*. New York: W.W. Norton.

————. 1992. *The Seminar of Jacques Lacan, Book 20*. New York: W.W. Norton.

Latour, Bruno. 1992. "Where Are the Missing Masses? The Sociology of a Few Mundane Artifacts." In Wiebe E. Bijker and John Law (eds.), *Shaping Technology/Building Society: Studies in Sociotechnical Change*. Cambridge, MA: MIT Press, pp. 225–258.

Lerner, Abba P. 1947. "Money as a Creature of the State." *American Economic Review* 37, no. 2. Papers and Proceedings of the Fifty-ninth Annual Meeting of the American Economic Association, pp. 312–317.

Levin, Hanoch. 1996. *Plays V: The Whore from Ohio and Other Plays* [in Hebrew]. Tel Aviv: Hakibutz Hameuhad and Tel Aviv Books.

Locke, John. 1823. *Two Treatises of Government*. Vol. 5 of *The Works of John Locke: A New Edition, Corrected*. 10 vols. London: Printed for Thomas Tegg; W. Sharpe and Son; G. Offor; G. and J. Robinson; J. Evans and Co. and R. Griffin and Co., Glasgow; and J. Gumming, Dublin.

Löwith, Karl. 1949. *Meaning in History*. Chicago: The University of Chicago Press.

MacIntyre, Alasdair. 1962. "A Mistake about Causality in Social Sciences." In Peter Laslett and W. G. Runciman (eds.), *Philosophy, Politics and Society*. Oxford: Basil Blackwell, pp. 48–70.

Marx, Karl. 1971. *Early Texts*. Oxford: Basil Blackwell.

———. 1973. *Grundrisse*. New York: Vintage Books.

———. 1975. *Early Writings*. New York: Vintage Books.

———. 1975. *The Poverty of Philosophy*. Moscow: Progress Publishers.

———. 1976. *Capital, Vol 1*. Harmondsworth, Middlesex, England: Penguin.

———. 1977. *Economic and Philosophic Manuscripts of 1844*. Moscow: Progress Publishers.

———. 1992. Capital, Vol 2. Harmondsworth, Middlesex, England: Penguin.

———. 1992. *Early Writings*. London: Penguin.

Mauss, Marcel. 1967. *The Gift: Forms and Functions of Exchange in Archaic Societies*. New York: W.W. Norton.

McCallum, Bennett T. 1989. *Monetary Economics: Theory and Policy*. New York: Macmillan.

McLuhan, Marshall. 1964. *Understanding Media: The Extensions of Man*. New York: McGraw-Hill.

Megill, Allan. 2002. *Karl Marx: The Burden of Reason (Why Marx Rejected Politics and the Market)*. Boston: Rowman and Littlefield.

Mitchell, Wesley C. 1950. *The Backward Art of Spending Money and Other Essays*. New York: Augustus M. Kelley.

Navot, Doron. 2009. "The Concept of Political Corruption." PhD diss., Hebrew University in Jerusalem.

Nelson, Antira. 1999. *Marx's Concept of Money: The God of Commodities*. London: Routledge.

Norris, Frank. 1900. *McTeague: A Story of San Francisco*. New York: International Book and Publishing.

Nussbaum, Martha C. 1995. *Poetic Justice: The Literary Imagination and Public Life*. Boston: Beacon Press.

Packard, Vance. 1957. *The Hidden Persuaders*. New York: David McKay.

Polanyi, Karl. 1957. *The Great Transformation*. Boston: Beacon Press.

Radford, R. A. 1945. "The Economic Organisation of a P.O.W. Camp." *Economica* 12 (November): pp. 189–201.

Ricoeur, Paul. 1984. *The Reality of the Historical Past*. Milwaukee, WI: Marquette University Press.

Samuels, Warren J. (ed.). 1998. *The Founding of Institutional Economics*. London: Routledge.

Schoenberger, Erica. 2011. "Why Is Gold Valuable? Nature, Social Power and the Value of Things." *Cultural Geographies* 18, no. 1: pp. 3–24.

Schudson, Michael. 1986. *Advertising, the Uneasy Persuasion: Its Dubious Impact on American Society*. New York: Basic Books.

Schumpeter, Joseph A. 1981. *History of Economic Analysis*. London: George Allen & Unwin.

Searle, John R. 1995. *The Construction of Social Reality*. London: Penguin.

Sebberson, David, and Margaret Lewis. 1998. "The Rhetoricality of Thorstein Veblen's Economic Theorizing: A Critical Reading of *The Theory of the Leisure Class*." In Warren J. Samuels (ed.), *The Founding of Institutional Economics*. London: Routledge.

Sen, Amartya. 1988. *On Ethics and Economics*. Oxford: Blackwell.

Shell, Marc. 1978. *The Economy of Literature*. Baltimore: The Johns Hopkins University Press.

———. 1982. *Money, Language and Thought*. Berkley and Los Angeles: University of California Press.

———. 1995. *Art and Money*. Chicago: University of Chicago Press.

Simmel, Georg. 1978. *The Philosophy of Money*. London: Routledge & Kegan Paul.

Smith, Adam. 1904. *An Inquiry into the Nature and Causes of the Wealth of Nations*. London: Methuen.

———. 1966. *The Theory of Moral Sentiments*. New York: Augustus M. Kelley Publishers.

Smith, Tony. 1990. *The Logic of Marx's Capital: Replies to Hegelian Criticisms*. Albany: State University of New York Press.

Sowell, Thomas. 1987. "Thorstein Veblen." In John Eatwell, Murray Milgate, Peter Newman (eds.), *The New Palgrave: A Dictionary of Economics*. London: Macmillan.

———. 2000. *Basic Economics: A Citizen's Guide to the Economy*. New York: Basic Books.

Spence, Michael. 1973. "Job Market Signaling." *The Quarterly Journal of Economics* 87, no. 3: pp 355–374.

Tversky, Amos, and Daniel Kahneman. 1981. "The Framing of Decisions and the Psychology of Choice." *Science*, New Series 211, no. 4481: pp. 453–458.

Veblen, Thorstein. 1898a. "The Instinct of Workmanship and the Irksomeness of Labor." *American Journal of Sociology* 4, no. 2: pp. 187–201.

———. 1898b. "The Beginnings of Ownership." *American Journal of Sociology* 4, no. 3: pp. 352–365.

———. 1898c. "Why is Economics Not an Evolutionary Science." *The Quarterly Journal of Economics* 12.

———. 1985. "The Limitations of Marginal Utility." In Daniel M. Hausman (ed.), *The Philosophy of Economics: An Anthology*. New York: Cambridge University Press, pp. 129–141.

———. 2007. *The Theory of the Leisure Class: An Economic Study of Institutions*. Oxford: Oxford University Press.

Warhol, Andy. 1975. *The Philosophy of Andy Warhol (From A to B and Back Again)*. Orlando, FL: Harcourt.

Weber, Max. 1958. *The Protestant Ethic and the Spirit of Capitalism*. New York: Charles Scribner's Sons.

White, Hayden. 1978. *The Tropics of Discourse*. Baltimore: Johns Hopkins University Press.

Wood, Allen. 1981. *Karl Marx*. New York: Routledge and Kegan Paul.

Zahavi, Amotz. 1975. "Mate Selection: A Selection for a Handicap." *Journal of Theoretical Biology* 53: pp. 205–214.

Zelizer, Viviana. 1997. *The Social Meaning of Money*. Princeton, NJ: Princeton University Press.

Žižek, Slavoj. 1989. *The Sublime Object of Ideology*. London: Verso.

———. 1992. *Looking Awry*. Cambridge, MA: MIT Press.

———. 1994. *The Metastases of Enjoyment: Six Essays on Woman and Causality*. London: Verso.

———. 1997. *The Plague of Fantasies*. London: Verso.

———. 1999. *The Ticklish Subject: The Absent Centre of Political Ontology*. London: Verso.

———. 2006. *The Parallax View*. Cambridge, MA: MIT Press.

———. 2011. *Living in the End Times*. London: Verso.

Zupančič, Alenka. 2008. *The Odd One In: On Comedy*. Cambridge, MA: MIT Press.

INDEX